Just Me an

40 Seasons of Supp

By Dave Small

For Dad,

without whom,

this would not

have been possible.

Literally.

Introduction

At the age of seven, I discovered I could actually play football. Not very well, but well enough to realise I loved it. The feeling of kicking a ball and being able to copy players I'd seen on the television was my new favourite thing. Every day after school I would go out in my back garden and kick my ball against the kitchen wall, before firing it into the imaginary goal that was our big tall double gate which stopped me from going onto the main road outside.

I would even commentate on myself, imagining I was at Wembley scoring the winning goal in the Cup Final. My mum would often think someone else was out there with me due to the amount of talking that was going on, so when it was nearly time for tea, she would call out that my friend would have to go now. I'd call back that there was no one else with me, "just me and my football".

At that point in my life, I fell in love with the game of football. It was my first ever love and one that will no doubt remain with me forever. Yes, it's been a long and winding road, with upset and heartache along the way, but isn't that why we love the game? The best part of breaking up is making up, and I've had to make up with my team on many occasions.

Football is, and always will be, a cruel mistress, or an errant child, to use the words of Peter Cook in his guise as Alan Latchley, the manager of Scunthorpe United, or Scunny as he affectionately calls them. "She can make you laugh; she can make you cry, she can bring tears to my eyes, and blood to my shoulders. Football is about nothing, unless it's about something!" She's certainly put me through the wringer, as no doubt she has done to us all.

But what she does do is connect us. Yes, what follows are my thoughts, my reactions, my reflections, my relationship with football, and my own personal memories are obviously very personal to me.

This book is about just me and my football. But not just me. The wonderful thing about football is that millions of other people all have shared memories too. Millions of people all saw the exact same images that I saw when watching football on the television; all our memories are interlinked. The important thing is that we can connect through these shared memories. I sincerely hope we do.

***

I write this the day after I, and millions of others, witnessed history being made. Yesterday Manchester City beat Watford 6-0 in the FA Cup Final, a week after securing back to back Premier League titles. They had started the season by beating Chelsea in the Community Shield season opener, before beating them again in February in the Carabao or League Cup Final. Everything they could win in the domestic competitions, they did win. They had done not just the domestic Treble, but if you count the Community Shield as legitimate, they did The Quadruple.

Never has it been done before, and possibly never will it be done again, except by the same team next year perhaps. The total and utter domination by one team in England became historic yesterday. Whilst watching the game on the television, to see the look of utter joy, disbelief and in some cases relief on the faces of the City fans, I have to admit that a bit of me was jealous.

I have a good friend, a Manchester City supporter, who had been to every trophy winning game in that season and also attended most, if not all, of the domestic Premier League home games. His Facebook post this morning was a picture of all the tickets and programmes he'd collected this season, with the caption, "If Carlsberg did football seasons!" And he's right, it has been the most glorious of seasons, one that he, indeed anyone, may never see again, and there came my slight pique of jealousy again. Why couldn't my team make me feel like that? Why did I have to watch others feeling like that? I wanted some of it. But I couldn't, and almost definitely never will.

Less than two weeks ago I also witnessed something incredible, something unbelievable, something truly staggering on a football pitch. Two nights running in fact. On the Tuesday, Liverpool had come back from 3-0 down against Barcelona to win 4-0 at Anfield and so 4-3 on aggregate to go through to the European Champions League final. The following night Spurs had come back from 2-0 down against Ajax, in Amsterdam, already being 1-0 down from the first leg, to win 3-2 and go through on the away goals rule. They won the game with literally the last kick of the allowed time. They would go onto meet Liverpool in the final. The most extraordinary two nights of footballing drama I've ever seen. Again, the faces of the disbelieving fans, full of tears and ecstasy, made me feel that increasingly stubborn pang of jealousy again. Well, a bit.

I've seen a lot of football, either being present at games, or on television, and these two matches on consecutive nights were nothing less than astonishing, incredible, unbelievable, stunning, and many other synonyms I can't be bothered to look up. The raw emotion and drama that was created over something as ultimately pointless as kicking and heading a ball around a field, trying to get it into your opponents' goal more times than they get it into yours, is what makes the game of football so exciting, passionate and intense.

Anybody who says that football is just pointless is absolutely correct. And yet that is why millions, even billions of people around the globe love it and consume it so richly. The spontaneous power and intensity of emotions created by football is far greater than the life changing events that you're meant to feel such emotion at. Yes, I cried at the birth of my children, but I certainly didn't leap around the birthing suite screaming with bulging, insane eyes, Marco Tardelli style.

Yes, I felt the most intense love looking into my wife's eyes as I married her, but I didn't take my shirt off and start swinging it round my head, revealing my Ryan Giggs style hairy chest, just as Giggs had done in 1999 after scoring the winning goal in the FA Cup semi-final. If I had done that, then it would certainly have made the ceremony more memorable for the spectators, if not deeply alarming and probably quite frightening for my unsuspecting new bride of the last ten seconds. That's what football can do. It can turn you into a lunatic, someone where the appropriate withholding of emotions in public places does not seem to work.

That's what I saw in the eyes of those Liverpool, Tottenham Hotspur and Manchester City fans' eyes, and many other supporters' eyes over the years.

My team has never, and probably will never, make me feel like that.

I support Preston North End.

Part One

Dad Before Me

1957-1977

Before you all start crying out that this is just a rip off of Nick Hornby's 1992 "Fever Pitch", then you are right. Why wouldn't I want to rip off something so great as that book? It has entertained and inspired me, indeed has been actually life changing for me, so I make no apology for the blatant copying of the format. With both books, there is an element of nostalgia. Quite a lot of nostalgia actually. But as we all know, books about nostalgia aren't what they used to be.

Hornby talks about how he sees life not in years, but in seasons. This is even more so for me, as the football season roughly equates to the academic year, give or take a month, and seeing as my whole life has been governed by academic years, as a school pupil, as a university student, and as a teacher my whole working life, then this splitting up of my life into seasons seems perfectly normal.

However, despite the format being similar, the fact remains that Nick Hornby is an Arsenal fan. Despite being humiliated in this season's Europa League Final, at least his team got to a final and at least had a chance of winning a trophy. If they had won, then they would have gone into the hallowed realms of the Champions League next season. His team, although not winning much at the moment, is still Arsenal, one of the biggest clubs in the country, one of the biggest clubs in Europe, where top-flight football is the norm. Finishing in the top six is expected for such a team.

Such wonders are just a pipe dream for me.

Hornby's book culminates with him having the most mind-blowing experience ever, one that will probably never be repeated for his team, winning the league with almost the last kick of the last game. It was truly astonishing, and to use the corny phrase, if a scriptwriter pitched that idea, then they would have been laughed out of the room, as it was just too far-fetched. I'm guessing that Nick Hornby will never ever feel that way again. Even if Arsenal win the

Champions League, it won't have that sense of catharsis, that utter and total joy.

The fact remains that the vast majority of football teams, players, and most of all, fans, never get to experience such wondrous things. This book could be about Plymouth Argyle, or Rochdale, or Cambridge United, or Oxford United, or Northampton Town, or Scunthorpe United, or Shrewsbury Town, or Exeter City, or Mansfield, or Torquay United. The list could go on to include at least half of all the teams in the whole football league, the point being that most teams never have a chance of winning anything, or getting anywhere near the Premier League.

Just to get into the Premier League and get beaten 5-0 every week would be at least something for teams like mine and all the others mentioned. At least we would have earned the right to get beaten 5-0 every week, rather than just in the vagaries of a cup competition where games against these giants occasionally happen.

***

I'm conscious of my use of the pronoun "we" here. I've had arguments with friends of mine when I use "we" when talking about my team. They complain and ask how can I say "we" when I was not playing, I'm not a part of the team etc. But all true football fans say "we" when referring to their team. That is because we are part of the club. If it wasn't for us then the club would not exist. Put simply "we" are the most important thing about any football club, and so I will unashamedly use the word "we" when referring to Preston North End.

"We" were one of the founding members of the Football League, along with eleven other clubs, and the first ever season was the one to be a Preston fan. Oh, the halcyon days of 1888/89! What a glorious season it must have been. Previously to this season we had beaten Hyde United 26-0 in an FA Cup tie, a record which still stands as the biggest win in an English first-class football tie. From these heady heights, we must have entered into that first season with a certain amount of expectation. Little did we know that by the end of that inaugural season, we would have done something that no one else would ever do. I know there were only twelve teams in the league, but we won the league that year without losing a game. It would take another 115 years for a team to do that. Sorry Arsenal (and Nick Hornby) but your "Invincibles" of 2004 were not the first or the original Invincibles. And to top it off, we also won the FA Cup that year without even conceding a single goal. The first ever season, the first ever league and cup Double, the first and original Invincibles.

To say that being a Preston fan has been downhill ever since is putting it mildly. We did retain the league again the following season, but it would not be until 1938 (the first ever televised Cup Final) that we won the FA Cup again, with a team that included the almost mythical figure of Bill Shankly, before he became a manager and turned Liverpool into the club they are today. Since then, absolutely nothing, zilch, zero. We have been promoted and relegated a few times, but since 1961 when we were relegated from the top division, we have never been back into what is now called the Premier League.

For us Preston fans, there has never been a club where the ultimate success arrived so early that it happened before anyone really cared.

Preston North End v Luton Town

April 30th, 1960   Deepdale

In those brief points in time where I find myself asking the questions, why did I have to be a Preston fan, why couldn't my dad have supported someone like Liverpool, Manchester City or even Manchester United? In those moments of slight jealousy, I remember the old phrase "You don't choose your club, your club chooses you." And that's the point. I had no choice as to whether I would be a fan of any other club. Those "fans" who tell me they chose to support a team rather than another one, I will always view with a certain suspicion. There has to be a reason behind why we support our teams, and as with most people, it comes down to their parents, and geography.

In the classroom when I proudly wear my PNE tie and the kids ask me why I support such an awful team, my answer is simple: my grandad supported them; my dad supported them; I support them. My daughter now supports them, and I would like to think that her children will support them too. It's as simple as that. "Yeah but they're rubbish, and they never win anything!" the kids reply, and at that point any thoughts of jealousy instantly vanish, and sheer pride wins out in my emotional battle. Yes, compared to those other teams, we are rubbish, but at least I support them despite them being rubbish.

Occasionally I then ask the kids who they support, and they respond with the usual mix of Premier League clubs just mentioned. I then ask how often they go to watch their team, and more often than not, they have never been to a single game. I've been to so many Preston games, and the vast majority of them have not brought me any sort of happiness; just frustration, boredom, and on some occasions, anger.

A few times I come back happy, hopeful, even exhilarated at times, but whatever the result, I always feel pride at supporting such a team. And for that, I have my dad to thank.

***

My father was born in 1946 and grew up in the small railway town of Carnforth, about seven miles north of Lancaster, just round the coast from Morecambe. Deepdale, in Preston, was the nearest league ground (Morecambe FC were very much a non-league team then; it wouldn't be for another 50 years or so that they would gain league status) and there was a direct bus route which would go all the way to Preston. As I said, geography chooses your team too.

My grandad and his brother-in-law, as with thousands of other working-class men, held a reverence for Tom Finney. Finney was without doubt one of the greatest footballers ever, and he just happened to play for Preston. He had fought in the war with men like my grandad, and after resuming his playing career, he created an affinity with such men.

Like the men who idolised him, Finney was working class and humble. He would often share the bus with the fans going to Deepdale after knocking off at his plumbing firm at lunchtime. This was way before the maximum wage was abolished, and instead of being a millionaire superstar, which had he played in a different era he would undoubtedly have been, he was more like those fans who were going to watch him. A typical working man who enjoyed his football, he just happened to be one of the most talented and gifted players ever. My grandad wanted to watch him not simply because of his footballing ability, but also because he felt a solidarity with him.

He and his brother-in-law would occasionally treat themselves to an afternoon at the football. Money was always tight; he didn't own a car and so had to rely on public transport, so occasionally he and his brother-in-law would go to Deepdale on the bus and watch the greatest player of his time (Blackpool fans would argue that it was Stanley Matthews, but in my totally unbiased opinion, they were wrong). And once he was big enough, my dad would accompany them too.

Back then, during the late 1950s, the crowds at Deepdale would regularly be in excess of 30,000, and when playing big local rivals who would bring many thousands of their own fans, the attendances would be almost 40,000. He has told me on many occasions how he was passed over the heads of the fans, as many of the younger boys were, down to the front where all these small boys aged between 7 and 11 would be sitting cross-legged on the side of the pitch, literally within touching distance of the maestro Tom Finney.

Preston's highest attendance of the 50s was 39,553 in 1954 against Bolton Wanderers, then a huge club with the great Nat Lofthouse playing for them. This may well have been slightly too early for my dad, but in 1957, he attended a match against Manchester United where 39,066 fans were there. This wasn't just any Manchester United team, this was legendary and doomed Busby Babes, including the now almost mythical figure of Duncan Edwards.

I can only imagine the excitement my dad must have felt sitting there on the side of the pitch watching Tom Finney, the greatest player at the time, and a player in Duncan Edwards, who most people say would have taken over the mantle of Finney, and would have become possibly the best player ever, rivalling players such as Pele, Cruyff and Messi. My dad saw him play, not just on the television, but from literally a few feet away.

But it was on Saturday April 30th, 1960, when my dad was 13 years of age, that the earliest programme in my collection comes from. I don't think it's an original, it's far too clean and unworn. It was probably bought by my dad at a later date as a souvenir replica and in the middle of the programme is Tom Finney's autograph, next to a picture of him about to put in yet another perfectly weighted cross from the right wing.

Below the picture the caption is *"Tom Finney makes for goal – one of countless impeccable memories of a legendary footballing wizard."* This is the programme from Finney's final ever game at Deepdale before he retired. The attendance that day was 29,781 and Preston thankfully won 2-0, allowing the greatest player my club, and possibly my country has ever seen, to bow out on a winning note. And my dad, and my grandad were there to see it.

The following season Dad was allowed to start going to games on his own. He used to save up his pocket money so that every other Saturday he would get the bus, a little fold up stool under his arm, and go and watch his team, the team that no longer had Tom Finney in it. A team that inevitably would never be able to replace such a player, a team that must have felt rather bewildered without their talisman, and a team that were relegated from the top division by the end of the season, in April 1961. My dad would never see them in the top-flight ever again. But at least he saw them in the top division. I have yet to do so, and may never do.

He also got to see them in the FA Cup Final, again something that I can only dream of doing. Dad's dream came true, sort of, when he was only seventeen, and what a day it must have been for him.

Preston North End v West Ham United

FA Cup Final   May 2nd, 1964

Wembley Stadium

After being relegated three seasons before, Preston managed to reach the FA Cup Final, despite being in the second division. The West

Ham team were captained by Bobby Moore and also included Geoff Hurst up front, and we all know what they both went onto achieve two years later in the same stadium. It's fair to say that Preston were the underdogs for this game.

My dad had left school at the age of 15 to become an apprentice joiner in a local firm, and by the age of 17 he was still regularly making the bus trip down to Deepdale, although the stool was no longer needed. He even got brave for one match and tested his new pride and joy out, his newly purchased Lambretta scooter, and drove it all the way down to Deepdale. He had never been further south than Preston, apart from visiting his grandparents who lived near Bristol, and so the prospect of going to the Cup Final, in a crowd of 100,000, in the huge metropolis of London, must have seemed pretty daunting for him. He hadn't even planned to go as he couldn't really afford it; London was just so far away and so big. But his own dad came up trumps.

On the Friday evening before the day of the Final, my grandad came home from work with a surprise for his son. A group of colleagues from the office had all got themselves tickets for the game, but at the last minute, one of them could no longer make it, and so my grandad presented my 17-year-old dad with what must have felt like a Willy Wonka golden ticket. My fairy grandfather said "Yes, you shall go to the match."

The following morning dad boarded a special Cup Final train which would go straight to Wembley station. No need to change trains and access the underground system. It was almost a door to door service. He walked up Wembley Way towards the iconic twin towers and went straight into the ground to soak up the atmosphere. What followed would not be the last time that West Ham would break Preston hearts. I would experience similar heartbreak much later.

14

Cup Finals happen every year, but not all of them are historic ones. This one was. A bit anyway. Howard Kendall, who would go onto win the league twice as manager of Everton in the mid-80s, would become the youngest ever player in a Cup Final, at the age of 17 years and 345 days, not much older than my own dad at the time. This record would be broken 16 years later and then again subsequently, but at the time, Kendall's appearance at least made the game historic. Kind of.

Preston's team would also contain many of my dad's early heroes. From Alan Kelly in goal (who would have one of the stands at Deepdale named after him), to Alan Spavin, a Lancaster lad who would open up a sports shop in Lancaster with his goalkeeper team mate. "Spavin and Kelly Sports" would be the shop where I got my first ever pair of football boots, Alan Spavin himself serving my dad as he paid for them. I remember my dad being slightly in awe of him, even though I had very little idea of who he was. He sold me a great pair of boots though.

There would also be two players who had come from the great Manchester United. After the tragedy of Munich, two young lads, Nobby Lawton and Alex Dawson would be a part of the rebuilding process, playing for Sir Matt Busby until the team was put back together and true replacements found. Both players found their chances in the first team limited, so moved to Preston in the early 60s, to go onto become club legends at Deepdale.

As for the match itself, after two early goals, one for each team, Alex Dawson, affectionately known as The Black Prince, went onto score just before half time, putting Preston 2-1 up. I have no idea why he gained that nickname, as he was neither black nor a prince. It was presumably something to do with his jet-black hair and rather haunting face underneath it. His goal just before half time gave my dad hope that his efforts to get down to Wembley would result in a win for Preston. Little did he, my dad, or every other Preston fan at the time know that this would be the last ever goal we would score in an FA Cup Final.

Early in the second half Geoff Hurst would equalise with a header that came down from off the underside of the crossbar and went in. Unlike two years later in the World Cup Final, this goal definitely, without any doubt whatsoever went over the line, although the ball only went in after hitting the keeper on its way back out.

The game must have been very tense and tight for the final half an hour, both sets of supporters getting themselves mentally prepared for extra time, before Ronnie Boyce headed the winner for West Ham with literally seconds to go. My dad's dreams were crushed by a bloke who sounded like an East End gangster.

Preston nearly won the Cup that day. But it was only nearly, and this is what life for my dad would be as a Preston fan: we would always be second best, never quite having what it takes to go on and win. But at least he saw them in the FA Cup Final at Wembley. It would be another 30 years before Preston, and my dad, would be there again, this time with me in tow. And it certainly wouldn't be in the FA Cup Final.

The final image from the DVD which he leant me is Bobby Moore, holding the trophy high above his head whilst being carried on the shoulders of his jubilant teammates. Now where would we see that again? But for dad, he was left with nothing but what ifs and an acute sense of disappointment as he travelled home. Such is life for a Preston fan.

***

Preston would continue to be a nearly team. The expectation of getting back into the top division gradually turned into a faint hope, before fading into a distant dream. We were relegated into Division Three for the first time in our history in 1970.

We managed to come straight back up though, so that by the time I arrived in the world in April 1973, Preston were struggling to stay in Division Two. We survived by the skin of our teeth that season, but succumbed to the inevitable the following season. Season 1973/74, the first full season that I was alive, ended in relegation, despite us being managed by none other than Bobby Charlton, who had left Manchester United to become player/manager with us. As is so often the case, truly great players do not become great managers.

We then tried Harry Catterick, the very successful manager of Everton in the 60s, but he could never quite get us over the line. In came another World Cup winner at the end of the 1976/77 season. Nobby Stiles actually got us promoted back into Division Two in his first season but could not take us any further. Preston would prove to be rather toothless under Nobby.

Little did I realise that when I started going to watch Preston with my dad, that we would have had two World Cup winners as our managers.

It would seem that winning the World Cup would be easier than winning anything with Preston, and nothing could help us in the early 1980s.

We were doomed.

Part Two

Dad and Me

1978 -1999

Nottingham Forest v Hamburg

European Cup Final

May 28th, 1980   Bernabeu Stadium, Madrid

Some of my very earliest memories of football are nothing to do with my beloved Preston North End. I have vague recollections of the 1978 World Cup finals in Argentina. Whenever Archie Gemmill's goal against Holland was replayed, my dad would always tell me that Archie used to play for Preston, which always gave me a certain sense of pride, even though I'd never heard of him at that point, as he'd played for Preston three years before I was even born.

The scenes at the 1978 World Cup Final, with the clouds of ticker tape everywhere, are seared into anyone's memories who saw them, but I do not remember a thing apart from that. I was far too busy playing with my Lego, or my Action Man, or my train set, or reading my Spiderman comics for football to take over my consciousness at the age of five. I was obviously aware of it and knew that silver or gold trophies were won during the months of May and July, but I didn't really know the rules properly. As far as being a football fan was concerned, then it would take a lot to pull me away from my remote-controlled car or Scalextric track.

Perhaps the first ever vague memory I have is of going to Anfield to watch the great Liverpool team of the late 70s. Well, when I say watch, I seemed to spend the whole match looking at the backs of other people's legs, apart from the times my dad would put me on his shoulders, but even then, I still couldn't see very much. My older brother has always been a bit of a glory supporter and obviously the team who got all the glory back then was Liverpool. (Funnily enough my brother's allegiance switched to Man United in the 90s). I was conscious of the fact that they had won the biggest of the silver trophies, the one with the massive handles when I was four and five in 1977 and 1978.

As a treat to my older brother, my dad took us all, mum included, down to Anfield. Apart from Wembley, my dad had never been to a big ground before, and he wanted to see this great stadium and team too, but as I said, all I remember is standing in one of the corner sections of Anfield, where it wasn't sloped and looking at the backs of people's legs. I don't know who Liverpool were playing, or what the score was, but hey, at least I can say that I've watched a game at Anfield, and seen what was then undoubtedly the best team not only in England, but all of Europe.

Again, my Lego and Scalextric were briefly interfered with by the 1980 FA Cup Final. I became very much aware of how big a game the Cup Final was back then, seeing as there was never any football on television, apart from Match of the Day which was way past my bedtime back then. There was certainly no live football shown back then, and so my parents would sit down to watch the Cup Final, whilst I would be building a new car or a spaceship with my big box of Lego. I vaguely remember Trevor Brooking scoring the winning goal in a very dull match to win the Cup for the then second division West Ham who remain the last ever team to win the cup from outside the top division.

I also remember my dad getting vey animated at the most cynical of fouls ever committed. Paul Allen, who by playing, would break Howard Kendall's record of being the youngest ever player in a final, was about to become the youngest ever scorer in a final. He was clean through with just Pat Jennings to beat before Willie Young scythed him down with no attempt to play the ball. What made it worse was that Young only received a yellow card, but this challenge would instigate the FA's decision to order referees to issue a straight red card for what would become known as the professional foul. At least it didn't affect the outcome of the match, the underdogs winning out on the day. I asked my dad why he wanted West Ham to win so much, particularly as they had crushed his dreams in the last minute back in 1964, and his reply was that if ever there was a match where he was completely neutral, with no affinity in terms of family members, or geography, then always support the underdog. This is a tenet I continue to follow.

A couple of weeks after the Cup Final we went away on holiday during the late May half term for a week in Llandudno. The hotel we stayed at, as was the case with all but the best hotels back then, did not provide televisions in each room. Instead there was a communal TV room, usually frequented by middle aged men who were escaping from their wives and families for an hour or so.

This was the week of the European Cup Final and my dad wanted to obviously watch it to see if Nottingham Forest could retain the trophy. Back then I did not realise just what a huge achievement it was for a small team like Forest to not only have won the League, but then go onto win the ultimate in European football the following season. All I knew was that Kevin Keegan would be playing against them.

Keegan had left Liverpool in the summer of 1977, to be replaced by Kenny Dalglish, and in the late 70s was a true superstar of the game, perhaps the biggest name in European, if not world football. He was European Footballer of the Year, having won it for the last two seasons, and he was English, so inevitably was quite prominent on my footballing radar. I naturally thought that whoever he played for was the team my dad, and so I, wanted to win, not realising that Hamburg were from Germany. I fully expected my dad to be of the same belief as we sat down to watch in the communal TV room, with a few other men who were prepared to forego the delights and temptations of the Llandudno night life.

My dad quickly picked up on my enthusiasm for Keegan and my desire for his team to win, and soon put me right. "Always support the English team son". Another tenet I have continued to follow. And that was that. Instantly my allegiance switched to Nottingham Forest. I have no affinity with the team, never have and never will, but that night, because my dad had told me to, I was a Forest fan, and was mildly pleased when John Robertson scored the winner and John McGovern lifted the big silver trophy with the massive handles again.

Being a Preston fan, club rivalries never come into the equation when a big game is being played. I know many Man United and Liverpool fans who want nothing more than their rivals to be beaten, even if it meant an English team didn't win. Not me. Always support the English team. But let's face it, Preston's arch-rivals are Blackpool, and the chances of them ever reaching a European final are even less than Preston's.

Looking back now, it is unfathomable really how teams such as Nottingham Forest, and a couple of years later, Aston Villa, were able to lift the Holy Grail of the European Cup. Gabriel Clarke's excellent documentary "When English Football Ruled Europe" covers the six consecutive seasons from 1977-1982 when English teams couldn't stop winning the European Cup.

Liverpool's three wins during those years, although huge achievements, were not particularly surprising as Liverpool were and still are a huge club with a massive global fan base, with the ability to buy some of the best players in the world. Indeed it is no surprise that they have gone onto win it now for a sixth time. But teams like Nottingham Forest and Aston Villa?

I would argue that it was easier to win the European Cup back then, before it became the Champions League. Ironically the "Champions League" is filled with teams who are not current champions of their country, and indeed never have been champions of their country, well not for 29 years now in the case of Liverpool, the current European Champions.

There are now many more better-quality teams in the competition than there used to be. The second, third and sometimes fourth placed teams from the big three leagues of England, Spain and Italy are better than the champions of countries like France, or Sweden, or Portugal, or Holland, or Norway.

When Nottingham Forest did the now unimaginable, the only teams that played in the European Cup were the champions of each country. There were no group stages and no seeding systems which meant that feasibly the best teams could knock each other out in the early rounds, leaving a much easier route to glory for the teams who had been drawn against the weaker nations' champions.

In 1977 Liverpool beat Borussia Monchengladbach, the German champions. The following year they beat Club Brugge, the Belgian champions. Forest's first win was against the Swedish champions Malmo. These three opponents have never appeared in a European Cup Final since, and probably never will, such is football now. Most kids who watch Champions League games in their Barcelona or Real Madrid shirts will literally have never heard of these teams. They may well not have heard of Nottingham Forest and Aston Villa too. And yet there they were, for three out of four seasons in a row, winning the greatest prize in club football. That would be unimaginable now. In fact, you might as well say that Preston have got more chance of winning the European Cup than Nottingham Forest now, which shows just how ludicrous the situation was between 1979 and 1982.

But Forest have never done the Double without losing a single league game or without conceding a goal in the Cup though have they? Come to think of it, no one has. Except Preston. I was still clinging onto these past glories as I entered my first full season as a Preston fan. Football was now winning the battle against Lego, and as much as I still enjoy Lego, it would be forever more in second place to football.

Season 1980/81

Preston North End v Swansea City

May 2nd, 1981   Deepdale

We all remember that moment; our first football match, holding your dad's hand as he slowly guides you up the steps into the gladiatorial arena of the stadium, all four sides of the pitch thronged with thousands of fans, all crammed into magnificent stands, all roaring and singing in anticipation. The vibrant green of the pitch, floodlit, making it almost glow in the dark night sky. You stand there amazed, overwhelmed, tingling with excitement. A moment you will truly never forget and hope to pass onto your own offspring when the time comes. Well guess what? Deepdale in 1980 was nothing like that.

My first match with my dad at Deepdale must have happened in the Autumn of 1980, but as for the thronging crowds, the swell of noise, the vibrant, glowing colours, all I can remember is how few people were there, the slate grey sky and the black cinder track around the pitch which made the stadium look about as majestic as a slag heap.

Deepdale is now a fantastic stadium, and thankfully I experienced "that" moment at Deepdale only very recently with a good friend of mine who had never been to a football match. I invited him to come to a game at Deepdale with me, and not just any old game against any old team: it was to be a big local derby against our Lancashire rivals Blackburn Rovers.

I knew the stadium would be full as Rovers would completely sell out their allocated end. It was late Autumn and so the floodlights were already on as we walked up the steps into the stadium. I hasten to add that he wasn't holding my hand though, we are both in our mid-forties after all, but I distinctly remember him stopping at the top step and being in a certain amount of awe at what he beheld in front of him. For once Deepdale was packed, with well over 20,000 fans inside, and he had "that" moment there and then which I never had as a boy. To top it off, Preston were 1-0 up after just two minutes, 2-0 up after ten, eventually winning the game 4-1. I had to explain to him that it wasn't always like that.

But back in 1980 Deepdale was not to put too fine a point on it, a bit of a dump. The terraces were slightly crumbling and all I remember was the amount of empty space on them. When I was bored, which was very often, I could literally run around at the bottom of the terrace, using the so-called crush barriers as climbing frames or balancing beams, swinging on them and occasionally being brave enough to swing right over and land on my feet the other side. They certainly weren't used to prevent crushes in the crowd, as the average attendance back then was just over seven and a half thousand in a stadium that had accommodated well over 30,000 a few decades earlier.

The "toilets" were simply a black painted cell, stinking of piss which collected into a gutter at the bottom, and would frequently overflow if there was some sort of blockage, making your shoes or trainers wet with other people's piss. I don't even remember actual toilets with doors on each cubicle. And as for hand washing facilities, there simply weren't any. It's no wonder very few women went to games back then.

And so it was into this great cauldron of footballing excellence that I would go to most games with my dad. My first game could have been against the mighty Grimsby Town or Wrexham, it might have been against Shrewsbury or Oxford United, it could also have been against Chelsea, Newcastle or West Ham, all Premier League teams now, as they were all in Division Two that season.

I definitely remember going away to Ewood Park on a snowy Boxing Day to endure a mind numbingly dull and piercingly cold 0-0 draw, possibly and very probably my first ever away game. I think I would have still preferred to have been sat at home playing with my new Lego set whilst Steve McQueen tried to escape from the Germans by jumping over barbed wire on his motorbike. But instead I was being tutored by my dad into the art of being a fan of Preston North End, a team that ultimately were not good enough in that first season of mine.

We had some decent players actually; Alex Bruce, the redheaded Scottish centre forward was my favourite simply because he scored most of our goals. However, there were not enough of them to keep us up. I vaguely remember Steve Doyle in midfield and Steve Elliot, a cast off from the European Champions Nottingham Forest, partnering Bruce up front, but they still couldn't score enough goals to keep us in the division.

The game I remember most vividly was our final home game of the season, against Swansea City, who had been in the depths of Division Four only three seasons earlier. If Swansea won, then they would be promoted to the top division for the first time ever, and relegate us to Division 3, which they duly did. In this one game I would experience the extreme juxtaposition of emotions between the two sets of fans, and mine would be of the negative kind. Swansea beat us 3-1 but it could have been five or six. Three was enough though. The Swansea fans were delirious with joy; ours were whatever the opposite of delirious with joy is, and as we trudged back to the car, I started to cry.

Preston would spend the next 18 years, all my childhood and a significant part of my adulthood, in one of the bottom two divisions. The realisation in that moment that Preston North End, my football team, were one of the three worst teams in the division and so didn't deserve to be in the same division next season made me cry. Not because of my deep emotional connection with the team, I hadn't been to enough games for that, but more because of my dad's face. He looked almost guilty for dragging me along to watch a team that really were not very good.

As we drove home, listening to Sports Report on the radio with James Alexander Gordon confirming the score for us, even though I was crying at being relegated, I certainly did not want my dad to feel guilty. The opposite in fact. I wanted to make him feel proud that I had become, by default, a Preston fan. Disappointment would be a staple part of my footballing life, and so I might as well accept it and get on with it. I wasn't going to change my team. I wasn't going to suddenly develop a love for another hobby or pastime. I was going to be a proper Preston fan from now on. And that meant accepting we were a bit rubbish, but if they were good enough for my dad, then they were good enough for me.

It wasn't just because of the football, in fact it had very little to do with the football. I remember very little about any of the games back then apart from asking dad how long was left, when there was always at least half an hour left. It was simply because my dad had asked if I wanted to go with him to the football. My dad was, and still is in many ways, my hero and if sitting on a cold wooden bench or standing in the freezing cold watching Preston play meant spending time with my dad, then that's where I'd be. I wanted to show him that he had somebody else to suffer with. If we were going to watch a crap team, then at least we'd watch our crap team together.

But then along came a couple of games of football which would help me get over my grief and disappointment of relegation, and restore my ability to at least dream of being any good.

Manchester City v Tottenham Hotspur

FA Cup Final   **May 9th, 1981**

FA Cup Final Replay   **May 14th, 1981**

Wembley Stadium

However much the BBC, or BT, or whoever has the rights to the FA Cup bang on about how the magic of the Cup has not and will never fade, I'm sorry but I don't believe them. They may put out inspiring trailers for the competition, but most football fans would agree with me; the FA Cup does not have the same appeal as it did before the might and power of The Premier League got going. Just as a juggernaut takes a bit of time to get going, once it does gain momentum, it will literally smash anything out of its way. The Premier League has smashed the once glorious FA Cup out of its way and without doubt it has been demoted to a less significant competition.

Most fans, like me, are not as excited about an FA Cup weekend if it means the normal Premier League fixtures are just not there. It's nowhere near as dull as an International break but the prospect of a lot of games where the outcome is so predictable is just not as appealing. Yes, we get the occasional shock or upset, and our faith in the old competition is restored for a short while, but this is very rare these days. Much as I love Gabby Logan or Dan Walker, a Match of the Day with either of these presenting, rather than Gary Lineker, is just not as good.

But back in 1981, I not only watched my first proper FA Cup Final, but absorbed everything about the game. This was when the FA Cup mattered, perhaps even more than the league. This was down to a number of factors: firstly, the amount of football on television these days is enough to sate and perhaps even saturate the most ardent of football fans. Live football can be watched every single day of the week, with two, three, four, even five games all being shown live on one single Sunday if you can be bothered to watch the games from the other European leagues as well. Back then, the FA Cup Final was the only live game shown all season, and I, with millions of others, was like someone roaming desperately around the desert, slowly dying of thirst before finding the oasis of the FA Cup Final, beamed straight into our front rooms for us all to drink in. We didn't just drink it in, we lapped it up, we bathed in it. It was our life saver.

Secondly, this was the only time, apart from England games, that Wembley was used. I understand why Wembley is used nowadays for the semi-finals too, but getting to Wembley meant so much more for the players back then. Very few players got to play there, whereas now with the play-off system, lower league and even non-league players get the chance to play there every season.

The more magic you show to people, the more likely the magic will lose some of its aura and mysticism. Getting to play at Wembley was the Holy Grail for many players, whereas now, so many more players get the opportunity. I'm not saying it's a bad thing, but inevitably the magic of the FA Cup final has been diminished.

Thirdly, the rewards for winning the Cup were much greater back then. Winning League Division One was great but the financial rewards were not particularly great. Nothing in comparison to today with the millions up for grabs for getting into the Champions League. It's no wonder that most teams would prefer to finish fourth in the league and qualify for the riches of the Champions League than to win the Cup and get to play in the Europa League. If Preston had any chance of finishing fourth in the Premiership, then no doubt I would be exactly the same. Why concentrate on the Cup if there is a chance of the Champions League? But back then, the Cup really mattered. A lot of teams would gladly finish second, third or fourth if it meant they won the Cup instead.

So, after the harsh reality of Preston's relegation the previous Saturday, I woke up on Cup Final day with the return of dreams in my head. If Preston were never going to play in the Cup Final again, then maybe one day I would. From that day on, when someone asked me what I wanted to do when I grew up, my answer would be to play in the Cup Final and score the winner. Not too much to ask.

I loved everything about Cup Final day. I drunk in every aspect of it. I jumped out of bed and went downstairs to assume my position for the rest of the day. I sat in my front room, as close to the television as I was allowed, and literally only moved to go to the toilet. Mum brought me my lunch and occasional snacks and drinks so I could be as undisturbed as possible.

The day started with Saturday morning TV, and as my parents disapproved slightly of the much more riotous and frankly fun Tiswas, Noel Edmonds' Multi-coloured Swap Shop it was. Between the usual bouts of Cheggers, Maggie Philbin, John Craven and of course the bearded one, we were given regular updates on the teams who would be playing later that afternoon. We were given access to their hotels before and after an episode of the awesome "Top Cat", before handing over to presumably Jimmy Hill for Cup Final Grandstand.

Looking back now to that first ever Cup Final I was glued to, the match and the coverage of it seems quite quaint now. We had the obligatory helicopter shots of both coaches leaving their respective hotels and travelling to Wembley. We had cheeky cockneys Chas n

Dave's video of their song with the Spurs team, Ossie Ardiles becoming an unwitting star of "Tottingham", the teams' pre-match walkabout on the pitch in their very snazzy suits, and what seemed like endless chat with the pundits in the build up to kick off. We also were treated to a little bit of the Scots' Guards marching band, another lovely and rather quaint tradition of the Cup Final.

"Abide with Me" was sung before the teams came out. It has always puzzled me why we should have a hymn being sung before a game of football, but even that had its charm and a certain innocence with the traditions being carried on from when it was first sung in 1927. I'm still not sure why that hymn is sung with its rather dark lyrics – "When other helpers fail and comforts flee, Help of the helpless, O abide with me." Maybe it was simply preparing the eventual losers of the forthcoming match to keep things in perspective.

And then the teams were led out, always from behind the right-hand side goal as we watched on the television. The noise was quite staggering, so what it must have been like in the stadium I could only imagine. The pre-match rituals of the coin toss and handshakes, and then we were ready. I did not care who won, despite Man City being the underdogs and from the North. My childish affections had been slightly swayed towards Spurs by Chas n Dave, but not to the point that I was on their side. I was on no team's side, so I could just enjoy the football without any emotional attachment.

I remember very little about the game apart from the two goals, both scored by Man City's Tommy Hutchison, the oldest player on the pitch that day. His first goal, in the first half, was a glorious diving header from the edge of the penalty area. After this goal, I assumed that only great goals were allowed to be scored in the Cup Final, but this assumption was put right in the second half when the same player deflected a free kick, which would have gone wide, into his own net to equalise for Spurs. It seemed so very unfair and was my first experience of football being such a cruel mistress. In John Motson's commentary, he says that Hutchison scored at both ends, and I remember being confused by this as he plainly did not score at both ends. He scored at the same end, but in different halves, but we all know what Motty meant.

The game went into extra time, and again I assumed that this was par for the course. Not only was I getting to watch a live football match in front of my own television, in my own front room, but this game came with a bonus extra half an hour attached. I was actually hoping, once John Motson had mentioned the possibility of a replay, that there wouldn't be any more goals, as then we would get to do it all again in five days' time.

And that's exactly what happened, the first ever time a Cup Final Replay would be held at Wembley. Two for the price of one. We would all be able to drink at the oasis again, and this time, it would be under the floodlights. Even better.

School dragged that week, crawling on until Thursday evening. No Noel Edmonds this time, thank God, and straight after my tea I settled down again. The anticipation was perhaps even greater this time as I knew what to expect. What I didn't expect was such a great game.

Everyone remembers the Ricky Villa winner where he twisted and turned, beating four of the City defenders, leaving a couple of them on the ground, but some of the other goals were brilliant too. The lead changed hands three times throughout the game, with Villa opening the scoring with a now completely forgotten goal, before Steve Mackenzie hammered in the sweetest of right foot volleys after only ten minutes or so. His is one of the truly great Cup Final goals which very few people seem to remember.

City then converted a penalty early in the second half to take the lead for the first and only time, before a much leaner than now Garth Crooks, levelled the scores and set the stage for Villa's winner. Ricky Villa's run at the City defence seemed to mesmerise the City defenders. It certainly mesmerised me.

There would be no need for extra time this time, but I couldn't be greedy, as the whole match was in effect, extra time. The Spurs' players climbed the famous Wembley steps, collecting an array of scarves on the way, and Steve Perryman lifted the trophy in the mid May dusky twilight. And that was that; my first proper FA Cup Final experience. You never forget your first time, and I certainly haven't.

All that was left of this season was for Liverpool to beat a proper team, Real Madrid, to win their third European Cup in five years, with Alan Kennedy scoring late on. Now we could all look forward to Ian Botham smashing the Aussies all around Headingley, and Prince Charles marrying Lady Diana Spencer. Fairy tales could still happen after all, but Preston's fortunes were about as promising as those of Charles and Diana. The future was rather ominous to say the least.

Season 1981/82

Preston North End v Oxford United

April 24th, 1982   Deepdale

Every fan welcomes the new season with a certain degree of hope. Hope of getting promoted in my case, seeing as we had never been in the top division. For the first time I couldn't actually say that this time next year we could be in Division One, as we were now in Division Three. For every fan, the hope either continues right to the end of the season, or it dwindles away into a different type of hope; hope that their team does not get relegated.

My hope this season was further compounded with the arrival of none other than Tommy Docherty as our new manager, who had won the FA Cup with Man United only a few seasons before. What could go wrong?

We got off to a great start, beating our arch enemies Blackpool 2-1 on the opening day of the season, but it wasn't long before the hope of promotion dwindled away. By December Docherty had been replaced by Gordon Lee, who had been at Everton for the previous four seasons, as we had won only five of our League games so far, one of which was against Portsmouth with Chris Kamara in their side, but I certainly don't remember anything unbelievable happening Jeff, just a dull 1-0 win. By Christmas the hope of promotion had definitely gone and had changed into the other type of hope – would we be able to avoid a second successive relegation?

My enthusiasm for the game, both as a fan and as a player, coincided with Preston's demise, which would end in ignominy a few seasons later with us finishing 91st in the whole League system, which would have meant in this day and age being relegated out of the actual League. Our club's motto of Proud Preston was to be severely tested over the next few seasons.

But this would also be the season that my own playing of the game would start to flourish, as much as an eight-year-old could flourish anyway. My school's House football competition helped immensely with this. Allow me to explain. Once you reached Year 3 and were no longer in the Infants, you would be put into one of four coloured Houses which would compete against each other at sporting events such as football, cricket and sports day, as well as various other more academic competitions.

We would be encouraged to support our teams and even chant from the side-lines. I was put in the Green team ("Greens, Greens, top of the teams!"), and would compete for the Greens the rest of my primary school days against the Blues ("Blues, Blues always lose"), the Yellows (randomly and simply because it rhymed "Yellows, Yellows, big fat fellows!") and finally the Reds ("Reds, Reds, pee their beds, put their nappies on their heads!") who seemed to be the Slytherin of the Houses for some unknown reason, hence the rather strange chant we created for them.

Only the Juniors were allowed to play, and because each team could never muster a whole team from the Upper Juniors of years 5 and 6, then the Captain of each team would have to scrape the barrel and include some of the Lower Juniors to make up the numbers. I had been drafted in for a couple of games the previous season when we were particularly desperate, my only contribution being to kick it away from our goal whenever I could, which I thought I did admirably.

I also remember vividly the first time I headed the ball that season as a seven-year-old little squirt. The ball had gone high into the air and was dropping almost vertically down. I was the only one near to it, so I simply positioned myself under it, closed my eyes and waited for the ball to hit me on the top of my head, which it duly did and went straight back up where it came from. I remember Mr. Hartley ("Fartley Hartley") the referee, laughing loudly at my rather inept clearance. But hey, it stopped the ball from going towards my goal. Mission accomplished.

Now that I was in Year 4, opportunities were becoming much more frequent. I played in quite a few games this season, even getting a couple of goals, which just fuelled my desire to improve and get better. This was when my endless practising in the back garden would start, as mentioned in the opening section of this book.

Kicking a ball against the back gate was becoming far more appealing than Lego by now. Learning to control the ball with one foot before firing it back against the gate took up hours of my time, and I was actually really proud of myself when I hit the same slat in the gate so often that it came loose and fell off, causing some, but very little grumbling from my dad, as I think he was secretly quite proud and impressed.

When it was wet or dark, which it frequently is in the North of England, then I would go into the front room and do the same with a sponge ball that I nagged my mum to get for me, this time using the long patio window curtains as my goal. I'd pile up the cushions and practise scissor kicks and overhead kicks over and over again, although my mum was less impressed when I broke one of her favourite ornaments from the mantelpiece with a wayward volley. I made up for it by saving up my 50p pocket money each week and replacing it with a similar little fancy, a little china horse, purchased from the local knick-knack shop on a Saturday afternoon when Preston were playing away, which she still keeps on her dressing table to this very day.

***

Preston's season dragged on, winning a few more games, drawing a few more, and losing a few more. My only other memory of that season, apart from the Oxford game, which I will get to soon enough, is of a Tuesday night game, possibly against Lincoln, or Doncaster, or Halifax, or some such giant of the game. My dad had asked if I wanted to bring my best friend along to keep me company on the sparse terraces, so I asked him and as he had no idea what he was letting himself in for, he accepted the invitation.

In the car on the way to the ground he'd been asking whether I'd ever touched the ball when it had gone out of play. In all the games I'd been to, the ball had never come anywhere near to me, usually because my dad took us into the old West Stand, but this time we were on the terraces, where there was more chance of being able to touch the ball. We were both leaning against the perimeter advertising hoardings a couple of feet from the nearest supporter, so if the ball went off for a throw-in, we might be able to lean over, pick it up and throw it back to whichever player was to be taking the throw-in.

Lo and behold the ball got kicked out of play and came straight for us. Well nearly. It was caught by the fan who was standing next to my friend, and just as he was about to throw it back, my friend who was quite tall, simply reached up and touched the ball with his index finger. His first ever game and he got to actually touch the ball, something I had never done and have still never done. The ball has always eluded me so far.

We all have dreamt of the ball coming towards us, and we watch it closely before delivering it back onto the pitch with a perfectly timed header, or even taking it on our chest and volleying it back, and I am always extremely jealous of those fans who do that, especially if it's on TV and gets shown to everyone else.

The nearest time since that one other occasion when my opportunistic friend touched the ball, was actually only a few months ago. A sliced clearance was coming straight towards where I was sitting. I readied myself. This was going to be my time for glory. But at the last moment the ball lost its pace and smacked an old fella smack in the face just two rows down from me, breaking his glasses and giving him one almighty shock. He needed to be seen by the medical staff as his glasses had been pushed into his nose and caused bleeding. To be honest, the exact same thing would probably have happened to me, and instead of gloriously heading it back onto the pitch, I would have just embarrassed myself in front of thousands of other fans and would quite possibly have needed a trip to the opticians for a new pair of specs.

If the fact that my friend touched the ball for a split second was a highlight of the season, then you can guess how Preston were doing. By the time my ninth birthday was due, at the end of April, we were in mid-table, with neither hope of getting promoted nor being relegated. Every game was a rather meaningless exercise, but on the Saturday before my birthday, my dad turned yet another meaningless exercise into something that I'll never forget. The result was still meaningless, a 2-2 draw against another team with no hopes for the rest of their season, but for this game I would be the team's mascot for the day.

Many Premier League clubs charge anything up to five or six hundred pounds for a "VIP Mascot Experience" as their glossy websites now proclaim. Even at Preston now it will cost £300 for a young boy or girl to be mascot for the day. According to the PNE website, the price will include: a choice of either the current home or away replica kit, three executive seat match tickets in the Sir Tom Finney Stand, photograph and mascot details in the matchday programme, complimentary copies of the match programme, guided tour of Deepdale, pre-match warm up on the pitch, pre-match meal and refreshments for the mascot and guests in the Greats' Room, walk out with the Preston North End team ahead of kick-off, official centre circle photograph with the team captains, presentation by the man of the match, and official photograph of the presentation. It actually sounds quite reasonably priced with all that's included. I don't know what my dad paid back in 1982, but we certainly didn't get the range of goodies on offer today. Some, but definitely not all.

I was meant to have my name and picture in the programme but someone in the office had messed up, so no picture, and I wasn't able to tell the rest of the fans that day what primary school I went to, who my favourite player was, and what I wanted to be when I grew up. To be fair, because of their mistake, the club gave me a wooden plaque with the club badge on, which stayed on my bedroom wall above my bed for many years. I got a signed football and programme, something that I treasure to this day, especially the autograph of Alex Bruce, who for the record, was still my favourite player, not that the rest of the crowd who had bought a programme knew it!

There was certainly no replica kit, pre-match meal or official photograph included, and the "executive" seats we were given were right behind one of the stanchions holding up the roof, giving us a somewhat limited view of the "action".

I did get a guided tour though, in fact I got more than I was expecting on this particular tour. My anticipation of meeting my heroes rose the closer we got to the team dressing room. Up to now these heroes of mine had been names on the back of the programme and faces that I saw from 20 yards away, but now I was actually going to get to meet them, shake their hands and ask them questions. So, imagine my surprise when my dad and I were shown into the dressing room to find my heroes in various states of undress, some, including Alex Bruce, stark bollock naked.

Remember I was still only eight years old and in your face, full frontal nudity was not something I was used to. Whenever I'd been swimming with my dad, we always had separate changing cubicles, so the sight of my hero's bare naked genitalia was a bit of a shock to say the least.

At least he put a towel round himself when I shook his hand and asked me if I was going to bring them luck. Or at least I think that's what he said. Alex Bruce had a very broad Dundee accent, and I literally did not understand what he said. My dad had to translate it for me, and I just mumbled a rather pathetic "Hope so" back to Alex.

I wasn't so much star-struck by meeting and actually being asked a question by my hero, more so that I was still reeling from the sight of so many bare-naked arses and pubic hair.

With the reddest of faces, I shook the hands of the other players, but was quite pleased when I was taken to a separate little room to change into my own kit, ready to walk out onto the pitch with our captain, Don O'Riordan. The roar of the crowd wasn't exactly deafening, more of an apathetic clap as we emerged out of the tunnel and onto the pitch. I kicked the ball around for a bit, trying to use all that practice I'd been putting in in our back garden, and I remember our keeper purposefully diving over the ball and letting the ball roll into the net so I could at least say that I'd "scored" at Deepdale, with a few fans giving me a rather sarcastic cheer. Now I knew what it felt like to be a Preston player, with ironic applause greeting my shots on goal. At least nobody told me that they could have thrutched harder than that.

I was called into the centre circle and shook hands with the referee and the Oxford United captain, before being given the 5p piece by the referee that he had used for the coin toss. And that was it. I ran off back to the tunnel where my dad had been standing taking photos of me with his new camera, before going up to our seats to watch the match from behind a large metal girder. No other memories remain. Four goals were scored but I remember nothing about them. We simply went home after the match and my dad put my treasured plaque on the wall for me above my bed. So much for the VIP experience. The only VIP treatment I got was Alex Bruce's Very Impressive Penis.

Preston's season petered out and we eventually finished 14th in the League, so successfully avoided any sort of excitement whatsoever, but let's face it, seeing my hero's cock and balls was more excitement than I could actually take. I could now look forward to the FA Cup Final again, which would obviously be as great as last year, or then again, perhaps not.

Tottenham Hotspur v Queens Park Rangers

FA Cup Final   May 22nd, 1982

FA Cup Final Replay   May 27th, 1982

Wembley Stadium

And so the day came round again, and my routine would be basically the same as last year, although I don't know what was on television in the morning as Noel Edmonds and his Swap Shop had finished only a few weeks before and Mike Read's Saturday Superstore would not start until the Autumn. I think the BBC just extended their Cup Final Grandstand from mid-morning, heightening the excitement and anticipation even further.

However, this time the game was rather a disappointment. I had absolutely no allegiances this year, both clubs being from London, although I did like Spurs' Cup Final song, again by cheeky cockneys Chas n Dave ("Spurs are on their way to Wembley, Tottenham's gonna do it again…") which may have swayed me towards them. QPR were managed by Terry Venables, someone who would have a much bigger impact on all of us 14 years later.

The game actually finished 0-0 after 90 minutes, with not a single memorable thing happening before Glenn Hoddle put Spurs ahead in extra-time with, for him, a not particularly clean strike. Spurs were showing their defensive weakness from set pieces, a theme that continues to this day, by allowing Terry Fenwick the chance to head in an equaliser from inside the six-yard box. And that was about it.

The replay offered even less drama, Hoddle slotting home a penalty after only six minutes which Spurs held onto for a 1-0 win. None of the glory and drama of the previous year, certainly no spectacular goals from Argentinians. Ossie Ardiles didn't even play, and Ricky Villa was fairly anonymous, which was understandable seeing as our country was actually at war with theirs at the time.

These two games did introduce me to the wonders of Glenn Hoddle though. He had not made a huge impact on me the previous year, but his two goals registered him on my radar and I instantly was entranced with him. He moved with such grace and poise, spraying passes all around the field from his central midfield role. He was like the hub that made the whole wheel of Spurs' team go around. Basically, without him, they would not have won, and I would go onto drool over him for ever more.

It has been said before, but worth saying again, that Glenn Hoddle was arguably the classiest, the most technically gifted, and yet the most wasted of all England players that have ever put on the shirt. Just go onto YouTube and watch some clips of him. He said himself that he wasn't a great goal scorer, but he was a scorer of great goals. His goals were certainly things of beauty.

He rarely smashed the ball into the net, but when he did, he did it with elegance rather than fury. Many of his goals were passed into the net, which is understandable as he is one of the greatest passers of the ball there has ever been. He could pick out 50, 60, even 70-yard passes and they would reach their target with pinpoint accuracy, the intended target never having to reach or stretch for the ball, and so slowing down the pace of the attack.

So, it was no wonder that many of his goals were passed into the net. If his intended target was the top left-hand corner or the bottom right-hand corner, he could put it wherever he wanted, sometimes with his back to goal. The simply sublime turn and chip against

Watford the following season, leaving Steve Sherwood completely perplexed as to what just happened, is something that very few, if any players, could have done. Those of you who know which goal I mean know exactly what I'm talking about. Those of you who don't, just watch it on YouTube and marvel.

Hoddle only won 53 England caps, which says a lot about English football in the late 1970s and 1980s. Looking down the list of most-capped England players, we get Peter Shilton at the top with 125 (and would have been at least 150, if not more, had it not been for the excellence of Ray Clemence in the great three-time European Cup winning Liverpool team). As for outfield players, players such as Emile Heskey, Gary Cahill, James Milner and even Glenn Johnson all have more caps. Hoddle has as many caps as Gareth Barry.

Not to degrade the efforts of these fine players, all of whom played a perfectly valid role in their respective teams, but I'm sure every one of these players mentioned would all happily say that they had nowhere near the class of Glenn Hoddle. As one of the most Hoddlesque of players, the great Michel Platini, said that if Hoddle were French, he would have won 150 caps.

Arsene Wenger adamantly calls Hoddle a truly world class player, but as I said, Hoddle's rather paltry 53 caps speak volumes for the way the English view such talent. Yes, he didn't "get stuck in", and track back as other midfielders would do, but that wasn't, and should never have been his role. Plenty of other players could perform that role.

Hoddle should have been the absolute focal point of any team he played in, as he was with Spurs, dictating play and running the game from his central midfield role. The French did it with Platini, and they won Euro 84, and again with Zinedine Zidane, winning the World Cup and European Championships in 1998 and 2000 respectively. But for some reason, pure class and skill have never been enough for English teams, be it club or country. The same would happen with the mercurial Matthew Le Tissier, and he even had a French name.

So, it was no wonder that Arsene Wenger, as manager of Monaco, bought Hoddle in the summer of 1987, with the intention of using him as the focal point of his team. Hoddle was simply not English enough to play in England anymore. His talents were far more suited to those continental poncey teams who didn't have the blood and guts of a "proper" player, and couldn't handle it on a cold, wet Tuesday night in Stoke.

I don't blame him for leaving England. As Butch Cassidy kept saying, "I got vision and the rest of the world wears bifocals." Hoddle truly did have vision, whereas English teams and English managers didn't just wear bifocals, they actually were blind to pure talent.

Maybe if they'd opened their eyes a bit more, then Hoddle would have become my ultimate England hero. As it was, that role fell to one Bryan Robson, who ironically was the player who prevented Hoddle from getting more England caps.

It didn't take me long to fall in love with Robson. About 27 seconds actually.

World Cup Finals – Spain 1982

England v France   **June 16th, 1982**

Estadio San Mames, Bilbao

My first World Cup Finals, and for anybody born after 1965, which was frankly a hell of a lot of fans, my first time watching England at a World Cup. I know we were in Mexico in 1970, but anyone who

44

was five and under in 1970 would struggle to remember that tournament. The bright radiant colours of that World Cup (the first one televised in colour) are now almost legendary – Pele, Jairzinho, Carlos Alberto's goal in the final against Italy, Bobby Moore's tackle on Pele, Gordon Banks' save from Pele, Moore and Pele swapping shirts, Jeff Astle's miss, Peter Bonetti's ineptitude as the third and winning German goal was smacked into the net, Germany's revenge for losing at Wembley four years earlier – we all know the 1970 World Cup, but anybody who saw that tournament would not have believed it possible that England, World Cup winners only four years previously, would not be seen at another World Cup until 1982.

My anticipation was almost overwhelming: live football matches, sometimes two or three times a day, almost every day for the next month. It was the gift that kept on giving, especially for a nine-year-old like me who had become obsessed with all things England and all things World Cup related. My mum and dad had bought me a very special book, all about the history of the tournament up to that point, and I devoured it. It was read from cover to cover, at least three times, and the pictures were photographically catalogued in my memory. The details of every tournament so far were ingested and learned by heart. I didn't even realise there was a country called Uruguay until reading this book. I now knew that they'd won the tournament twice already and even who scored for them in each final.

I learnt about the great Ferenc Puskas and how the great Hungarian team of 1954, the one which had humiliated England 3-6 at Wembley only the previous year, were beaten by West Germany, and denied possibly the most romantic of World Cup wins. This was my first realisation that Germany mostly win, and how sentiment in football doesn't register with the Germans, something I would experience again much more acutely in 1990 and 1996, but that's for later chapters.

I learned of the genius of Pele and how he burst into the world's footballing consciousness when he won the tournament in 1958 at the age of just 17, and then again in Chile the following tournament. I also learned how he was literally kicked out of the tournament in 1966. I read the section on 1966 again and again until I could have told anyone who cared to ask (although surprisingly no one ever did) the names and positions of every English and West German player in the final, the times each goal was scored, by whom, and probably what size boots they were wearing too.

I also learned of the disappointments of not qualifying in 1974 and 1978, the demise of Sir Alf Ramsay, the fiasco of Don Revie, and the FA's decision not to appoint Brian Clough. I frankly didn't care. Ron Greenwood had got us to Spain, and I was about to watch my heroes grace this tournament for the first time in my life.

So, after school finished at 3.30pm I ran home as fast as I could, got myself a drink, a bag of crisps and a handful of custard creams, and sat cross-legged in front of the television for the kick-off at 4pm. My parents had also got me a book, it may well have been a pull-out from the daily paper, all about the current England team, so I could get to know them as intimately as possible. My favourite player before the match was Ipswich Town's Paul Mariner, as he was the top scorer in qualifying. It soon changed.

A Steve Coppell throw-in into the box, a nod on by Terry Butcher, before Bryan Robson acrobatically turned the ball into the net with his left foot. 27 seconds into my World Cup experience and we were already 1-0 up. We weren't playing an outsider either. This was France, a team that included Michel Platini, Didier Six, Patrick Battiston and Jean Tigana. They would go onto the semi-finals of the tournament and should probably have got to the final if Germany's Harold Schumacher hadn't brutally launched himself at Patrick Battiston's head, knocking him out cold. The keeper didn't even get booked, let alone sent off, when quite frankly he should have been charged with assault and locked up. And to make matters worse, he was still on the pitch to save the penalty in the shoot-out which ultimately won the semi-final for the West Germans. It would not be the last time the West Germans would break hearts in a World Cup semi-final penalty shootout.

So, we were 1-0 up against France in less than half a minute. I just assumed this was the norm in World Cup games. However, the French came back and equalised before half-time, and it was evenly matched until mid-way through the second half. But then Trevor Francis delivered a beautiful cross from the right-hand side into the penalty area, which was just asking to be put away. With one of his trademark late runs into the box, Robson leapt like the proverbial salmon and executed the most perfect header I had ever seen. His body shape, the way he hung in the air before powering the ball past the keeper, and the way he had rolled his socks down to show his shin pads hypnotised me.

From that point on I would always roll my socks down and show off my own shin pads when I played because that's what Bryan Robson did. His first minute goal was enough to give him hero status; his second transported him into almost the realms of a deity with me. From that point on I was frankly in love with him. Paul Mariner (who?) went onto score a third for England late on to clinch the game, but his idol status had been displaced for another.

Frankly it was all downhill for England from then on. After scoring three against France, we scored two against Czechoslovakia, but could only manage one against the lowly Kuwait, easily qualifying for the second phase group system where we would have to play West Germany and the hosts Spain.

Neither team were the powers they would become, and we should have beaten at least one of them to get to the semi-final. But we could not muster a single goal in two games. I challenge anyone to remember anything about the West Germany game, I certainly don't recall anything of any interest or of any consequence in this game, but we all remember the game against Spain where Ron Greenwood rather desperately put the recently injured Kevin Keegan and Trevor Brooking on with a quarter of the game left in the hope of getting that vital goal which would have put us through.

Brooking had a glorious chance with his left foot to win it, shooting straight at the keeper, before Robson, his socks rolled down again by this stage of the game, floated a ball into the area, only for Keegan to skew his header off target. This was Keegan's only appearance in a World Cup Finals, a whole 26 minutes of frustration. If only it had been the other way around, with Keegan crossing it for Robson to replicate his salmon-leap header against France, we would have been in the semi-finals, and who knows, maybe the final.

England's tournament was over, and just like Preston, we were a nearly team, a team that could, and possibly should have done better. It didn't stop me from idolising Bryan Robson though. I begged my parents for the now iconic Umbro England kit, the one with the blue and red sections on the upper chest. They gave in and my mum even sewed a number 7 on the back, as Robson had now replaced Keegan in the central midfield role. This was back in the days before iron-on numbers were a thing, and she must have spent ages hand stitching my beloved number 7 onto not just that shirt, but subsequent England shirts I got for birthdays or Christmas.

I even wrote a letter to his boot sponsors, New Balance, to explain my devotion to him, and they sent me back a signed poster of my hero, which obviously took pride of place on my wall above my bed, maybe even shifting my Preston plaque along a bit. When the new season started and I was allowed a new pair of boots, my mum gave into my incessant nagging, and instead of getting the usual pair of

Puma boots, she relented and spent a little more on a brand-new pair of New Balance boots. This was the season I would try and emulate Bryan Robson in every possible way. Well, that was the plan anyway.

Brazil v Italy   July 5th, 1982

Estadio Sarria, Barcelona

The thing that struck me most about any Brazil team were how cool their names were. They weren't just foreign and exotic; they were almost serene. Whereas the teams of the 60s and 70s had Pele, Jairzinho, Rivellino and Garrincha, the Brazilian team of 82 had Falcao, Junior, Socrates and Zico. Forget the ancient Greek philosopher, Socrates was the first and best in my mind. But it was Zico who really captured my imagination. If Bryan Robson was my England hero, then Zico would quickly become my other favourite player.

I first saw him and his Brazil team play against Scotland in their group game. The Scots had the temerity to go 1-0 up, with a beautifully struck shot with the outside of the right boot from David Narey. This simply annoyed Brazil and they went on to trounce Scotland 4-1, Zico scoring a sublime free kick into the top corner.

He then went onto score twice against the minnows of New Zealand (their one and only appearance in a World Cup Finals), with his first being particularly special. The ball was crossed in from the right and Zico, from about eight yards out, executed the most perfect scissor kick to slam the ball home. He'd obviously been watching me practise mine with the sponge ball in my front room. I'd never seen anything like it before and from that moment I was entranced by the Brazilians and their golden shirts, long flowing hair, and exquisite football.

So, when they met Italy in the so-called Group of Death second round phase, with Argentina, Maradona and all, already having been disposed of, it was a winner takes all match. In fact, a draw would have done for Brazil as their margin of beating Argentina was greater than Italy's. They had also managed to wind Maradona up enough to get himself sent off for a ridiculously crude challenge. Even better. The Brazil v Italy game was to be a truly great game, easily the best of that tournament, and possibly the best of any tournament.

This time I didn't watch the game at home though. It fell on a Monday and my mum worked later than usual on Mondays, so every week my gran would pick me and my brother up from school and take us to her house. We would always stop at the local corner shop where we were allowed a bag of sweets and a chocolate bar. It was always a quarter of midget gems and a Texan bar, a big slab of nougat and toffee, covered in chocolate, sadly no longer available. And so, with my usual choice of confectionary, I settled down about two feet away from the television, cross-legged again, and became utterly engrossed and enthralled.

I vividly remember the way the pitch had been mown into diagonal stripes. Before then I didn't realise football was ever played on pitches that weren't brown and muddy, even at the beginning of the season. The pitch at Deepdale was somewhat less exotic than the one I was watching now. This one was lush, verdant and gleaming in the bright sun, something else you rarely ever saw in Preston.

Even though they were brilliant as an attacking force, this Brazil team were lacking somewhat in their defensive qualities, which ultimately proved to be their downfall. Italy took the lead after just five minutes, and we all knew we were in for something special as Brazil would have to attack. They duly equalised only seven minutes later with the philosopher Socrates being put through by Zico, before coolly passing the ball into the gap between the keeper and his near post.

Brazil were back in the game and would surely go onto win it now. But no. Rossi would get a second after 25 minutes after yet more defensive frailties and would hold the lead until the 68th minute. Up stepped Falcao to hammer home a pile driver of a left foot shot to equalise again. He ran away in celebration with those mad eyes that Marco Tardelli would take to an even more insane level in the Final.

Surely there was only going to be one winner now. And of course there was, the Brazilian defence forgetting to mark Paulo Rossi who was lurking in the six-yard box, who slotted the winner and his hat-trick goal home. Brazil could not come back for a third time and went out of the tournament at the same stage as England, but at least they gave us some entertainment in the second group phase, unlike the hapless England.

It was a quite breathless game of football. If only it had been the actual final. Instead Italy went onto comfortably beat the West Germans, which everyone, apart from the German fans, was extremely pleased about due to the villainous Schumacher's antics in the semi-final. Rossi would score yet again in the final to claim the Golden Boot and Dino Zoff (another cool name) would lift the World Cup to end a month of footballing heaven.

I wasn't quite sure how I would survive without football for the next few weeks. I'd just have to practise my Robson inspired salmon leap headers, and my scissor kicks, or "Zicos" as I now called them, if I was going to get a starting place in the Green team once we went back to school.

Season 1982/83

Year 5 v Year 6   Every Morning Playtime

Carnforth North Road Primary School

The 82/83 season was for me a varied one. Lots happened in terms of football, but sadly nothing of interest as far as Preston were concerned. We were a club going nowhere – quite literally; Preston would finish 16th in Division Three for the next two seasons. The average attendance at Deepdale was now below 5000 for the first time in our history, us fans turning up dutifully to watch our team huff and puff.

Again, we won our first game of the season against Millwall, but then lost the next four, and that's how the season panned out; a few wins being nullified by a few more losses. My dad and I went along to as many home games as possible, but the already muted atmosphere was becoming increasingly moribund. It was as if we all knew that success was just a pipe dream now. We were actually in danger of going down, but a late good run pushed us into mid-table safety, only losing one game from the middle of March.

Preston's demise seemed to reversely parallel my own footballing abilities, which were improving week by week – all that practice seemed to be paying off. I was now in Year 5, the second highest year in primary school and I had now become not just a regular, but quite a crucial part of the Green team, playing an attacking midfield role in the same vein as Bryan Robson, or at least that's what I told myself. I was scoring regularly in our lunchtime House fixtures and now that I was in Year 5, was allowed to play football in the playground during the morning twenty-minute playtime session.

The unofficial law of the playground was that only Year 5s and 6s were allowed to use the concrete pitch marked out with coloured lines, and the biggest and hardest Year 6s, as the senior kids in the school, ruled the roost. They decided who could play, and who they would play against. There would always be eight or nine Year 6s who would want a competitive game against decent opposition, someone who would at least give them a game. However, this did not stretch to the point of ever possibly losing. They would allow eight or nine Year 5s, picked by them, to play against them but never allow their opponents to be good enough to actually beat them.

I was one of the select few to be allowed to play against them and us Year 5s would lose every day. Even if we scored a perfectly good goal, the Year 6s would come up with a variety of reasons why the goal should not stand, even though they had just scored a goal in similar circumstances to ours. It was either offside, even though they weren't exactly sure of the rule; or it was handball, despite the ball never being near anyone's arm or hand; or it had gone out of play or not quite crossed the line. Even if the ball had blatantly gone in, the pile of coats acting as goalposts would mysteriously get shifted across and so prove that the ball could not in fact have gone in.

It felt a bit like we were playing against a whole team of PE teachers from the film "Kes", all played by Brian Glover who would bend the rules in their favour. They were basically cheating, but us younger ones just had to get on with it and accept their decision, otherwise they would either beat us up, or not let us play again the following day. We didn't stand a chance and so just accepted it – up to a point. I was determined to score a goal so awesome that nobody could question its legitimacy. My practising of Zico style scissor kicks was about to pay off. We all have our moments of brilliance and glory, and this was mine.

The greatest goal I ever scored happened sometime in September or October 1982, in the first half-term of Year 5. This particular playtime, as usual, us Year 5s were trying manfully, or rather boyfully, to compete, and were playing really well, already having had two perfectly good goals disallowed for some reason by our year older opponents, whereas they had scored twice, with their goals obviously standing. In my mind the score was 2-2 and there was only about a minute left before we would all be called back into our classes.

I received the ball on the halfway line and pushed forward into their half. I knocked it up to our main striker just inside the penalty area, who laid it back to me at a rather awkward waist height, too high to control and pass it, and too low to head. I instinctively leapt up and scissor-kicked the ball, connecting perfectly with it, into what would have been the top right-hand corner of the goal. It wasn't close enough to the post for them to say it had missed, and not too high to say it had gone over the bar. In fact, it was fairly close to the keeper, but I hit it so well that it flew past him before he even saw it.

It wasn't exactly like Zico as I wasn't horizontal in the air and didn't fancy landing on the cold, wet, hard concrete. If anything, and I realise how this might sound, it was more like Paulo Di Canio's famous goal for West Ham, the ball rifling into the net off the outside of his right boot. I remember the Year 6s being rather bewildered and trying desperately to come up with a reason why my goal shouldn't stand, but they simply couldn't think of one. It was a brilliant goal, if I do say so myself. I actually heard one of them mumble to his teammate that that was the best goal he'd ever seen.

At that moment the bell went and so the game ended with us still 2-1 down, but in my head the previous two goals that should have stood made my scissor-kick the winning goal. In an instant my reputation in the school playground shot up, the Year 6s now holding a rather disgruntled admiration for me. They still kept disallowing every other goal that we scored though; I couldn't keep producing Zicoesque Di Canio strikes every playtime, but they would never be able to take that one away from me.

54

***

My confidence in my own ability and my enthusiasm was growing so much that I decided that I wanted to sign up for one of Bobby Charlton's Soccer Schools (similar to the one where David Beckham was discovered). Charlton himself was doing a favour to his former colleagues at Preston, Alan Spavin and Alan Kelly, who if you remember, had a sports shop in Lancaster. They had asked Bobby to make a personal appearance in the shop to drum up trade, and also so he could promote his Soccer Schools in our area.

My dad took me along one Saturday morning with my PNE autograph book clutched in my hand, and we queued up to get the great man's autograph. He noticed who I supported from my autograph book, and he and my dad had a brief conversation about how we could do with someone like him back in charge. He signed my book and asked if I'd like to take part in his Soccer School. Of course I said that I would, and so clutching my autograph book and the form that I would have to fill in, off we went to have a look around the shop, and plan which boots I would ask for when my feet had grown out of my present ones. I also drooled at the red England away shirt, the one that Bryan Robson was wearing when he scored his 27 second goal against France only a few months before.

The Soccer School was to take place in Blackpool and a coach would take all those from my area back and forth for the five days of the half term holiday at the end of October. This perturbed me slightly as I felt a bit uncomfortable about wearing my Preston kit, as I knew I would get abuse from the other kids who would, more likely than not, be Blackpool supporters, our hated local rivals. I had the home England kit, the one with the number seven stitched on, which would prevent abuse, as everyone supported England, but I wouldn't be able to wear that every day without mum washing it every evening (she hadn't done that since I was four, when I became particularly attached to a cowboy outfit I'd got for my birthday, refusing to wear anything else).

I needn't have worried though. On the Saturday before I was due to start at the Soccer School, my parents treated me to that iconic red Umbro shirt, and so I would be able to alternate between home and away England kits and not give my mum a laundry dilemma.

So, with my New Balance boots and my England away kit, I was ready to be Bryan Robson, and show the rest of North Lancashire what I could do.

After the first hour on the Monday morning, I realised that what I actually could do was nowhere near as good as most of the other boys in my age group. I fell into the 9-11 age category, and only having turned nine the previous April, I was one of the youngest in my group of around thirty boys. The vast majority of my group was in Year 6 or even Year 7 and had already started secondary school. I immediately felt out of my depth, and as a result performed more like Bryan Ferry than Bryan Robson. I have no idea what standard of football the lead singer of Roxy Music plays at – he may be brilliant for all I know, but you get the point.

Each morning we would do proper training sessions before lunch, and then have a game in the afternoon, finishing with some sort of competition, either a penalty shoot-out or keepy-uppy contest. My confidence grew throughout the week, doing fairly well in the penalty competitions but I frankly embarrassed myself at the keepy-uppies. I'd simply never practised them before and could only manage a few before I lost control of the ball and it clumsily hit the ground.

I had to watch in awe at some of the other lads who were able to juggle the ball with ease, using both feet, both knees, and sometimes even their shoulders and head. Our coach showed off his own skills and caught the ball on the back of his neck, before allowing it to roll down his back, back-heeling it over his head and volleying it into the net. To be fair, it wasn't just me who watched him in awe, and I resolved to teach myself the same skill at some point.

By the end of the week, I'd got into double figures with my keepy-uppies but was still woefully below the standard of a lot of the boys. On the Friday afternoon, we had an awards afternoon where little trophies were handed out. Most, if not all of us, received some sort of trophy, and I suppose I should have been more pleased when my name was called out to receive the Most Improved Player award. I was aware of the double-edged nature of such a prize, which basically meant that I was crap to start with, and not quite so crap by the end, but at least it was a reward for showing the coaches that I was learning, listening to their advice, and putting it into practice.

One morning we actually got to meet Bobby Charlton himself. He jogged over to our group in his tracksuit and everybody was rather starstruck. He said a few words of encouragement and inspiration to us all and then after he asked if there were any questions, most boys simply asked if he could give them his autograph. Without him having a pen, or any of the boys anything for him to actually sign, he promised he would leave some signatures near the changing rooms for us to collect later. I stood rather smugly, knowing that I'd already got his autograph, in pride of place in my PNE autograph book. He'd signed it personally for me and not just left it to be collected later. It was as if I knew him on a deeper level than the other lads as he'd actually spoken to me individually. To them he was Bobby Charlton; to me he was my mate.

Bobby then went over to the older group of boys, the 12-14 age group but then another man made his way towards us – Jimmy Armfield. A lot of the other lads had no idea who he was, but I knew him from conversations with my dad, particularly as he was a

Blackpool legend. He was to Blackpool what Tom Finney was to Preston. Some Blackpool fans would say that Stanley Matthews was their greatest ever player, and they are probably right, but he played a huge part in Stoke City's history and there is a statue of him outside Stoke's stadium, whereas Armfield, like Finney, played his whole career at one club. It is Armfield's statue that stands outside Bloomfield Road, just as Finney's stands outside Deepdale. And here he was, walking over to our group.

Again he said some inspirational words to us all, and as we were working on our headers that morning, he asked us all what makes a good header. My hand shot up and after another lad had given his answer of "power", Jimmy pointed at me and I confidently said "direction". A quick word of praise from Jimmy before someone else said "make sure you keep your eyes open and look at the ball" (something I'd failed to do in that game for the Green team a couple of years earlier). We were all encouraged to put all three answers into practice and off he went.

From that day I've always had a great affection for Jimmy Armfield. The way he spoke to us calmly with his encouraging and motivating tone, and the way he believed in us as young lads, even though he didn't know any of us, has stayed with me to this day.

In his later years, he'd frequently be commentating for BBC Radio 5Live on a Saturday afternoon, usually with the brilliant Jon Murray. I always used to love his enthusiasm for the game and the way he always used to quantify his thoughts by using the adverb "really". For example: "I think he's a great player. I really do", or "He should have hit that first time, he really should." His knowledge and insight, along with his boyish enthusiasm and sense of humour made listening to his commentary such a pleasure.

I'll always remember one afternoon a couple of years or so before he died, when he and Jon Murray were commentating on a Burnley match which included their midfielder Scott Arfield. My appreciation for Jon Murray was already high, but it went to the next level when he said to the listeners, knowing full well that Jimmy would pick up on it, something along the lines of "And now it's Scott Arfield on the ball, who's one letter away from being a truly great player." Jimmy chuckled quietly in the background and carried on with the commentary. Pure class from both men.

When Jimmy Armfield passed away in January 2018, Preston paid a heartfelt and moving tribute to him. Even though our two clubs are fierce, and at times, quite nasty rivals, Jimmy Armfield's humility brought us all together. I genuinely miss him. I really, really do.

Tottenham Hotspur v Brighton and Hove Albion

December 28ᵗʰ, 1982   White Hart Lane

Just after Christmas of that year, my family went on a little sightseeing trip to London, seeing all the usual sights. We went to the Tower of London, Madame Tussauds', the Planetarium, took in a show on New Year's Eve at the London Palladium before heading into Trafalgar Square to watch people jump around in the fountains as Big Ben struck midnight. None of the fancy fireworks of today but it was entertaining all the same.

We also went on a tour of Wembley stadium, the hallowed ground that I'd only ever seen on the television before, and the scene of my dad's early heartbreak in the 64 Cup Final.

This was the definite highlight of our trip as far as I was concerned. Why queue up for hours just to see some Crown Jewels, or almost wet yourself with terror in the Chamber of Horrors at Madame Tussauds' (I was only nine still), when you could go into the dressing rooms of Wembley and sit in the same seats as all those players who

I so wanted to emulate? We got to walk out of the tunnel, wander around the ground, and climb the steps to lift a not very similar trophy to the FA Cup. That trophy would have to wait. I was still dreaming.

In the changing rooms, our guide wanted someone to volunteer to have some treatment done on an imagined injury. My initial reaction was to shrink away behind my mum, but he caught my eye before I could hide. Before I knew it, I was up on the treatment bench having some sort of cold spray administered to my lower leg in front of the thirty or so other people on the tour. At least I could say that I'd been treated for an injury in the Wembley dressing room, which would be the closest I ever got to being a real footballer.

It was a great day out and I'll treasure the memory forever. The atmosphere inside the stadium was obviously very quiet and actually quite eerie. It just made my thirst to experience a Wembley Cup Final even greater, and I think my dad could see it. He'd had that awesome experience, watching Preston, his own team, despite the ultimate disappointment of losing. He also knew that he certainly wouldn't be taking me to watch our team there again anytime soon, such were our dismal fortunes at that time.

At that point my dad wanted to give me as many footballing experiences as possible. Not just for me, but for him too. He'd been to very few away grounds at that point, Wembley excepted, and so in the next couple of years we went to many different grounds. I think this coincided with Simon Inglis' excellent book "The Football Grounds of England and Wales" being published, which he got himself a copy of. I remember us both poring over this book, taking in all the pictures and reading it word for word. I remember the picture of Deepdale was of our old West Stand, with its wooden stanchions proudly holding up a handsome old stand with its benches running along the length of it, curving around towards the Spion Kop end. The rest of the ground was conveniently not in the picture, and it did make me feel quite honoured to sit in that same stand every other week, even if it was to watch my team play not very well.

Over the next few years we would go to a lot of grounds in the North West of England, not just to watch Preston, but any others we could get to if we were in that part of the country for whatever reason. And so, on our second day of our trip to London, my dad noticed that Spurs, the present FA Cup holders, in fact the only team to have won the Cup since I became addicted to football, were at home against Brighton. We'd had a busy day sightseeing and I think my mum was happy to have a break from him. I'm not sure whether she went somewhere else with my brother, but when my dad suggested going to watch Spurs, Glenn Hoddle and all, my answer was of course yes.

Up Tottenham High Road we went and got seats quite high up in one of the stands. Apart from Ewood Park in Blackburn, this was the first ever away ground I'd been to, and definitely the first for a Division One team. The score apparently was 2-0 to Spurs (I had to look it up) with Chris Hughton, who would go onto manage that night's opponents, and Ricky Villa scoring the goals. The Spurs team was basically the same as the one from the Cup Final only seven months before, with Ray Clemence in goal behind Graham Roberts and Steve Perryman, the last man to lift the FA Cup on those Wembley steps I would soon be going up. Hoddle, Villa and Mickey Hazard in midfield, with Garth Crooks and Steve Archibald up front. Not a bad team at all actually. I wonder what they'd be worth individually as players now.

I don't remember anything about the game, apart from it being cold and damp, except two blokes sitting behind me and my dad who never stopped moaning about their own team, especially Steve Archibald. Here they were, watching their team, a team who hadn't lost an FA Cup tie for two whole seasons, effing and blinding about them, all within perfect earshot of my innocent little ears.

It was a constant stream of "Fackin' 'ell Archie" or "Fer Fack's sake Archie" whenever the Scottish international got near the ball, let alone when he actually touched it. I don't recall him having a particularly bad game, but I do remember my dad getting very annoyed and protective of me. After yet another volley of sweary cockney abuse down our ears, he turned around and asked them politely if they wouldn't mind not swearing. They gave him a look as if to say who the fack is this northern prick giving them orders. They mumbled an apology and didn't swear again for a whole five minutes.

At half time my dad noticed there were some spare seats a few rows further back, so we moved there for the second half, and could watch Steve Archibald play without the running commentary on how awful he was and what a waste of fackin' money he'd been. He must have been doing something right as he would move to Barcelona at the end of the 83/84 season and win La Liga with them, the first time Barca had won it for eleven years.

I have nothing against criticising and being angry at players if you don't think they're doing their job well. Us fans pay a lot of money, and if we feel the players who we help pay the wages of are not performing up to standard, then we have the right to let them know. But when criticism just becomes mindless abuse for the sake of it then that is counterproductive. Anyway, I'm guessing that Steve Archibald didn't give a fack what those two fans thought of him as he relaxed in his Spanish villa after winning La Liga. He'd finished his first season with Spurs as Division One's top scorer and helped win the FA Cup twice for those fans, something that I could only ever fantasise about, and there they were, just shouting out mindless abuse at one of their own players.

From the point of view of someone who supports a team that doesn't win games very often, let alone be in Division One and win FA Cups in successive years, I cannot stand the amount of moaning from so-called supporters of big teams. The amount of abuse, particularly on social media these days, that fans of teams like Arsenal and Man United give to their own players and manager angers me. I get that with big clubs come big wages and thus big expectations, but I wonder what they'd be like if they supported a team like Preston, or one of all the other lowly clubs who never taste, or even have the opportunity to taste success at the highest level. I'd give my left arm (not my right, it's far too useful) to have the opportunity of losing to teams like Arsenal and Man United. But I suppose these fans have never experienced their team losing to Mansfield, or Bury, or Hartlepool, or Walsall, or any such team. Maybe it would do them good if they did experience that. Then they might just be a bit more grateful and appreciate what they do have.

Apart from that, me and my dad had a great night at White Hart Lane, despite the cold and the damp. We certainly didn't moan.

Little did I know at the time, but only a few hundred yards from where I was sitting that cold night in December 1982, in her home, a little terraced house on Church Road, just off Tottenham High Road, would be my future wife. Little did I know that that 12-year old girl would change my life completely fourteen years later. But more of that in due course. I had to go to Wrexham first.

Wales v Bulgaria

European Championship Qualifier   **April 27th, 1983**

Racecourse Ground, Wrexham

As Preston's season trundled on and we eventually got into mid-table safety, my dad got free tickets to my first ever international game, but not as an England fan. Well not directly anyway. My dad owned his own small joinery firm back then and one of his main suppliers of timber was the company owned by the then manager of Wales, ironically named Mike England. As a valued customer, my dad was given complimentary tickets by the Welsh manager, and so on my tenth birthday, a Wednesday evening, a school night at that, me and my dad set off straight after an earlier than usual tea down the M6 to the mighty Wrexham's Racecourse Ground.

What surprised me most was how ordinary their stadium was, and here it was, hosting an international game of football, with some of the best players in the country on display. Wrexham were then in the same division as Preston and so it shouldn't have been a surprise to me that their ground was similarly run down, if not more so than ours, but this was way before The Millennium Stadium, now The Principality Stadium, was even conceived of, let alone built. Wales played their home games either at Wrexham or Cardiff City's old stadium, Ninian Park, and so here I was watching Wales, courtesy of (Mike) England, at a ground where Preston had lost 3-1 only a few months before.

My dad always liked to get to matches early, especially away games, so we could wander round the outside of the ground, read the match programme and generally get used to our unfamiliar surroundings. Looking at the match programme now, there are some players such as Jeremy Charles, Paul Price and Nigel Vaughan who I certainly do not remember. But also in that same Welsh team that night were

64

three of the greatest players of the 1980s: Neville Southall and Kevin Ratcliffe, arguably the best goalkeeper and centre back respectively of that decade, lynchpins of the Everton side who would go onto win the FA Cup the following season and then win the league, ousting their Merseyside rivals as Champions the season after that.

There was also probably the greatest striker of the 1980s playing for Wales that night. Ian Rush, the Liverpool striker was pure class back then, and without him Liverpool simply would not have dominated way they did. His partnership with Kenny Dalglish was devastating, and here he was playing in Wrexham on my birthday.

One of the other reasons why my dad liked to arrive early was to see if we could get a glimpse of the players arriving and maybe get a few autographs to add to my growing collection. Sure enough, our early arrival paid dividends as on the front of my programme, above a picture of him being challenged by his own club teammate Phil Thompson, whilst playing against England, is the signature of Ian Rush himself. It was his own personal birthday present to me, even though he had no idea I had just hit double figures that very day in terms of years being alive.

A crowd of just over 9000 turned up to watch a dull game, won by the scrappiest of goals from Swansea City's (I had to look it up) Jeremy Charles. The Bulgarian side, who I remember being fascinated that every single one of their players' names ended in "ov" apart from two rogue "ev" players, was a long way from becoming the side that would do so well eleven years later at the World Cup of 1994, humbling the then holders Germany, with their truly world-class talisman Hristo Stoichkov and the balding Yordan Letchkov, who looked about 50 even though he was only 26 at the time, scoring a brilliant free-kick and diving header respectively.

The Bulgarian side that night had no one I'd heard of, and would hear no more about for ever more, and Wales got a deserved victory, but as usual eventually missed out on qualifying for a major Finals tournament, pipped by Yugoslavia.

But at least I got to watch Wales win, for free, and got Ian Rush's autograph thrown in, and I could bask in the glory of probably being the only boy in the whole world who got to watch Bulgaria play in Wrexham on his tenth birthday. I was living the dream.

Manchester City v Luton Town

May 14ᵗʰ, 1983   **Maine Road**

I include this game because of one player, and one player only, and it had nothing to do with his footballing ability. I didn't go to the game; I have no affiliation with either club and frankly couldn't have cared less who won it. It was a winner takes all relegation battle on the last day of the season. Whoever won would stay up. Whoever lost would go down into Division Two. Preston were away that day, so my Saturday afternoon was spent watching Grandstand and of course the vidi-printer scores as they came in as the full-time whistles around the country blew. The BBC were not allowed to show any of the game itself until later that night on Match of the Day, but they were certainly allowed to show the scenes as soon as the final whistle blew.

We all remember David Pleat, the Luton manager, skipping hysterically onto the pitch, desperately trying to do his beige jacket buttons up whilst also rapturously celebrating, later to be hilariously parodied by David Baddiel and Frank Skinner in one of their "Phoenix from the Flames" sketches on Fantasy Football League in the mid-90s. The first player Pleat ran to and hugged was Brian Horton, and he is the sole reason this match is rather nebulously included.

I've always held a strong affection for Brian Horton, not because of his footballing ability, but simply because a few days before this match, the sticker with his face on it completed my Panini sticker album for the 1982/83 season. For the previous couple of seasons, I, along with loads of other boys at school, became obsessed with our sticker albums, and this was the first year I had actually completed it before the end of the season.

Those sticker albums were not just immense fun, watching the gaps getting filled in gradually over the course of the season, but also really good sources of information. Us boys got to know each player for each team, which ground they played at, how many fans each ground would hold, and even who the chief executives of the FA were, Ted Croker and Bert Millichip rather bombastically having their own page all to themselves.

Every week throughout that season I would use my pocket money to buy as many packets of stickers as I could, and whenever either of my grandmas offered to treat me, the only thing I ever wanted was yet more packets of stickers. Every Saturday morning would be spent opening each packet very carefully, to be sure not to rip the treasured prizes inside, finding the gap where each sticker would go, before carefully sticking it in its designated place, making sure it didn't look wonky and thus destroy the aesthetics of each page.

The stickers that you already had went into your swaps pile, which would then be taken everywhere with you, and swapped with other collectors, mainly at school playtimes and lunches, when we weren't playing football that is. Two words were said to each other whilst flicking through each other's pile of swaps, either "Got" or "Need", and the more you completed your collection, the fewer times you were able to say that magical word "Need".

By April my pile of swaps was huge, as obviously the closer you got to completion, the more swaps you stacked up. My pile was about three inches high by this point, and it was a good day at school if you came home with three or four stickers to add to your album. Some boys were tempted to frankly cheat and write off to Panini, telling them which number stickers they needed, which would be sent back to them, for a small fee of course. But I was determined not to do this; I was going to do it properly.

However, my hopes were fading away as I had literally one sticker to get: the extremely elusive Brian Horton of Luton Town. More pocket money was spent, but all that happened was my pile of swaps just got fatter. I was giving up hope and considering the cheating option, but one morning playtime, I was doing the usual rounds of swapping with the other collectors, when there he was. It took me a second or so for his face and his name to register with me, as I thought I would never get to see who this Brian Horton was, but once it did register, I shouted at the top of my voice "NEED!" and made whoever I was swapping with very happy as I simply exchanged my whole pile of swaps for that one precious piece of shiny paper.

Brian Horton was put very carefully in a book I had in my school bag, and he was protected as though I had a few fifty-pound notes in there. At the end of the school day I ran all the way home and had, quite frankly, an almost sacred moment as I stuck Brian in the one remaining gap in my album. The sense of satisfaction was quite overwhelming. This goal I had been steadily working towards for the past nine months had finally been achieved. The only problem was I wouldn't know what to do with myself on Saturday mornings and school lunch times anymore. Until next season anyway.

So, here's to Brian Horton; a fairly decent player, a fairly ordinary manager, but one who will forever be one of my all-time heroes. Cheers Brian.

Manchester United v Brighton and Hove Albion

FA Cup Final   **May 21st, 1983**

FA Cup Final Replay   **May 26th, 1983**

Wembley Stadium

For this year's end of season showpiece, I was in a bit of a quandary as to who I would be supporting. Man United were from the north and they obviously had my hero Bryan Robson playing for them, but Brighton were huge underdogs, already having been relegated from Division One, finishing bottom of the league. Their team also contained a striker called Michael Robinson, who had started his career at Preston, leaving in 1979, just before I remember him playing, but my dad had fond memories of him, so his presence probably just pushed my allegiance over to The Seagulls.

I also loved the way Brighton arrived at Wembley. Every other team in every other Cup Final had got a coach to Wembley, but not Brighton. They were determined to enjoy their day whatever the result and arrived via helicopter, flying over the stadium in which they would be playing a few hours later. Extravagant maybe, but I certainly didn't hold it against them. And they almost pulled off one of the biggest upsets in Cup Final history – almost. Again I would be supporting a nearly team that day.

Bryan Robson led his team out, which included the 18-year old Norman Whiteside, who had burst onto the scene at the previous summer's World Cup, becoming the youngest player ever to appear at a World Cup Finals, younger even than Pele in 1958. Alongside Robson was the Brighton captain, the very impressively bearded Tony Grealish. His was one of the best beards on a footballer I'd ever seen. His beard had nothing to do with Brighton actually taking the lead in the first quarter of an hour, and they managed to hold on until half-time.

United's manager, Big Ron Atkinson, must have had a right go at his team in the dressing room at half time, as they came out much better after the restart. They equalised after 55 minutes before Ray Wilkins put United in front after scoring one of the most sublime curling left foot shots you could wish to see. Everyone assumed that United would pull away and go onto win it easily, but Brighton had other ideas. With only three minutes of normal time remaining, they equalised after sloppy marking from United in their box left Gary Stevens free to slam the ball home and take the game to extra-time. Three years in a row there would be an extra thirty minutes for me to enjoy.

Half an hour of tension with very few opportunities ensued, before my man, ex-PNE player Michael Robinson, slotted the ball through to Gordon Smith with only the keeper to beat. This was Brighton's chance to write their names in the history books. With what would have been the very last kick of the final, Smith fluffed his lines, and shot straight at the United keeper. The fairy-tale ending was there for the taking, but as I said, Brighton were a nearly team that day. An oh so nearly team in fact. I can't remember another team ever having such a glorious chance to win the Cup. The chance evaporated and another replay it would be.

By now I just expected all FA Cup Finals to have a replay on the following Thursday night, this being the third one in a row, but this time there would definitely be no fairy-tale. Brighton weren't even a nearly team in this game, they were an absolutely not team this time. A ruthless United weren't about to let them have a sniff this time around, and were 3-0 up by half time, Robson opening the scoring with a beautiful left footed drive into the bottom corner, reminding me why I fell in love with him a year ago. Norman Whiteside then became the youngest ever scorer in a Cup Final with a darting header five minutes later, before Robson killed the Seagulls' spirit with another goal on the stroke of half time.

United went on to add a fourth in the second half, completing the trouncing that Brighton should never have allowed them the opportunity of giving them. Bryan Robson, now captain of England as well as his club, number seven on his back, his socks rolled down again, climbed the Wembley steps to lift the first major trophy of his career. He wouldn't have to wait too long to do it all again, but next time, I would be there too.

Season 1983/84

Torquay United v A N Other

August 1983 Plainmoor

With no World Cup to watch that summer, my dad was chomping at the bit to get his football fix. My season started with a trip to Torquay for a pre-season friendly that didn't even include Preston. If we had made the 616-mile round trip just to watch Preston in a pre-season friendly, then I could be called not just a proper fan, but also a rather over-obsessed and slightly unhinged fan. Of course, there are fans out there who travel the length and breadth of the country every other week, sometimes midweek too, taking time off work to do so, to support their beloved team, but I suspect that only a handful would go to Torquay from North Lancashire even for a league game, and those that would do it for a pre-season friendly need to have more going on in their lives. But each to their own.

My family were spending our summer holiday in Paignton, Devon that year, and when my dad spotted a potential football match only a few miles from where we were staying, then that was our evening sorted. I recall very little, if anything of the game. I have no idea which players were playing, what the score was, or even who Torquay's opposition was. Maybe I was looking out for the Sydney Opera House, or the herds of wildebeest sweeping majestically across the plains that Basil Fawlty had mentioned to his hard-of-hearing guest in one of those classic episodes of "Fawlty Towers".

I saw neither. Nor apparently did I see anything in the game to have stuck in the far recesses of my memory. But it was another away ground to have ticked off. If I was ever going to join the 92 Club, those who have visited every league ground in the country, then I was going to have to go to Torquay at some point, so it might as well be whilst I was staying just down the A3022.

My trip to Torquay wouldn't even count now as they have since been eliminated from the Football League. It's no surprise really considering their geographical location. There's only so many potential fans in that part of the world. I have no idea what the attendance was for the pre-season game I went to, but for one of their final home games at the end of the 83/84 season, against Chester, there were only 967 spectators watching. Not only are there not many home fans available, but how many away fans are going to travel to Torquay?

If there was ever a committed, dedicated and frankly slightly deranged fan, then it's a Torquay United fan who travels to every away game. Every round trip will be over 100 miles, with most being well over 300, and quite a few being over 500 or even 600 miles long. To go and watch Torquay play away at Hartlepool, which they did for many seasons, meant a trip of 732 miles. That's a hell of a lot of your life spent travelling to watch a team that will probably not reward you for your efforts with even a draw, let alone a win.

As Maximus shouts out to the crowd in "Gladiator", "Are you not entertained?" well I'm guessing that for a lot of Torquay fans, the answer would be a resounding no, and yet they still keep on travelling to be unentertained.

So, for those about to travel to Hartlepool from Torquay, or vice versa for that matter, we salute you!

Greens v Yellows

March 1984 Carnforth North Road Primary School

I was a big, hard Year 6 now, and one of those who had the playground power to beat up any Year 5s who had the temerity to think they'd scored against us Year 6s. I wasn't like that – well I didn't beat them up anyway, although I may have argued that at least one of their apparent goals would have hit the post if we'd have had one, and so disallowed it.

I had power in more ways than one, as now, by default because of my superior age, I was made captain of the Green team – House football champions for the past three seasons – our chant of Greens, Greens, Top of the Teams was certainly true, and I wasn't about to let our grip on the Cup slip in my season in charge. I now had the power to select the team, decide on "tactics" and basically boss people about. I loved it. In fact, this may have been the seed which ended up with me becoming a teacher twelve years later.

Our goalkeeper had left and gone onto secondary school, so my first decision was who was going to be my Peter Shilton. The player who I chose has ended up being my longest and closest friend, living with him in London for a while after university, and being his Best Man at his wedding twenty-five years after asking him to don his goalie gloves for the Green team. That's if he had any goalie gloves to don, which he didn't. I soon rectified this.

He was one of the oldest in the year and so his birthday fell just as the footy season was about to start. So, when he invited me to his eleventh birthday party, I knew exactly what to get him for a present.

Another trip to Spavin and Kelly's sports' shop in Lancaster to get him a fancy pair of gloves which he was extremely happy about. He was so grateful for being given the chance to be in the team that he would go out of his way to impress me with how much practice he was putting in.

Goalkeepers are a strange breed. Just listen to Peter Crouch's podcast about how Rob Green, the ex-England keeper, would be so weird that he would even read a book on coach journeys to and from matches. My mate was no exception. Keepers can't just kick a ball against a wall to practise their control or shooting as us outfield players can. I suppose they could just go out and dive around like a lunatic if they really wanted to, but keepers need someone to practise with, unless it is their kicking, either out of their hands, or goal-kicks. And that is what he would do.

When there was no one else out on the playing field at the end of his road, he would simply go and kick his ball and see how far he could get it towards the other end of the field. Then he would run and get it, turn around and do exactly the same thing back to the other end of the field. He must have looked like some sort of dog that could throw its own stick, but it kept him happy and he would proudly tell me the next day at school how far he was able to kick the ball now.

As far as his kicking ability was concerned, I had no worries, but as for his saving capabilities, I was less confident. But now he had his new gloves, that would sort that problem. At least now he could blame it on the dodgy cheap gloves I'd got for him if he let the ball slip through his fingers into the net.

He didn't let me down though. He was one of the stalwarts in a season that would prove to be not just victorious, but very nearly invincible. We had won or drawn every game until well after Christmas, and it became a real possibility that we might be able to go all the way and avoid defeat until we broke up for the Easter holidays when the football season would end, and we would switch to cricket for the summer term.

The Green team were way out in front with only a few games left to play. We had to play each team about four times throughout the season, and we had beaten every team at least twice by March. Maybe it was over-confidence on my part, or even cockiness, but in one of our last few remaining games, this time against the Yellows, an early mistake from our defence allowed them to score, and even though we had so many chances, we just could not equalise. I should have scored at least twice, but it was as if I had my slippers on that day and it just would not go in.

So when Fartley Hartley blew the final whistle, my dream of emulating the 1889 Invincibles of Preston North End was gone. We still won the league comfortably and convincingly, but I was so annoyed that we nearly became invincible. Again, a nearly team. Or maybe I'm just being a tad over-dramatic.

Rochdale AFC v Preston North End

February 22nd, 1984   Spotland

How many blokes come home from a hard day at work on a bitterly cold and wet February evening and say the magic words, "Do you fancy going to Rochdale tonight?" My dad did. Well, my homework would just have to wait as I simply could not resist the temptation of a trip to Rochdale, whatever the weather. Preston's season had, as usual, gone downhill by now. We started off looking something like The Invincibles, not losing until our seventh league game. But then we lost eight in a row around October/November, and by February were in our usual mid-table anonymity. What better way to beat the long winter blues than a trip to watch The Associate Members' Cup

First Round against a team in the division below us? It wasn't even a league game.

This competition was in its inaugural year, and would change its name seemingly every season, depending on whichever company was sponsoring it. I remember it being The Auto Windscreens Trophy at one point and the LDV Vans Trophy too, but now it is simply known as the EFL Trophy and is "the third most prestigious cup competition in our country"! Who could resist an offer like that? Certainly not me, so off down the M62 we went.

I think my dad's thought process was that surely, we couldn't lose to a team like Rochdale, and whatever happened, it was another step closer to the 92 Club. With Wrexham, Torquay, and now Rochdale, my dad was really spoiling me with fairly rubbish away grounds, and this would continue over the next few seasons with, in no particular order, Prenton Park in Tranmere, Springfield Park in Wigan, Boundary Park in Oldham, Burnden Park (Bolton's previous ground, with half of one end being taken up by a supermarket), Brunton Park in Carlisle, Gresty Road in Crewe, Valley Parade in Bradford, Turf Moor in Burnley, Ewood Park in Blackburn again and Bloomfield Road in Blackpool.

They weren't all rubbish though as we would go to a few bigger and much more impressive stadiums too, such as Hillsbrough and Bramall Lane in Sheffield, Goodison Park in Liverpool, Maine Road and Old Trafford in Manchester, and dad even went to the Stadio Olimpico in Rome when he and my mum went for a supposedly romantic few days away a few years later. But you know, when in Rome…

I don't know what my mum did whilst he was watching AS Roma play against AC Milan. Maybe she told him she didn't mind leaving her alone in a strange city, went to The Mouth of Truth instead, and had her hand bitten off. Gregory Peck certainly didn't come and rescue her. I can't really blame him for going really. The prospect of watching AC Milan in the Olympic Stadium in Rome was just too tempting. I would have given my right hand to do that - just like Gregory Peck did with Audrey Hepburn.

I would continue this tradition of going to watch Preston at rather rundown grounds once I moved to London and started my career as a teacher. My dad was very proud of me when I told him that I'd been to Underhill in Barnet, The Abbey Stadium in Cambridge, The Priestfield Stadium in Gillingham, Brisbane Road where Leyton Orient play, and he was particularly pleased when I told him that I'd taken my new wife of just over two weeks for a post honeymoon trip to Kenilworth Road in Luton. I certainly know how to treat a lady. Like father, like son. (Just for the record my marriage survived and twenty-one years later we are still going strong. I just needed to test it first.)

Spotland, Rochdale's unfortunately named stadium, was a proper dump. Deepdale looked palatial compared to this. The icy wind was blowing, there was a constant dampness in the air; definitely a two pairs of socks and long-johns kind of night. With very few other fans willing or mad enough to attend this particular football feast, we could stand basically wherever we wanted to that night. We opted to be as close to Preston's dugout as possible to see if we could hear some tactical wizardry going on.

We certainly didn't get any sort of wizardry; more like the sound of teeth chattering with cold. I remember how primitive compared to these days our dugout was. None of the comforts that players, coaches and managers luxuriate in nowadays. The substitutes, the coaches and the manager were all squeezed onto one wooden bench, trying to stay out of the cold, and they had one of those awful, thin, nylon sleeping bags unzipped across their legs. They looked like a load of grannies trying to keep warm; I think there may even have been a tartan flask with tea involved too.

I also remember how much they all swore. I thought managers were expected to behave in a manner more befitting to their stature, but obviously not. It was like being back at White Hart Lane.

My dad wasn't going to ask our own manager to cut down on the profanities, so we moved to another part of the ground for the second half – there were plenty of places to choose from. The swearing must have had some effect though, as Preston ended up winning 3-0. We were into the next round and one step closer to Wembley glory. "Wem-ber-ley, Wem-ber-ley, we're the famous Preston North End and we're going to Wem-ber-ley."

Our dreams were dashed by the mighty Doncaster Rovers in the next round, and that was the end of that. Ah well, at least we'd given Rochdale a spanking.

We decided not to go to Doncaster's ground, The Belle Vue Stadium (before they moved to the Keepmoat Stadium), for the next round, which was probably for the best, losing 2-1, although it would have been another ground ticked off the list. Having never been, I can only suggest that Belle Vue is the least appropriately named ground in the country. I'm not sure there is any view in any part of Doncaster which is particularly belle, but I may be wrong. My sincere apologies if there is.

My list of visited football grounds was expanding, but dad thought it was about time I went to some proper stadiums. I would soon be going to two of the biggest and best stadiums in the country; to watch an England game in one, and the current FA Cup holders in the other.

England v Italy

UEFA Under-21 Championship Semi-Final, First Leg

April 18th, 1984   Maine Road, Manchester

The two weeks between April 18th and May 2nd, 1984 would prove to be very significant in my footballing education. When my dad said we were going to watch England, I was ecstatic. When he told me it was the under -21s I was slightly less ecstatic, but we were going to Maine Road, the then home of Manchester City, one of the biggest stadiums in the country, one that had hosted many FA Cup semi-finals, and one which saw the highest attendance ever for an English league club.

Way back in 1934, almost 85,000 fans crammed in to watch City play Stoke in an FA Cup quarter-final, a game which would feature Sir Stanley Matthews for Stoke and Sir Matt Busby for City, although they weren't Sirs by then of course. It had become known as The Wembley of the North due to its capacity, and I was hoping for that moment which Deepdale had let me down on, "that moment" when you walk up the steps to see the pitch and stand there, amazed and awe-struck by the scene in front of you.

Unfortunately, I was let down again as Maine Road that night was way less than half full – probably only about 10,000 fans were there in a stadium that could hold well over 40,000. The Wembley of the North felt only slightly more full than the real Wembley had on my guided tour the previous season. I remember the vastness of the old Kippax Stand and could only imagine the noise when it was full to bursting.

As usual, we arrived early and hung around, collecting autographs from young players arriving at the ground. Looking at my programme from that night, and the signatures scrawled on the front cover, I recognise very few names, but the team list on the back cover proved to be more interesting. Back then, I don't think I'd heard of many of the players from either team, but looking back now, it's interesting to see how those young internationals fared later on in their careers.

England's team contained Peter Hucker as keeper, who, as the QPR keeper, Glenn Hoddle had scored against in the 1982 Cup Final. Mel Sterland, Nick Pickering, Paul Bracewell, Dave Watson and Mark Chamberlain would all go onto play for England at senior level, and Chamberlain would also produce his son Alex, part of Jurgen Klopp's present Liverpool team.

The team also had Howard Gayle in it, Liverpool's first ever black player, who had actually helped them win the European Cup in 1981. The captain of England that night was Tommy Caton, who had played for City in the 1981 Cup Final at the age of just 18. And on the bench as reserve keeper, was a little known David Seaman, then with Peterborough, who would of course go onto become the second most capped keeper for England, only Peter Shilton having won more caps. More on both of them later no doubt.

The Italy side contained a 19-year-old Roberto Mancini, who played for the great Sampdoria team of the 80s and 90s, and would go onto become the current manager of The Azzurri. At the then home of Manchester City, I wonder if he had any inkling at all that he would be back as their manager, this time at a new stadium, The Etihad, and win them their first Premier League title with Sergio Aguero's famous injury time winner in the last seconds of the last game of the 2011/12 season. I suspect not.

Also in the Italian team was Giuseppe Bergomi (except the programme had spelt his name wrong) who was an actual World Cup winner. He had played in the victorious Italian team of the 1982 World Cup at the tender age of just 18, and would go onto captain his country in both the 1986 and 1990 Finals. He would also become one

80

of Inter Milan's longest serving players, playing his whole career for the Italian giants and basically be one of Italy's greatest ever defenders, from a country that has produced a hell of a lot of great defenders.

Bergomi's defensive skills didn't help much that night as England won it quite comfortably, 3-1, though I can't recollect any of the goals. They went onto lose the second leg in Italy but still won on aggregate. They would then beat Spain in the Final, both home and away, winning 3-0 overall to win the 1984 Under-21s European Championship. A pity their seniors couldn't emulate them, not even qualifying for that summer's tournament in France, denying me the chance of watching players like Bryan Robson and Ray Wilkins. I would only have to wait three more days to see them though.

Manchester United v Coventry City

April 21st, 1984   Old Trafford

My dad and I were getting a taste for big stadiums now. Perhaps dad could sense that I was yearning for "that moment", or maybe he just wanted to see some of these grounds as well. After all, he'd been to very few away grounds too. Maine Road had been a great experience, but with it only being a quarter full, it was never going to provide "that" moment. As Preston were away that weekend, he surprised me on the Saturday morning by announcing that we were going to Manchester again, but this time to Old Trafford, The Theatre of Dreams. Surely I would get "that moment" there. It did not disappoint.

United at that time were full of confidence, having just beaten Barcelona 5-0 on aggregate in the Cup Winners' Cup, and had just drawn against Juventus. As usual back in the 80s, they couldn't keep pace with Liverpool, who went onto win not only the League, but also the League Cup and with Bruce Grobbelaar's spaghetti legs, their fourth European Cup. But still, there would undoubtedly be a huge, vocal crowd at Old Trafford to give me "that moment".

The journey to Manchester took over twice the time it did to Deepdale, so again we set off early. Dad had no idea where to park or where to get tickets (tickets were still available to buy on the day back then). A proper matchday at Old Trafford felt so different to Deepdale. We could feel the atmosphere building the closer we got to the ground, the pavements and streets packed with chanting fans all making their way to their place of worship.

I was used to clusters of Preston fans ambling towards Deepdale at about ten to three, pretty much expecting to be let down by their team, but in Manchester, even at 1.30pm we could feel the expectation. These fans expected not only to win, but to win well. I think my dad felt slightly out of his depth, particularly when we had parked the car and a group of lads, probably younger than me, demanded some money to "look after" the car. My dad knew that they were liable to scratch his car if he did not partake of this service, and so he chose to accept their kind offer and gave them a few quid.

The ground was huge as we walked towards it, and dad bought me a United scarf from one of the many street sellers lining the way. That was another massive difference – the only place to get a scarf at Deepdale was the tiny little club shop in a portacabin near the players' entrance. Here, the smell of the burgers, the shouts from the street sellers, the constant buzz of chatter, the smell of beer and the chanting coming from all directions were quite intoxicating as we bought our tickets and went through the turnstile into the underbelly of this great stadium.

And then, I finally got it – that moment I'd been hoping for, and it was probably better than I expected. The Stretford End away to my left was packed, the fans swaying and chanting, and the whole ground seemed to be pulsating with energy, excitement and anticipation. Well I certainly was. To use another comparison to "Gladiator", I was like Maximus as he looked around in wonder at the Colosseum for the first time – a mixture of awe and disbelief. At least I wasn't about to be attacked by a horde of bloodthirsty Legionnaires on chariots.

Coventry were the lambs to the slaughter that day and United soundly beat them 4-1. The win included a goal from United's Maximus, Paul McGrath, his first ever at senior level, and a first ever brace from a young Mark Hughes, who was quickly making a name for himself in his first season for United. He'd thrust himself into the team and become a regular first team player by April, gaining a reputation for being powerful and a scorer of explosive goals, something he would continue to do for some time.

My only disappointment was that I would not be seeing my hero Bryan Robson in action as he had picked up yet another of his frequent injuries which plagued his career due to his combative and high energy style of play. But I would see Ray Wilkins. He scored the other goal, not only scoring, but completely controlling the whole game, dominating midfield with a true Captain's performance. My dad said Wilkins' performance that day was the best he'd ever seen from a midfielder, and the rest of the stadium seemed to agree with him. With Wilkins' job being done, after securing the three points, he was substituted after 77 minutes or so and the whole ground rose to their feet (those who weren't standing already) and gave him the biggest ovation I'd ever seen. Even the Coventry fans were standing and applauding in appreciation too. They knew they'd been beaten by the better team and had witnessed a truly great performance from one of the finest midfielders England had produced.

He probably didn't need to come off, he wasn't injured or anything, but I suspect that Ron Atkinson knew what sort of reception he'd get and gave him that moment to bask in the glory of 40,000 fans' applause. Wilkins didn't exactly bask as he walked off the pitch – he actually looked quite humbled as he turned and applauded back to the fans. He knew he'd done his job well, and maybe he also knew that he wouldn't be at Old Trafford for much longer, as AC Milan would buy him for £1.5 million at the end of the season. He would always be remembered for that sublime goal in the Cup Final only eleven months earlier, and the United fans know a great player when they see one. Wilkins was certainly one of these.

On the drive home I was exhilarated. I'd just seen a truly great performance in a truly great stadium – something I don't think I'd ever experienced at Deepdale before. My exhilaration was slightly tempered with pangs of guilt and a certain sense of betrayal. United were not "my" team – they had not chosen me; Preston had. So, the following Tuesday night I was back to where I belonged to watch Preston play Scunthorpe United. It was like going from the sublime to the ridiculous; the contrast in games and stadiums was huge, but it was strangely comforting to be back at Deepdale, cheering my team on and helping them get a narrow 1-0 win in front of all 3,413 (minus a few Scunny devotees) loyal PNE fans. My guilt was gone for now, but would soon return.

Manchester United v West Ham United

April 28th, 1984   Old Trafford

My birthday came around again, and another game of football played a significant part in my celebrations. I'd got the Preston players' autographs for my ninth birthday back when I was mascot, and this time I would get the Man United team's autographs, as well as a few others.

For some reason Preston had two away games on consecutive Saturdays, whilst United had two home games. Preston were almost 300 miles away in Exeter, whereas Old Trafford was only 60 miles away. There was no choice really, and we had been to Deepdale in midweek, so it wasn't as if we'd chosen United over PNE.

For some reason we set off even earlier than the week before, even though we now knew the route, where to park, and how much to pay to not have our car scratched by a load of kids from Salford. The atmosphere, if anything, was more intense than the previous week as West Ham, with all due respect, are a much bigger club than Coventry, and brought more supporters, swelling the crowd by another 8000 or so.

The match programme confirmed my suspicions that Bryan Robson would still be injured, and so I would have to wait even longer to see him play in the flesh. However, little did I know when we walked through the turnstile that I would actually get to meet him in person in the next hour – well sort of.

I don't know whether my dad had planned somehow what was to follow, or whether he had just been opportunistic and slipped the guy on the door a tenner and had a quiet word with him about it being my birthday, but I then realised why we had arrived so early. Somewhere near to where we had entered the ground was a door, a magic portal almost, which led into a corridor where the Players' Lounge and the changing rooms were. It certainly became my magic portal anyway.

Dad had said that if I stood at the doorway I might be able to get a glimpse of some of the players, and maybe get some autographs on the front of my programme. I didn't expect much, but for the next hour or so I was allowed to enter Wonderland through my newly found rabbit hole. Whenever a player or group of players came out of the Lounge or out of the changing rooms, I was allowed to shuffle up and politely ask if they wouldn't mind signing my programme please. Everyone I asked was all too happy to oblige.

I basically was able to get all the United team's autographs scrawled onto the front of my programme, which included Ray Wilkins, Paul McGrath, Frank Stapleton, Mark Hughes and Kevin Moran. The seemingly always injured Steve Coppell's name is on there too. He would soon have to announce his far-too-early retirement a few months later due to his dodgy knee.

Big Ron Atkinson also obliged, as did some of the West Ham players, which, according to the team sheet included Paul Allen, who was still the youngest ever player to appear in an FA Cup Final, along with their captain, West Ham legend Billy Bonds, Tony Cottee and the great Trevor Brooking. ITV were covering the match for their highlights show so as well as the players, I also got Brian Moore's signature, the voice of ITV football.

I'd given up hope of seeing my hero, Bryan Robson, but just as we were going to leave and take our seats in the stand for the game, he emerged from the Lounge, and I pounced. Nervously, and with wonder in my eyes, I approached him, practising what I was going to say to him. I wanted to ask him how long he would be out for, and whether he'd be ready for the start of next season, but at the crucial moment I fluffed my lines. Well, I didn't just fluff them, I just didn't even say them. I must have been so overwhelmed with the prospect of actually talking to the man I had idolised for almost two years now that all I could do was proffer my pen and programme to him.

Maybe he was used to star struck young fans being slightly over awed in his presence, but he knew what to do, and gladly signed the right-hand side of my now very full programme. I did at least mumble a thank you to him before he went off into the Lounge, or up into the VIP area of the stand. The moment must have taken all of 10 seconds, and his signature was almost like his birthday present to me, even though he had no idea who I was and that it was my eleventh birthday the day before. I was totally made up, and went into the stand with my dad feeling almost blessed by the footballing deities. My dad had come up trumps yet again. As for the game itself, United's confidence and swagger of the previous week seemed to disappear and the game ended in a very frustrating 0-0 draw, but I'd already been a winner that day thanks to dad.

Did the fact that I was disappointed by United's failure to win mean that I was becoming a proper United fan? They were certainly becoming a large part of my footballing affections, but as I said previously, United didn't choose me. I was a Preston fan at heart. I am now, and always will be. It was always Preston's result that I would listen or look out for first. Preston were my bread and butter, with United providing a very nice, rather exotic garnish on the side.

Most, if not all of us hundreds of thousands of fans who support teams from the lower leagues have a favourite Premier League team. Manchester United were becoming mine. It wasn't as if I was glory supporting. United won nothing that season, as did Preston. My dad just wanted to watch a team that had the chance of actually winning something, as well as his own team, one that had no chance of winning anything. The two clubs' fortunes would take very contrasting trajectories over the next two seasons, and we would both be there to witness most of what would unfold.

Wales v England

Home Nations' Championship

May 2nd, 1984 Racecourse Ground, Wrexham

Another year, another couple of complimentary tickets from Mike England, but this time to actually watch the senior England team, and not just the Under-21s. What with a trip to Maine Road, two to Old Trafford, a trip to Deepdale squeezed in, and now another trip to Wrexham, my cup had certainly runneth over in the last two weeks.

The Home Internationals, that now obsolete competition between England, Scotland, Wales and Northern Ireland, was a tournament which frankly nobody really cared about. This was especially so for Scotland when we beat them, but they very definitely cared about if they beat us. Whatever it was, it was still a chance for me and my dad to watch some great players.

In England's team that night was not just one European Cup winner, but four. Alan Kennedy and Sammy Lee had been in the victorious Liverpool team of 1981, and both would soon be playing for the club's fourth win, in Rome, a few weeks after this rather irrelevant match. Peter Shilton and Tony Woodcock had both been in the Nottingham Forest side of 1979 which had beaten Malmo.

In the Welsh team again was the formidable Ian Rush, with Neville Southall in goal and Kevin Ratcliffe in front of him. May 1984 would be quite a big month in all these players' lives, a life changing month in fact. This game was simply being used as a warm-up for the much bigger club games that would follow.

England were the favourites, despite Bryan Robson still not being fit enough to play, but one of his United teammates, Mark Hughes would be making his international debut in this game. I felt slightly torn with my allegiances. I felt almost duty bound to support Wales seeing as their manager had given us our tickets, but I was, and still very much am, English, and I was still revelling in the magnificence of Ray Wilkins' performance for United only ten days ago, so England it most definitely was.

I should have supported Wales instead, as they ended up winning 1-0 with Hughes scoring on his debut and a rather lacklustre England side not caring enough to try and equalise. Hughes' goal was well taken, but it wasn't exactly explosive. It was nothing like the goal he would score in a quite extraordinary 3-0 win for Wales against Spain the following season in a World Cup qualifier, the most brilliant of scissor kicks which rocketed into the top corner. Maybe he'd been watching Zico too in the previous World Cup. In fact, he out Zicoed Zico himself with his scissor kick, as Hughes' strike was from the edge of the penalty area, and still gave the keeper absolutely no chance. If only my dad had got tickets for that game instead of this one. Not that I was complaining.

And so, my season which had started at Torquay would end again in Wrexham, but those last two weeks had made my season quite extraordinary. I'd finally had "that moment", been to some magnificent stadiums, met my hero, and watched some great players perform.

All that was left was to watch the remaining two Finals of the season, both being won by the two Merseyside rivals. Everton comfortably beat Watford 2-0 in the FA Cup and so no replay was required this year. I remember feeling slightly cheated on the Thursday evening after the final the previous Saturday, I had got used to a replay always following the first match, and so would have to wait until the European Cup Final to finally round off this season.

In that Final, Phil Neal became a four time European Cup winner, the only Liverpool player to appear in all four of their wins in the late 70s/early 80s, and by scoring Liverpool's goal that night, became a member of a very select group of players who have scored in more than one European Cup Final, in amongst some truly great players, not that I'm suggesting Phil Neal was not a truly great player. He must have been doing something right if you look at how many trophies he won over the course of his career.

We all know what happened in the penalty shoot-out which eventually won it for Liverpool, and how Bruce Grobbelaar's goal line antics meant he didn't even have to save the penalty that AS Roma would miss, as whoever it was that took it blazed it over the cross bar, allowing Alan Kennedy, who I had seen playing for England only a few weeks before, to slot home the winning spot kick.

And that was that. Little did I know that the following season would bring for me some of the highest highs, the lowest lows, and for all football fans, the most tragic of tragedies.

Season 1984/85

Preston North End v Telford United

FA Cup Second Round

December 8th, 1984 Deepdale

To say that both my teams would have contrasting fortunes would be an understatement this season. I use the word "both" with a certain reticence, but this season I went to watch more Preston matches than any other season before, as well as watching quite a few at Old Trafford as well. I still felt a certain amount of guilt about going to watch United. They were not my team, and it wasn't as if I'd abandoned Preston. I remained faithful to my first love, but was having a bit of an exotic dalliance with a frankly more exciting mistress. My use of the pronouns "we" and "us" will always be reserved for Preston, as I am a part of "our" club. Always have been and always will be. Manchester United were mine and my dad's adventure into something bigger, something more vibrant and something with at least the prospect of some success. Preston were not going to give us anything along those lines for the next two seasons – the complete opposite in fact.

My season began with watching Preston lose 3-0 at home to Rotherham. This result did obviously not bode well, and over the course of the season it carried on in the same vein, getting worse if anything.

In contrast, my first game at Old Trafford was a UEFA Cup first round tie against a team called Raba Vasas ETO Gyor. I'd never heard of them then, and I've just had to look them up now to discover they are a team from Hungary. Give yourself a sticker if you knew that already. It was my first ever experience of a European match, and also my first ever under the floodlights at Old Trafford.

It was also the first time that I would get to see Bryan Robson, having recovered from his injury at the end of the previous season. Robson did not disappoint and United won comfortably 3-0, in front of a rather sparse crowd of just over 33,000. This last phrase, including the word "sparse" when used with the figure 33,000, says it all about the contrast in my football viewing at that time. Preston were averaging just over a tenth of this rather "sparse" crowd for their home games, with their lowest attendance of the season being just over 2,500. I told you the contrast was huge.

I would go onto watch United draw with Watford, lose against an awesome Everton team in the League Cup in front of over 50,000 fans, comfortably beat Luton, Norwich, QPR and Ipswich, lose to Sheffield Wednesday and Coventry, beat another rather unknown Hungarian team, Videoton, in the fourth round of the UEFA Cup, before actually going out of the UEFA Cup in that round, losing 1-0 in Hungary and then losing the subsequent penalty shootout. My last game at Old Trafford that season, but my penultimate game watching United, was a thumping 5-0 victory against Stoke. United would end up fourth in the league though, their inconsistency, as ever, being to

91

blame for yet again not winning the title. There would be one more game to come for me, but at the time I had no idea about it.

In stark contrast, after seeing Preston early in the season being humiliated at home by Rotherham, we would go onto lose 25 more league games, quite a few by at least three or four goals. By the time my birthday came around again in late April, we were clinging on by our fingertips to survive relegation.

On my past few birthdays, I had been Preston's mascot, watched an International game involving the League's best striker, and a match at Old Trafford in which I met my footballing hero. This year's treat would be a dour 0-0 draw at home against Gillingham, which would confirm our relegation for the first time ever into the bottom division of the English League system.

We were already on our third manager of the season, and no amount of managerial changes would help. We were down, eventually finishing second from bottom with a goal difference of minus 49. It had been a truly awful season, but the lowest point, apart from relegation being confirmed on my twelfth birthday, was our FA Cup Second Round tie against non-league Telford United, which would lead to us getting rid of our manager Gordon Lee just before Christmas.

The previous season, Telford had finished mid-table in the Alliance Premier League, now the National League or Football Conference, and were a semi-professional team who had had a few decent FA Cup results, reaching the fourth round the season before. Never in a million years did my dad and I think that we would come away from Deepdale that day in December 1984 having watched our team not only get beaten, but humiliated 4-1.

There was a good crowd in there that day, over 6000 turning up, expecting an easy win to give us all an early winter boost before the tough schedule of the Christmas period. We got the exact opposite, and instead of giving us the boost we were looking for, we came away feeling bewildered, dejected, and also angry. My dad has never been one for chanting and singing along whilst watching football. He prefers to study the game closely, but occasionally he would shout out words of encouragement or advice, his favourite phrase being "Come on Whites, get a grip!"

Dad's anger was bubbling under the surface the further behind we went, and as Telford scored their fourth goal that afternoon, and completed our abject humiliation, I looked at my dad's face and saw him at the most exasperated I'd ever seen him before at a football match. He finally could keep quiet no longer and he stood up and bellowed out "This is an absolute disgrace. You're professionals. Have some pride and self-respect!"

I was shocked at my dad's uncharacteristic outburst but could understand his frustration. Here was a man who had started watching Preston in the days of Tom Finney, who had been to watch them at Wembley in the FA Cup final, who had spent a lot of his hard-earned money supporting them, and effectively helped to pay these players' wages.

He has always had a very strong Methodist work ethic, and when he saw professional players not even putting the effort in to earn their wages, then that was the final straw which led to this sudden paroxysm. I think we may have even left early that day as he felt the team were not worthy of his support – the one and only time I remember doing that. It certainly was the worst day in our history and would be the catalyst for our season's demise and ultimate relegation. Not a word was said to each other in the car on our journey home; I thought it was best to just leave him to his own thoughts, and probably prayers.

It certainly didn't stop us from going to watch our team; true supporters go through thick and thin, and this was definitely the thinnest period in both our lives as Preston fans. We lost the next home match against York 4-2, ensuring our Christmas period got off to the worst possible start. We would not win another game until the end of February, and that was against the only other team who ended up below us in the league that season, Cambridge United. My dad's spirit was revived to an extent, so we travelled away to Valley Parade to watch them against Bradford, but were again thrashed 3-0 by the eventual Champions. We would see them lose 4-1 at home again, beaten by Hull City this time, just before my birthday.

From that point on, our fingertips could no longer cling on, conceding five to our local neighbours Wigan Athletic in our final home game of the season, and so falling into the pandemonium of League Division 4. If we thought this season was bad, then the following season would see us being tormented as never before.

Carnforth High School v Castle School

Lancaster and Morecambe District Under 12s' Cup

March 27th, 1985   Giant Axe Stadium, Lancaster

All this turmoil at Deepdale coincided with my greatest season as a player. I was now at my local Secondary School, Carnforth High, and after my success at primary school, I was obviously keen to carry on my own footballing journey. After playing rugby for the first time between September and Christmas, I was glad to get that over with and start the school football season, which would run until Easter.

On a freezing cold January afternoon, all the boys who wanted to be considered for the Year 7 football team had to attend training. This was the afternoon we would all show our teacher what we could offer to the team and what our favoured position was. We'd all come from different primary schools, and although we all knew each other by now, we weren't sure what each other's footballing abilities were.

I was hoping to get a midfield role, still trying to emulate Bryan Robson, and I think I performed quite well. But would it be good enough to get into the A Team (not the one with BA and Hannibal) or would I have to slip down into the B Team? Our first game against one of the other local schools was the following Saturday morning, and all those who attended training spent the rest of the week anxiously waiting for the team sheet to be pinned up on the Thursday.

I hoped and possibly suspected I'd be good enough for the A Team, after all I had been Captain of my primary school team, but there were a lot of good players who'd come from other primary schools, and so places would be limited. Thursday came around and we all crowded round at morning break to see our fate. My name was on the A Team sheet, but I was only sharing the game with another lad who was vying for a midfield role too. I would play the first half, whilst he would play the second. I couldn't help but feel rather disappointed, but would just have to impress with my performance in the first half.

The lad who I was sharing the game with has since become one of my closest and oldest friends, and ever since then we've always had a healthy competitive rivalry, but at that moment he was more than a rival. He was the one stopping me from getting a full place in the team.

Our teacher was basically using the first game we played as a yard stick, to allow him to pick the best team for the rest of the season, and we both must have done well on the Saturday as the next game the following week, both our names were in midfield, this time for the full match. I was to play on the right side of midfield, with him

95

on the left, flanking our best player, who controlled the middle of the pitch in the same way that Ray Wilkins had done for Man United.

I was really pleased for my other best mate, my goalkeeper from primary school, who had also been given half a game for the first match, before winning that mini rivalry and becoming our team's first choice keeper. I think he still had the gloves I'd bought him over a year ago. Maybe he still has them now, thirty-four years later.

Our season was going well, beating most of the other teams in the local area, only losing to the largest comprehensive, Morecambe High. There was no organised League competition, but there was a knockout cup competition, where the final would be played at Lancaster City's ground, Giant Axe. It was, and still is, a very small stadium, but to play there would mean playing on a full-size pitch that actually had a stand for the spectators.

We thought we might have a chance of doing well in this competition, especially after the favourites, Morecambe High, the school who had already beaten us, went out in the second round in a shock result. This upset gave every other team hope that they could actually win the competition. We sailed through our quarter-final, but just before our semi-final, I came down with tonsillitis and had to stay home from school for the week before the game. I knew I wouldn't be able to play and so had to just hope that not only would we win, but also that my replacement wouldn't play well enough to keep me out of the team for the final.

Thankfully, both happened and so in the final we would be playing against a school from Lancaster, the school who had beaten the favourites back in Round 2. We'd already beaten them in our usual Saturday morning "league" match, but neither team could call themselves favourites. It was going to be a close-run thing.

The big day arrived, and I just had to get through five lessons before we would get into the minibus and drive to Lancaster. My French, English, Maths, and double Woodwork lessons seemed to drag on longer than usual that day, but as soon as the bell went for the end of the day, we rushed down to the PE department and waited eagerly for our teacher. As soon as he arrived, we all piled into the minibus with our bags and got to Lancaster. There was no helicopter journey for us, as Brighton had done two years previously, and not even any helicopter camera footage of us as we drove the seven miles into Lancaster. But once we arrived at the ground and got into the changing rooms, we felt as near to proper footballers than any of us had ever done before.

My dad said he'd be able to get away from work early, so as soon as we came out onto the pitch, I scanned the perimeter for him. Sure enough, there he was, with his trusty camera. I so wanted to make him proud and him being there meant the world to me. Even if Preston had given him absolutely no chance of winning anything that season, at least his son might win something.

The game was predictably very tight, nerves getting the better of both teams, until after only about fifteen minutes, my best mate in goals was adjudged to have taken the ball out of the penalty area as he went to deliver one of his many practised kicks up the pitch. Maybe he should have practised not just his kicking, but also had his eyesight checked as he failed to see the line he carried the ball over. I still wind him up to this day about how he nearly lost us the Cup Final in Year 7.

It was a very harsh decision, and from the resulting free kick, right on the edge of the area, our opponents scored with an excellent direct hit into the top corner. Postage stamp in fact. We felt very hard done by, but within ten minutes we were level. I picked the ball up in midfield and automatically looked for our very quick right winger.

He didn't have to beat players with skill, he would just knock it past them and outsprint them, which he again did, getting to the by-line, before delivering a cross right onto the head of our big centre forward who powered it into the back of the net.

So, it was 1-1 at half time, and the game continued to be very tight. Either side could have snatched it to be honest, but with only fifteen or so minutes to go, my other best mate, the one who I had had to share the first match of the season with, received the ball a few yards outside the area on the left hand side. He dropped his shoulder, went past one defender, and then hit a shot which crept inside their keeper's far post. It didn't exactly get smashed in, but in it went and we were 2-1 up. Glory was within our grasp.

After some late scares in our own area, my mate made a great save to make up for his earlier error, and we just about managed to hold on and become District Champions. The crowd, well my dad anyway, went wild at the final whistle. He didn't actually, but the look he gave me as I received my Winner's medal and held the cup aloft told me that I had played well and that he was immensely proud of me. He managed to get some great photos of us all after the game, as we crowded around the trophy in our dressing room. All that was missing were the bottles of champagne and the Instagram posts.

We had done it, and whatever happened to Preston that season, there was nothing that would take away the feeling of joy I had that evening. At the end of term Awards' Assembly, a few members of our team were singled out to receive a certificate for their Outstanding Achievement in Football, and I was lucky enough to be one of them. It was a really special moment as I went up on stage in front of the school to receive my certificate from the Headteacher. A lovely juicy cherry on the top of the icing.

Unfortunately, that would be the pinnacle of my footballing career at school. In the next few years the team broke up, a couple of the farmer lads, including our prolific centre forward, had to help their dads on the farm and so couldn't commit to playing anymore. Another couple, including our central midfield Ray Wilkins type, decided to make more of their rugby and joined the local team, which prevented them from playing on Saturdays too. We got to the semi-final the next year but were soundly beaten and would never again reach the heights of that first year at secondary school. But at least we had reached those heights once.

That wouldn't be the last final I experienced that season, but first came something which would shock everyone in football, and would put Preston's relegation into the most awful of perspectives for me.

Bradford City v Lincoln City

May 11ᵗʰ, 1985   Valley Parade

As Preston's dismal season was coming to an end just 45 miles away up the A64 in York, Bradford City were having what should have been the most glorious final day of the season. They had won League Division 3 the previous week and so the whole crowd were in celebratory mood. It was a beautiful Spring day, and the team were presented with the trophy just before kick-off, their first piece of silverware for 56 years, and over 11,000 fans had come along to be a part of such a wonderful spectacle, almost double their average for that season, with 3000 fans in the main stand.

We all know what happened next, or if we don't, then we should.

Just before half-time a small fire broke out underneath the main stand after a fan had dropped a cigarette on the floor, but before he had time to put it out with the underside of his shoe, it had fallen through a gap in the wooden floorboards, landing on a pile of litter which had accumulated there over the past few months. He saw a small fire break out below him so poured some of his coffee through the gap, which seemed to put it out. A minute or so later, the apparently extinguished small fire got going again, and so the man went to inform a steward. By the time they returned, the fire had taken hold properly.

Some spectators could feel heat rising from underneath them, and so someone went to find a fire extinguisher, but there were none available. A police officer shouted for an extinguisher, but his call was misheard, and instead the fire brigade was called.

If such a simple measure as ensuring working fire extinguishers were readily available, what happened in the next few minutes would have been dealt with quickly. Instead, 56 people died, with many others left with life changing injuries, in the most careless, preventable and, quite frankly, criminal of tragedies we had ever seen in this country.

Due to the age of the wooden stand, which was also covered with highly flammable roofing felt, the fire raged and raced its way along the stand as the fans fled, many getting onto the pitch to escape danger. If there had been perimeter fencing to prevent fans from entering the playing area, then the tragedy would undoubtedly have been even worse. Because it was just before half-time, many fans had already gone underneath the stand to get their refreshments, and so were oblivious of the danger they were in until it was too late.

There was no way of getting back up and onto the pitch due to the flames and the choking smoke, so the only way to escape the flames was to go through the doors next to the turnstiles they had used as they entered the ground an hour or so ago. As it was nowhere near the end of the game, these doors were padlocked and so scores of people were trapped. They attempted to smash the doors open, and eventually did so, with one other door being frantically prised open by people outside, but for many fans, it was simply too late. Most of the victims died as the flames consumed them whilst trying to escape through these locked doors.

On the pitch, many fans were clambering over each other, desperately trying to get onto the pitch, children being thrown over barriers to get them to safety. We all remember the images of the policeman with his hair on fire after he had been helping people get onto the pitch. I'm sure there were much worse images which could have been shown, but the television producers chose not to.

For those of us who were not there, we can only imagine the scenes that day. It must have been like something from a horror film. Some fans were found dead sitting upright in their seats after the tarpaulin material from the roof had fallen on top of them and prevented them from moving.

By the time the fire brigade arrived, there was nothing left of the stand for them to put out. The whole stand took less than four minutes to be engulfed in deadly flames. It was truly astonishing in its rapidity and virulence.

***

You may wonder why I include this chapter: I was not at the game; I have no allegiances to either of the teams involved. It did have a profound effect on me though. Indeed, I was at Valley Parade only a few months earlier watching Preston lose. The disaster that unfolded that day could have happened during that game instead of this one. I could have been there to witness the dreadful scenes. I could even have been injured, or killed, as two of the Lincoln City fans were.

There were so many young kids with their parents there that day, just as I had been with my dad a few months before. Reading the list of the victims' names, there were fathers there that day, who had taken their boys to watch something that should have stayed with them forever, who died along with their sons. One mother lost not only her husband, but both her sons, aged 11 and 13. Probably just after they'd finished their lunch, she said goodbye to them, hoped that they'd come back with a win to tell her about, and never saw them again. My mum used to do that for me and my dad most Saturdays.

Every time me and my dad sat in Preston's grand old West Stand, I used to feel a real pride about our ground. It was a great piece of Edwardian architecture and took pride of place at Deepdale. I thought nothing of the fact that it was made of wood. I thought nothing of the fact that people casually smoked in it, and discarded their cigarettes even more casually. That was just how it was back then. At no point did I ever think that I was sitting in a potential tinderbox which could kill me. Tragedies like the one at Valley Parade could have happened at many of the football grounds up and down the country. Quite frankly, it was a case of when, and not if, such a fire would happen.

I wrote earlier that this tragedy at Valley Parade was not just careless and preventable, but probably also criminal. The club had been warned less than a year before the fire that their ground safety was woefully below standard. Not only had the build-up of litter been noted, but a county council engineer had said that the problems should be rectified as soon as possible and that a carelessly discarded cigarette could give rise to a fire risk.

The club were less than swift in their response, and only took delivery of steel to improve their stand in March of 1985, less than two months before the fire. They had planned to install the steel and carry out further improvements, such as replacing wooden terracing with concrete, the following season after they had been promoted.

A complete lack of basic fire safety equipment such as plentiful fire extinguishers and easy to open fire doors, along with wretchedly inadequate stewarding meant that this tragedy was not simply an accident. It was more a case of criminal neglect.

As usual, it is only after the event that new legislation was introduced which would have prevented such a tragedy in the first place. The Popplewell Inquiry led to the banning of wooden grandstands at all UK sports grounds, the immediate closure of other wooden stands deemed unsafe, and the banning of smoking in wooden stands – procedures we would not only expect nowadays, but are part and parcel of the fabric of modern-day stadiums. Never has there been a case that such apposite recommendations should have been carried out much earlier.

Or maybe not actually. 32 years later, similar recommendations were ignored which led to a fire consuming a block of flats in West London called Grenfell Tower. We learned a dreadful lesson that day in May 1985, but obviously not enough of a lesson to prevent other such needlessly preventable tragedies from happening, as in the case of Grenfell Tower.

It seems to me that both these tragedies are linked. A football stadium in the mid-80s, and a tower block in which mostly immigrants live, are both filled with people who the government do not really care much about, and so can't be bothered to ensure their safety. It is not just the local council's or the football club's responsibility to ensure the safety of those people who populate such structures; it is also the government's responsibility to enforce such safety procedures.

Blame has to be apportioned to many different organisations who failed the victims and their families that day. The Bradford City fire, and subsequently the Grenfell Tower fire are not only national disasters, but also national embarrassments which we should be appalled by, and thoroughly ashamed of.

With a certain macabre irony, one of Bradford's most famous sons, J.B. Priestley, wrote in "An Inspector Calls", way back in 1946, "We don't live alone. We are members of one body. We are responsible for each other. And I tell you that the time will soon come when, if men will not learn that lesson, then they well be taught it in fire and blood and anguish."

I think he makes my point better than I ever could.

Everton v Manchester United

FA Cup Final May 18th, 1985

Wembley Stadium

I mentioned earlier that even though I'd paid my last visit of the season to Old Trafford, it would not be the final time I would watch Manchester United. The FA Cup Final would be the final time.

United had got through after a tense semi-final against arch-rivals Liverpool. After a 2-2 draw at Goodison Park, the replay would be held at Maine Road. United went in at half time 1-0 down, but an equaliser from Captain Fantastic Bryan Robson, and a winner from Mark Hughes meant that they would be going to Wembley to meet Howard Kendall's Everton, who themselves were going for the Double after trouncing everyone in the League, finishing thirteen points clear of their Merseyside rivals. Liverpool's only chance of a trophy this season would be yet another European Cup – sounds quite familiar.

I had no idea that I would be going to the game at Wembley until only two days before. All week at school I had been getting more excited as the big day got closer. This year I would definitely have a preferred winner – I'd been to a lot of games at Old Trafford this season and so had earned the right to call myself a United fan. My footballing allegiances had been expanded since United's last appearance in the final two years before, and let's face it, Preston were definitely not going to give me the opportunity of watching them in the final, as they had done for my dad 21 years earlier. My dad knew this too but still wanted to give me the chance to experience something he had done as a young lad.

Nowadays there are strict guidelines on obtaining Cup Final tickets, only using recommended ticket agencies affiliated with either the clubs involved, or the FA. Back then, ticket touts could very easily buy a load of tickets and flog them on for a profit. At almost the last minute, and on a whim, my dad rung the ticket office at Old Trafford to see if there were any tickets still available. Obviously there weren't, but the very nice lady on the other end of the phone told him that there were a few touts outside the ground offering tickets for a certain price.

He drove all the way down to the ground and managed to get a couple of tickets at a reasonably marked up price. He didn't mind. Not only was he going to be able to take his football mad son to Wembley, but he could relive his visit to watch Preston. This time he may even see a win for the team he was supporting.

He kept it secret all day from me and then, as he came in from "work" that day and sat down as usual for his tea, he told me that unfortunately I wouldn't be able to watch the Cup Final on Saturday as we had to go somewhere. I was distraught. Where could I possibly have to go which would mean missing the most important match of the season? From his pocket he casually placed the two tickets on the table and watched my face turn from disgruntled annoyance, to a bewildered disbelief. After a couple of seconds, it sunk in. I was going to the FA Cup Final, the Holy Grail of football matches, and one that I'd been obsessed with ever since I could remember.

At school the next day, word got around that I would be going to Wembley the following day, so I had a few mates, and also older kids from further up the school, asking me if I could bring a programme back for them, which made me feel extremely lucky, but also very conscious of others feeling jealous of me. My dad had given me something that no one else's dad in the whole school had given to their kids. My first hero had given me the chance of watching my second hero, the captain of Manchester United, lift the cup.

All United had to do was to beat Everton, not only the runaway League Champions, but also the winners of the European Cup Winner's Cup, which they had secured the day before my dad surprised me with the tickets, beating Rapid Vienna 3-1.

Everton were a brilliant team that year. They had basically won everything they had competed for, apart from the League Cup since winning the FA Cup the previous year. They were certainly the favourites to beat United, but United had a knack of upsetting the odds, particularly in Cup matches.

Dad woke me up early on the Saturday morning, probably around seven o'clock as we had to get to Lancaster to catch the train down to London. I gave mum strict instructions to video the whole of the build-up to the game, on our newly acquired Ferguson Videostar, as well as the game itself, in the vain hope that I might be able to see myself on screen. This was going to be a day I would need to keep on tape forever.

I knew this was going to be a big day, as at 7.45 am there was already quite a large group of United fans waiting on the platform at Lancaster station, already drinking beers and already being quite vocal. We got on the train and settled down for the three-and-a-half-hour journey. The group of United fans were in the same carriage as us and the songs and chants were starting to get going.

At each stop we made, more fans got on and joined in the songs, mostly about how much they hated not Everton, but Liverpool. These were fans who probably went into the Stretford End every week, something my dad had never done with me, preferring a quieter, more family orientated place to watch. I had never been in such a riotous atmosphere on a train journey before. It was fun and felt slightly mischievous. My dad winced whenever one of the chants included swearing, although he did enjoy the one to the tune of "She wore, she wore, she wore a scarlet ribbon" in which the famous Man United were going to Wem-ber-ley. There was no swearing in that one. He may even have joined in.

As we pulled into Euston and joined all the other fans who were now streaming out of the carriages, my excitement grew. I could see banners and flags draped around the shoulders of the fans as we all made our way into the underground to get the tube up to Wembley Park station. The chanting got louder as we went deeper into the Tube system, and I was conscious of everyday Londoners getting annoyed with us Northerners who seemed to have taken over their city.

It was by now just after midday and we emerged from the Tube to be greeted by the magnificent sight of the Twin Towers of the great old stadium welcoming us, almost luring us towards them. By now there were fans from both teams congregating, and the atmosphere was actually very jovial and friendly as we got ourselves some lunch from a sandwich stall, and sat and watched the interactions between the groups of fans.

There wasn't the hatred between United and Everton. If anything, there was a certain amount of respect towards the Everton fans as their team had knocked Liverpool from their perch as Champions. I'm not sure the atmosphere would have been quite so friendly if United had been facing Liverpool.

The chants were not really aimed at Everton or Liverpool, but were certainly derogatory about the city of Liverpool. This was the mid-80s after all, a time of huge unemployment on Merseyside. This was post "Boys from the Blackstuff", in which Yosser Hughes had become so famous for his catchphrase "Gizza job". Unemployment was running at over 20% in Liverpool in 1985, double the national average, and the Mancunians were not about to let them forget this.

They would sing the tune of "You'll Never Walk Alone", but change the words to "You'll Never Get A Job, sign on, sign on, with hope in your hearts…" At the time, my innocent twelve-year-old self found this chant quite funny, and as it didn't have any swearing and was easy to learn, I found myself joining in, to my dad's annoyance. He didn't like this song as even though it was clean, it was too cruel.

I now realise that this was the cruellest chant of all. Fair enough to be singing about how bad the other team was, or how great their team was, but United had been in both Merseyside club's shadow for a long time. United hadn't won the league for eighteen years and had to watch their greatest rivals win it many times, along with four European Cups. Now Everton were starting to do the same, so the only way they could feel superior was to attack their fans' social standing.

A man's ability to work, to earn money, to provide for his family gives him not only a sense of worth and pride, but also a sense of identity. This chant targeted the very essence of being a male working-class football fan. It attacked his self-respect, not his football team. It made the Everton fans feel powerless, something which their football team made up for to an extent, but it was still aimed at their metaphorical solar plexus. I understand why the United fans sang the song; it was their only way of feeling superior. It was up to their football team to make them feel that way now.

The last time I'd been to Wembley it was empty and eerie. This time it was the complete opposite, packed full with 100,000 vibrant, noisy, expectant fans, easily the biggest crowd I'd ever been a part of. The United fans were all in the end opposite the tunnel, and eventually me and my dad managed to get a decent view, with me perching on one of the crush barriers, him holding onto me, making sure I didn't slip off into the melee.

The whole situation seemed surreal to me. I'd seen crowds like this only on the television. Here I was, in amongst a seething mass of football fans, all seeming to need a piss at the same time, which ran down the terraces, singing along to "Abide With Me", cheering wildly as the two teams emerged from the tunnel, belting out The National Anthem before the players were introduced to The Duke of Kent, and generally being in a state of utter excitement, waiting for the game to start.

Strangely I remember very little about the game itself. Lots of players who have actually played in the FA Cup Final say they also don't remember that much, and I understand why now. There is simply so much to take in, so much sensory overload that your brain can't process it all and it becomes all a bit of a blur. I do remember Peter Reid hitting the post in the first half after a poor clearance from a corner, but the only other incident I recall from the ninety minutes is the one that this final became historic for. And it wasn't a goal.

Never before had there been a player sent off in an FA Cup Final, but this changed in the seventy-eighth minute. Peter Reid was clean through on goal with only Gary Bailey in United's goal to beat. It was the clearest of clear scoring opportunities ever. United's centre back, Kevin Moran, had to take drastic action. He attempted to take the ball, he really did, but was woefully late, and scythed Reid down. In today's game, it was a straight red card all day long, but back then, professional fouls were still rarely punished with a yellow card, let alone a dismissal.

The United fans went mad, as did the United players. They felt that Peter Willis, the referee that day, was being over officious and wanted to make a name for himself. I could see their point. It was an honest challenge, but just a very late one. Frankly it looked worse than it actually was, Peter Reid flying up into the air such was the pace he was going, but he was not in any way hurt by the challenge. Kevin Moran was in tears as he eventually left the pitch, after desperately attempting to make the referee change his mind, but to no avail. He had just become the first ever player to get sent off in an FA Cup Final.

This could easily have affected United. They could have lost their heads and allowed Everton to nick a winner in the final ten minutes, but instead their resolve was strengthened. They had suffered an injustice and were determined to put it right. The ninety minutes ticked by, still goalless. This was the first FA Cup Final I had ever seen where neither team had scored in normal time, but that would change with only ten minutes of extra time left.

I was preparing myself for the disappointment of neither team scoring and started wondering whether we would have to come back down the following Thursday, if indeed we would be able to come back down. Probably not actually. My first ever experience of a Cup Final would also be the first ever one played at Wembley which had ended goalless. A certain young man named Norman Whiteside would put an end to those fears.

There are certain goals/incidents I remember because of the commentary on the TV. We all know the most famous piece of commentary ever, Kenneth Wolstenholme's iconic, "They think it's all over; it is now", and we all know which goal it describes. For me there are a few others. Let's see how many you can get:

1. "Oh. My. Word, have you ever seen anything like that?"
2. "Look at his face, just look at his face!"
3. "Name on the trophy!"
4. "What a save – Gordon Banks!"
5. "Whiteside shoots – it's there!"

6. "Agueroooooooo!"
7. "Oh, you have to say that's magnificent!"
8. "And Solskjaer has won it!"

The answers, in no particular order, are: Gordon Banks' wonder save - England v Brazil 1970; Teddy Sheringham's equaliser – Man United v Bayern Munich 1999; Diego Maradona's second goal, scored with his foot rather than his hand – England v Argentina 1986; Francis Lee on his return to Maine Road – Manchester City v Derby County 1974; Eusebio's thunderbolt at Goodison Park – Portugal v Brazil 1966; Ole Gunnar Solskjaer's winner – Man United v Bayern Munich 1999; Sergio Aguero's last second winner – Manchester City v QPR 2012.

The remaining answer is Norman Whiteside's winner in the 1985 FA Cup Final, and ironically, I didn't hear the commentary as I was there in the crowd. I subsequently have watched the goal countless times and so has become rooted in my memory (my mum was true to her word and taped the game for me.)

By the second period of extra time the game was becoming very stretched, with wide open spaces appearing. Players were going down with cramp, and Robson had his socks rolled down yet again. Mark Hughes received the ball in his own half, and just knocked the ball up into a big space on the right-hand side where Norman Whiteside picked it up. He had no passing options as all the United players were mostly still in their own half. He would have to do something very special if he was to score, and that is just what he did.

The Everton full-back closed him down as he pushed on towards the corner of the penalty area. One little stepover before he saw the slightest of gaps to aim for and released a perfect left-footed shot which curled around the full-back, just out of reach of Neville

Southall's desperately outstretched right hand. "Whiteside shoots – it's there!"

The noise was just mind-blowing. Remember that I was used to being in crowds of usually around 4000, so when 50,000 fans, give or take, exploded into euphoria, it really was quite overwhelming. Everyone was just jumping up and down with bulging eyes. I was surrounded by 50,000 Marco Tardellis and it literally brought tears to my eyes.

After such a long wait, with the first ninety minutes, and then the first extra time I had ever experienced, my brain was so bombarded with noise and ecstatic bewilderment, that tears just poured down my face. I think my dad may even have let out a few tears too, not simply because of the goal, but also because his son was getting to experience this beautiful madness. He never had such a feeling when he was at the Cup Final in 1964, quite the opposite in fact when West Ham scored their last-minute winner.

The next thing I remember was how long the final few minutes felt. No one seemed to know how long was left. Some people said 10 minutes, other were saying only two. It felt like at least 20, but eventually the clock ticked down and the whistle blew. Cue the madness again.

I literally do not remember much else about the day. I must have watched Bryan Robson lead his team up the steps and lift the Cup. I watched it so many times again in the days and weeks after the game, but the actual event does not register in my mind. What did register was that the cheering and celebrating all seemed to stop when the referee climbed the steps to receive his medal. The cheers turned to boos and the atmosphere became quite ominous for a few seconds, before returning to celebratory joy.

112

We must have left the stadium, got back on the tube, got to Euston station, and got on the train to head back up north, but again, I do not remember it. My mind had taken in about as much as it could. It must have been completely saturated.

All I do remember is that the train was absolutely crammed full, to the point where no seats were available, and all the aisles were filled with standing fans too. Me and my dad sat on the floor next to a luggage compartment, and suddenly a suitcase looked extremely comfortable. The next thing I know, we were arriving in Lancaster, probably around 11.30. I don't know whether my dad had fallen asleep too, or whether he had kept an eye on me the whole journey after I passed out into exhaustion. I suspect the latter.

We got home about midnight and even though I had just slept for four hours, I instantly fell into another deep sleep as soon as I crawled into bed. It truly was a most wonderful day, one which I'll never forget, and one which I will always be thankful for.

The next game I'd watch would be also one I'll never forget, but I certainly wouldn't be thankful for it.

Juventus v Liverpool

European Cup Final

May 29th, 1985   Heysel Stadium, Brussels

Every single evening after the FA Cup Final, I was out with my mates playing football on our old primary school field. I was trying, without success, to replicate Norman Whiteside's goal, but my left foot has always been rather embarrassing compared to my right. We would be playing until around nine o'clock every evening, usually playing a game of wally, which was kind of like squash but without the side walls. Each player took it in turns to hit the wall with the ball, and we had to hit it first time, no controlling touches allowed. Once someone missed, then they went on the wall and became a goalkeeper, or more appropriately, a wallkeeper. This meant that if there were eight of us playing, the final two would have to beat six keepers to win. It was great practice and great fun.

This night we would all leave the game early as we all wanted to go and watch the European Cup Final. It was almost a given by now that there would be an English team in the final, and usually that team would be Liverpool. And so it was again this season.

At about half past seven, we all drifted home to settle down to watch what would probably be Liverpool's fifth win. They were up against the mighty Juventus team which included Michel Platini as captain, the great polish midfielder Zbigniew Boniek, and also two scorers in the 1982 World Cup Final, Paulo Rossi and our old friend Marco Tardelli. Despite these great players, Liverpool were probably slight favourites, and I had no doubts that they would win England's eighth European Cup in the last nine years.

I got in, and mum and dad were already in the front room with the television on, but there were no pundits chatting in the build-up to the game. Instead the TV screen just showed scenes of confusion, carnage, violence, and most horribly of all, death.

I'd sadly become accustomed to scenes of crowd violence at football matches, although never experiencing it myself at a stadium. The appalling scenes at the FA Cup quarter final only a couple of months before between Luton and Millwall are seared onto anyone's memory who witnessed it, having been broadcast on the BBC's Wednesday evening Sportsnight programme. That night Millwall had asked Luton to make the match all-ticket to try and reduce the potential for trouble, but the home team did not heed the warning.

A huge number of Millwall fans made the trip up to Bedfordshire, more than twice the average home attendance at Kenilworth Road, and basically went on the rampage, smashing shop windows in the town centre, before breaking turnstiles at the ground, or climbing over fences to enter the stadium.

They then tore up seats to use as missiles to bombard the Luton fans. The police were helpless in the face of such numbers. And this is the point; the police should never have been helpless. There seemed to be no forethought, no coordination, no assistance, no common sense from the FA which could have prevented such trouble. And so it was absolutely inevitable that there would be trouble, which indeed there was.

I am not singling out Millwall fans, or Liverpool fans. Most teams back then, my own included, had a hardcore number of "supporters" who followed their team not for the football, but for the fighting. I would need to write a whole book on why hooliganism became such a part of football culture, indeed British culture in the 1970s and 80s. Many books already have been written. Socio-economic factors, club tribalism, and a system which actually seemed to encourage fans to get drunk and cause havoc, were all stubbornly ignored by the authorities. Not just in England, but to a lesser extent across Europe too.

Potential for trouble between fans was a fact of football back then, and nobody seemed to know what to do about it, and instead of trying to prevent or solve the problem, the authorities just carried on regardless. It was only a matter of time before the violence became fatal.

Whichever set of fans caused the trouble in Brussels that night, and ultimately the deaths of 39 people, is disputed. Liverpool blame the Italian fans for goading their fans, but let's be honest, if the Liverpool fans had not taken the bait, if indeed they needed any bait, they would not have ripped down the flimsiest of fences separating the two sets of opposing fans, and rushed towards the Juventus fans, who only naturally retreated towards the crumbling wall which would then collapse.

I am in no way excusing the Liverpool fans for what happened that night, but yet again, the police were needlessly helpless in that situation. They should never have had a situation like that to deal with. UEFA knew the potential risks but chose to stubbornly carry on as they always had. In fact, on this occasion, they actively facilitated the potential for trouble and ultimately deaths.

To choose a stadium which was not just in a poor state of repair, but literally falling to bits, was their first major error. The President of Juventus and the Chairman of Liverpool had both urged UEFA to choose another venue, especially as the game would involve two of Europe's biggest teams, with huge numbers of fans who would travel to the ground, whether they had tickets or not. UEFA's inspection of the ground had lasted just thirty minutes, so whoever signed the inspection off has blood on their hands too. Lots of it.

Fans who did not have tickets were able to literally kick their way into the ground, as part of the outer wall was made from cinder block. Once in the ground, the opposing fans were separated by a temporary chain link fence, and a central thinly policed no-man's land. The crumbling stadium actually provided missiles in the form of broken bits of concrete for the fans to throw at each other.

UEFA did not only facilitate the violence; it would seem that they actually encouraged it. There had been no restrictions on the consumption of alcohol, no screening of known hooligans, no attempt to ask for advice from British police. It was a complete and utter shambles; the least amusing farce ever.

Inevitably, tensions between the fans reached a crisis. The fence was ripped down, the wholly inadequate number of police were overpowered, and the terraces became a free-for-all. The Italian and also many neutral Belgian fans naturally ran away after being confronted by a large group of marauding scousers.

The fleeing fans were then pressed up against the perimeter wall, which gave way under the pressure. Most of the 39 deaths and hundreds of injuries were caused not by the wall collapsing, which actually relieved pressure, but by being trampled or suffocated in the melee. As soon as bodies were seen being laid out, the Juventus fans at the opposite end of the stadium started to riot in retaliation, adding to the mayhem. It kind of looked like a war zone with the blood red flares adding to the hellish atmosphere.

Some sort of order was eventually restored after both teams' captains were asked to appeal for calm. Phil Neal must have felt completely out of his depth. He should never have been put into such a position, and it showed just how inept the policing was that evening. Resorting to asking the players to basically beg for order and calm is a damning indictment of the police's lack of authority, lack of resources, and lack of control.

As for the game itself, it should never have taken place. The authorities feared a further escalation of chaos if the game was postponed and so, with bodies still waiting to be taken away outside the ground, both teams were put in an impossible situation.

No one remembers anything about the game, apart from the penalty which Michel Platini converted to win it for Juventus. The fact that the game was played at all is just another disgrace in a long line of disgraces that happened that night. I'm sure the Liverpool players could not care less that they had lost the game. They were in no way to blame.

But who was to blame for this deeply shameful absurdity? Without doubt, some Liverpool fans played a large part, some Juventus fans played a smaller part, and the police did not exactly cover themselves in glory either. But ultimately the blame lies with UEFA, for the most incompetent and amateurish organisation of the biggest game in club football in the world.

Instead of taking any responsibility themselves, UEFA simply blanket-banned all English clubs from competing in European competitions for an indefinite period. Another complete fudge. Liverpool's ban was to be for a further three years after the other clubs were reinstated. Eventually English teams were allowed to compete five years later, with Liverpool only having to wait a further year.

Apart from the obvious human tragedy that night, there was a footballing heartbreak too. I have no doubt that Liverpool would have won the match if the circumstances were in any way normal, and poor old Norwich City, who had won the League Cup and so would be eligible to compete in the UEFA Cup the following season, were denied their first ever foray into European football.

Similarly, the magnificent Everton team who had won the League easily, were prevented from attempting to win what their Merseyside rivals had won four times already, the European Cup. They would have done very well, and possibly would have won it in 1986, to continue the English domination of Europe's greatest club competition. It didn't feel like Europe's greatest club competition that night in Brussels. It felt the most shameful of competitions.

We would all have to wait another fourteen years and a change of name for the competition to see another English victory, and it certainly wouldn't be Everton, nor indeed Liverpool who would win it next. But of course, that pales into insignificance next to the real tragedy of that night in May. A tragedy which is still the most indelible of stains on European football's history.

Season 1985/86

Manchester United v Everton

FA Charity Shield

August 10th, 1985   Wembley Stadium

As always happens, football carried on. The new season began as usual and Heysel, though not forgotten, faded away at the prospect of football being played again. After such an awesome day in May watching the Cup Final, my dad wanted the rest of the family to experience something that he and I had done. An exact repeat of the Cup Final would be this season's traditional opening match, with Cup Winners United playing against League Champions Everton. Gary Lineker had just signed for Everton, and would play just one season for the Blues, before getting snapped up by the mighty Barcelona. Other than that, the teams were basically the same as those who had fought out such a tight game in May, apart from the exclusion of Kevin Moran in the United defence, as he had been suspended following his historic sending off in the Cup Final.

No train this time as my dad drove down to London, with my mum and brother in tow. To be honest, the whole day lacked the excitement or the buzz of the Cup Final. It didn't feel as special as it wasn't just me and my dad, and of course there was nothing really at stake. It was simply a chance for my mum and brother to see what Wembley was like when it was full, rather than the empty experience of the guided tour, but as Woody Allen said in "Annie Hall", "As empty experiences go, it's one of the best."

Even though the stadium was packed full of fans who had been starved of football for over two months, with no summer tournament that year, the atmosphere was still empty. There was just no intensity about the game, which is often the case with the Charity Shield match, or Community Shield as it is now known. The game is basically just a glorified friendly match, where the managers of both teams are still working out what their best team is, ready for the following week when the season starts properly. As a result, there was no repeat of the drama and tension of the Cup Final, and Everton ran out easy 2-0 winners.

I literally don't remember anything about the game at all as it was so tame and boring. Apparently, Trevor Steven and Adrian "Inchy" Heath each scored a goal in each half, but I doubt even the most ardent of fans of either club could describe either of the goals now. It was just all so flat and tepid. If I hadn't had the mind-blowing emotions in May, then maybe I would have been blown away by this experience. But I had, and so I wasn't.

We were all waiting for the real football to start the following Saturday, and again, Preston and Man United's fortunes could not be more drastically different. As with the previous season, I would watch both teams as often as my dad could take us, but for the first time ever, Preston would be in the bottom division, whereas United were genuine title contenders in Division One.

You may be thinking that I must have come from a rich and privileged background to be able to go and watch two teams for most of their home games, as well as a few away games, with a couple of trips to Wembley thrown in in the past year. I understand why you may think this with today's prices being so high.

If I were doing now what me and my dad were doing for two seasons in the mid-eighties, it would cost a small fortune. Today, it would easily be the best part of £100, if not more each game for me to take my son or daughter to Old Trafford. Tickets, petrol, parking, refreshments, match programmes; all these add up to a sizeable amount. To do the same at Deepdale today, it is still well over £60 pounds to watch a mid-Championship team, including all the other sundries. If I were doing now with my son or daughter what my dad did with me back then, it would easily set me back around £400 a month, and if I wanted to take my whole family, then the price would instantly double. This is simply not viable for the vast majority of fans.

My dad came from a completely working-class background, left school at fifteen to take an apprentice as a joiner, and eventually started his own business. We were comfortable, but certainly not well-off. Money was never plentiful, and yet he could still afford to do what he did for me, the point being how the game we love has become inaccessible to a lot of ordinary people. Some kids get treated every now and again to a football match, but they certainly do not go most weeks, as I did. Most people simply do not have the money.

From its working-class roots, football has become elitist, with only a certain section of society being able to afford to follow their team week in, week out. The irony is that with more money than ever flooding into the game, fewer people have the opportunity to be true supporters. It was affordable back then, before the behemoth of the Premier League became such a colossal money-making and money-taking machine. This filters down into the lower leagues and prevents a lot of people from watching their team, who may be in League One or League Two.

I'm not blaming or making accusations at anyone. It's just the way it is now. There are plenty of books dedicated to the change in the game with all the billions of pounds being pumped into it, but this book is not one of those, and I am certainly no expert on the finances of the game. What I do know, is that I cannot do for my own kids what my dad did for me, and that's a shame.

Sheffield Wednesday v Manchester United

November 9th, 1985 Hillsborough

Having just ended a chapter about the vast amounts of money flooding into the game at the moment, with the numbers only ever going to increase, and the TV coverage getting even more ubiquitous, it seems absolutely alien to the modern football fan that there was a time in the mid-eighties that football simply was not on the television.

At the start of the 85/86 season the TV companies could not come to an agreement with the FA and so for the first part of the season literally no football was shown on our screens. Can you imagine life without Match of the Day, Football Focus, Super Sunday, Gillette Soccer Special, all the games on BT Sport now? It would be awful. And yet life went on without football on the television. Football needs television, but television does not need football. Maybe that's why my dad took me to so many games this season, as we didn't even have Match of the Day to feed our addiction.

The contrast between United and PNE could not have been more absolute, and for us Preston fans, more grim. I'll deal with the Good first, before going onto the Bad and the Ugly later.

For once, United got off to a flyer, and looked like a team who could, and indeed should, go onto win the league. They won their first match of the season 4-0 against Aston Villa, and would go onto win their next nine league games, dispatching Ipswich, Arsenal, West Ham, Nottingham Forest, Newcastle, Oxford (yes, they were in the top division then), Man City, West Brom and Southampton, before the mighty Luton held them to a 1-1 draw.

I went to watch five of these games at Old Trafford, and saw United score ten goals, whilst conceding none. They would remain unbeaten for the first fifteen League matches and were miles ahead of everyone else by the start of November. They were playing some of the best football they had ever played, and would ever play, even in the glory days of Alex Ferguson. If they could avoid defeat against Sheffield Wednesday at Hillsborough, then they would break the record for the longest unbeaten start to a season (apart from Preston's Invincible season of course.)

My dad had never been to Hillsborough before and as it was only a two-hour or so drive away, he fancied going to one of the biggest club grounds in the country. It was another ground to be ticked off and I would be going to watch history being made. That was the idea anyway.

Hillsborough was huge. In the early eighties I remember how vast the uncovered kop was which held the Sheffield Wednesday fans. It seemed to go on and on. The club put a roof on this swathe of concrete in May of 1986, so I never got to see the seething masses in their full glory, but from the opposite end, the now infamous Leppings Lane End, where me and my dad were sitting, the home end still looked vast and quite daunting.

Adding to this feeling of doom, the weather was grey and overcast, and in this hard as nails city of steel, I could feel that it was going to be a real test for United, and one which they ultimately could not pass, losing 1-0. People go on about how tough it is getting a result on a cold, wet night in Stoke, well believe me, a cold, wet Saturday in Sheffield is about as tough as the steel they make there, and United were gradually beaten down and hammered into submission. So, I didn't get to see history being made, but I was glad to get out of deepest darkest Yorkshire, and home to the slightly less dark loveliness of Lancashire.

This defeat well and truly burst United's imperious bubble, and they did not win any of their next three games. Their belief was sagging and by Christmas they were still top, but in nowhere near the seemingly unsurpassable position they were in only a month or so earlier.

Bryan Robson, still my hero and United's talisman, had got injured yet again and would play very few games for the rest of the season. They were away at Everton on Boxing Day, and dad took me to Goodison Park to see if they could repeat the heroics of the Cup Final. They had just been beaten by Arsenal and needed a good result against the champions to go into 1986 with some of the confidence they exuded in the early part of the season.

Everton beat them quite easily 3-1 and without Robson to inspire them, United just drifted away, only winning another seven games in the second half of the season, eventually ending up fourth in the table, with Liverpool restoring the previous natural order, pipping Everton to the title by just two points. Liverpool would also go onto complete the double, rubbing their superiority into Everton's faces by beating them 3-1 in the Cup Final, and so becoming only the fourth team to win the double, after Preston (oh sorry have I mentioned that we won the double in 1889?), Spurs and Arsenal.

From a season of such promise, United won nothing, and the board and the fans were getting angry, especially as their fiercest rivals up the M62 were lauding their success over them. But at least they ended up fourth in the top division.

Preston did not even finish fourth from bottom in the bottom division.

Preston North End v Chester City

October 12th, 1985   Deepdale

Whilst United were sweeping aside everyone they played in the early part of this season, Preston were doing the exact opposite. They began the season by conceding four goals at home against Peterborough in a 4-2 defeat and would also lose 6-0 away to Northampton a few weeks later. By the time Chester came to Deepdale the two teams I went to watch regularly were literally at opposite ends of the whole league; United stretching their lead at the top of Division One whilst my beloved Lilywhites were becoming cast adrift at the bottom of Division Four. It really was a case of polar opposites, and yet me and my dad kept on going to watch both teams.

Chester were a decent team that season and would eventually get promoted, finishing second only to the runaway leaders Swindon Town, who won the title with 102 points. Chester scored six goals against us that afternoon. Six! However decent Chester were, they should never have been able to put six goals past us on our own ground, but that is what they did, beating us 6-3 in a frankly bizarre game. Off the top of my head I can only think of two other games in which the home team conceded six or more, both games ironically involving Man United, when they beat Forest 1-8 in their Treble winning season of 1999, and also their humiliating 1-6 loss in 2011 to their Manchester rivals City, Mario Balotelli and all.

I suppose I could also include Brazil's 1-7 loss to Germany in the World Cup semi-final of 2014, as technically Brazil were the home team that day. The embarrassment, the shame and the general gnashing of teeth for the Brazilian fans that day must have been something like the way me and my dad felt against Chester, but at least we had scored three, not just one. But then again, Brazil had lost to the eventual winners of the World Cup, and not to a team who ended up second in the English League Division Four.

This was the first and probably the only time I had seen a team score six against us, home or away, and it definitely signalled the start of literally the darkest time in our history, as not only were we dim and dismal on the field, but our floodlight pylons were deemed unsafe too, which meant that our games throughout the winter months kicked off at 2pm and then 1.30pm so that we could finish the game before whatever sunlight there was faded away. Our midweek evening matches became midweek afternoon matches, resulting in our Freight Rover Trophy match against Bury on Wednesday 29th January 1986 being watched by just 768 supporters, our all-time record lowest attendance, one of whom was a good friend of mine who to this day is proud of being part of that paltry crowd. His presence at that particular game is like a badge of honour for him. It really was the bleakest of bleak midwinters for us.

By that point in the season we were already onto our second manager, with Tommy Booth leaving just before this match against Bury, and Brian Kidd, a European Cup winner with Man United in 1968 taking over. From the glories of lifting club football's greatest prize in front of 100,000 at Wembley against Benfica, to managing his first ever game in front of 768 people on a cold Wednesday afternoon in late January against Bury must have seemed surreal for Kidd. No wonder he only stuck at it for nine games, leaving in March, with no hope for Preston by that point.

Our only aim by then was not to finish bottom, which we just about managed to do due to Torquay being even more awful than us. Good old Torquay. Ever since I went to watch them in that pre-season friendly a few years before I've had a soft spot for them. Little did I realise then that they would help us out by being the only team in the whole 92 team league that would finish below us.

My birthday treat this year was our final home game of the season against Exeter, a 2-2 draw on the day before my thirteenth birthday. At least we got a point. The following week our season ended appropriately with a 4-0 humiliation away to Aldershot, and we had to apply for re-election to stay in the League, a League which we were founder members of, a league which we dominated in those first ever seasons, a league which in this day and age we would have been relegated out of, into the void of the non-league pyramid (no disrespect to all those non-league clubs and supporters out there; I have huge admiration for you all).

And so, along with Torquay, Cambridge and Exeter, we had to go on bended knee, with cap in hand, to ask the other League clubs at the AGM whether they deemed us fit to remain a part of the Football League. The last three teams deemed unworthy to be a part of the league anymore were Southport, Workington and Barrow, clubs like us from the North West of England. Thankfully the other league members took pity on us, and we were allowed to try and be less crap next season.

This would be the last time the re-election process would happen, as automatic relegation was introduced the following season, with the bottom club in the league definitely getting kicked out with no chance of any reprieve. It is now the bottom two teams who go, and so we would have been one of those kicked out if the present system existed back in 1986, something that is unimaginable to anyone who is a fan of Proud Preston, a motto which seemed completely incongruous at the end of the 85/86 season in which we finished 91st out of 92 clubs. It was the lowest point in not just mine or my dad's football watching life, but the lowest point for any fan of Preston North End.

Langdale v Coniston

February 1986   Carnforth High School

In secondary school, the House system was basically the same as primary, but this time each house was named after an area of the nearby Lake District. There was Fairfield (Reds), Coniston (Blues), Rydal (Greens) and the house I was put into, Langdale (Yellows). Did this mean that I was now a big fat fellow? Maybe I'm a little more portly now, but I wasn't then at the age of twelve.

For our house football competitions each house had to get a team together from those available. Each house would have a few players who played in the school A Team, a few from the B Team, and then the numbers would be made up from any others who were willing to get involved.

As a member of the A Team, I was given the task of picking the team for the Round Robin competition which would take place over the course of a few weeks after school. Each team would play each other once so we only had to play three games. Fairfield were easily the best. They had more A Teamers available to them, and some decent B Teamers too. Our school team captain, the Ray Wilkins/Bryan Robson all rolled into one central midfielder, who had led our school to glory in the District Cup Final the previous year was in Fairfield, along with quite a few of our best players. They were always going to win the competition. It was just who could finish second.

Rydal were awful, with only a couple of A Teamers, and so they were always going to finish last, but Coniston and my house of Langdale were fairly evenly matched. The match between us two would basically decide who would finish in second place. I would be up against my old mate, our school team goalkeeper, who probably still had the pair of gloves I'd bought for him when we were still at primary school. I so wanted to get one over him to ensure I would be able to wind him up about it, but it was going to be a close-run thing.

Each team had two or three players who could win a game on their day, along with some solid B Team players who knew what they were doing. Only a couple of players on each team were complete numpties who had no idea really what was going on, and they were under strict instructions to just pass it to one of the better players if they got the chance. This game was to be my game. I was determined not to let us lose and so only be able to say we'd beaten the frankly dire Rydal team.

The afternoon of the match was fairly blustery, cold and grey; standard weather for a February day in North Lancashire. We got off to a great start, our school team centre forward scoring with one of his trademark headers, similar to the one he'd scored in the Cup Final the previous year. We were looking comfortable as half time approached, but then one of our numpties, instead of passing it to one of our team, passed it to one of their team, who promptly scored to equalise.

Straight after the restart we went behind to a good goal by their best player, another one of my school teammates. We were trailing because of a stupid mistake by one of our players, not because our opponents were a better team. I was not going to let us lose because of this.

Time was ticking down and there was only about ten minutes left, with us still 2-1 down. We managed to scramble a corner and I waited on the edge of the box, hoping for a knock down from someone. The corner was delivered into the six-yard box and my mate, their keeper, came and punched the ball out, but it looped up and fell to me, waiting on the edge of the penalty area. I controlled it on my knee and then volleyed it into the top corner to draw us level. Please do not think I'm bragging, but it was a peach of a goal, one of my very best, and the whole team believed again that we could now go on and win this game.

The game looked to be heading for a draw, which meant that second place would be decided on goal difference, which would then depend on how many we beat Rydal by in the next match. I didn't want to have to rely on that.

As the game entered the final minute, Coniston were putting us under huge pressure, looking for a winner themselves. After another attack by them, the ball broke to me on the edge of my own penalty area. There were very few options available to me as only our big centre forward was up the field. I took the ball up towards the halfway line and knocked the ball out wide on the right-hand wing for our centre forward to run onto. I knew that if he could square it back to me then I would only have the keeper to beat. The cross was good, but not perfect, giving their keeper, my best mate, a chance to come and clear it before I could hit it.

We were both bearing down on the ball, and it was a race as to who would get there first. Unfortunately, he had more pace than me, and he got there just before me, but instead of clearing it over my outstretched foot, he hit it against it and the ball looped back over him towards the goal. We were both on the ground, on the edge of the area, watching as the ball bounced towards the goal-line and nestled in the back of the net.

I had done it. I had almost single-handedly got us back into the lead, a bit like David Beckham had done for England against Greece in 2001, except his astonishing last minute free-kick had only drawn England level that day to get the point we needed to qualify. I had actually won the match for Langdale, and that game remains one of my finest moments on a football pitch. I'd like to think it was a true captain's performance, one that Captain Marvel, Bryan Robson himself would have been proud of. I know it was only a school game between a bunch of twelve and thirteen-year-old lads, but to me it felt very special.

Preston North End v Exeter City

April 26th, 1986   Deepdale

I only include this match as it was the nearest game to my thirteenth birthday, that awkward point when a young lad becomes a teenager and wants to desperately fit in with something. Teenage years have a knack of making you feel alienated and different, until you grow out of them and become the adult you will hopefully blossom into. Football gave me something to feel a part of. Whenever I was on a football pitch, be it a proper game, or just a kickabout with mates, I always felt comfortable; I belonged there with my like-minded friends, all just playing footie, as it was what we all enjoyed so much. And yet it was these mates who would make me feel the most alienated and different I had ever felt, with a little help from my parents.

After watching the game at Deepdale, and watching us draw with a fellow team who would have to go onto apply for re-election the following week, I'd got home, had my tea, and as usual went out onto the field opposite my house to play footie with my usual set of mates, ranging from eleven to fourteen year olds. My house was opposite my old primary school, and back then the gates were always open, unlike the Fort Knox security that schools have to have these days, and we could go and play wally on the concrete if it was wet, or have a proper game on the grass if it was dry. Most evenings we would be out playing, and that is where I felt the most comfortable.

A lot of my mates had joined the local Sunday league team by now and were always nagging me to sign up too. I would have got in the team no problem and would have been an asset, so it was a mystery to them as to why I hadn't joined. The answer was that it was out of my control; in fact, it was all down to God.

Both my parents are Christians, with a real living faith which they live their lives by. My dad was even a Methodist lay preacher, which meant he would preach at local churches most Sundays, sometimes twice as he often delivered his sermons in the evenings too. They had seen the film "Chariots of Fire", in which Eric Liddell had refused to run on a Sunday as it was reserved as a day for the worship of God, and my parents, particularly my dad, whose own mum was even more devout, were completely set against me playing on a Sunday.

I'd had to explain this to my mates on several occasions, with varying degrees of embarrassment, and would have to take the consequences from them. As young lads are wont to do, they took the piss. If I was in their position, I would have taken the piss too. I was frequently called a God Squadder or a Bible Basher, but I was used to it by now, and let my football do the talking, except on this one morning, the morning of my thirteenth birthday, at the apex of my awkwardness.

Every Sunday morning, my parents and I would walk to church, Bibles in hand, wearing our Sunday best. To get to church, we would have to walk past the field where my mates and I would play footie. Usually they were not there by 10am so I would be able to get to church without being seen by them, but this morning, a beautiful Spring day, they were all out earlier than usual. The teams had been picked, the jumpers were down for the goalposts, and the game had already started when my parents and I strolled out of our house.

I had to wear a shirt and tie, some smart trousers, and polished shoes, and compared to my normal football top, tracksuit bottoms or jeans and muddy trainers, I felt as though a huge flashing sign was stuck on my head, calling all my mates to stop their game and just stare at me. Some sniggered, some whispered to each other, but all of them stared. I was mortified and just wanted the ground to swallow me up. As I got further past them, out of earshot, I looked over my shoulder to see them all cracking up. I knew that the Bible Bashing slurs would be in full flow the next day at school.

Not only did I have to go past them on the way to church, but I knew that they would all be there on my way back too. After the church service, my parents always chatted to other members of the congregation, leaving me the option of getting home myself. Instead of praising the Lord for an hour, I spent the whole service planning a very convoluted route home which would mean not having to go through that excruciating ordeal again.

My route would have to include the canal towpath, climbing over a fence into the coal yard which backed onto the end of our garden, and negotiating a path through said coal yard, without getting any of my Sunday best dirty, so I could climb over our back garden fence and in through our back door. It was like something out of "Mission Impossible", except without the excitement, and I just about managed it, with only a slight bit of coal dust getting onto my best trousers, which could be brushed off before my mum got back. It certainly made for an eventful thirteenth birthday.

***

I've been an English teacher ever since I left University, and one of the poems I had to teach in my early career was by a British/Pakistani poet called Moniza Alvi. Her poem, "Presents From My Aunts in Pakistan" captures perfectly that feeling of awkward anxiety, that feeling of so wanting to fit in with the other teenagers, but family not allowing you to do so.

As a teenager herself, attending her local school in England, wearing the same Uniform as everyone else, Alvi felt as though she fitted in. However, for her birthdays, her family back in Pakistan would send her beautiful, brightly coloured saris and salwar kameez for her to wear at the weekends with her family.

Just as I was expected to get into my Sunday best at the request of my parents, so she was expected to don her newly acquired garments. Whenever her friends came around at the weekend, she would feel so different and so out of place from the role she cultivated for herself with her school friends during the week. She says she felt "Alien in the sitting room", and how her "costume clung to me, and I was aflame" with embarrassment at her "weekend clothes".

Whenever I taught this poem I always used the analogy of me in my Sunday best being sniggered at by my footie mates as a way of trying to convey the depth of Alvi's sense of otherness, her acute embarrassment, when all she wanted to do was to fit in with her friends. She understood why her parents wanted her to wear the weekend clothes, and how they wanted her cultural roots to be celebrated and not forgotten about, but it didn't stop her from feeling different and awkward.

My own parents too were proud of their faith and wanted to nurture in me the same sense of belonging to a community as they did. It was just hard to explain to them that kicking a ball about with my mates at the age of thirteen gave me much more of a sense of belonging than church would ever do.

There is a certain religious element to football. Us fans go as a congregation at the end of the week to worship at our churches. We sing songs of praise and adoration and can almost feel a certain redemption after a match. We feel we belong in that congregation. My dad's enthusiasm for the real church congregation has never waned, whereas I have fallen by the wayside, shall we say. I'd rather be worshipping God by kicking a football around.

And speaking of God, or in this case the Hand of God, it was the World Cup again that summer, and a certain Diego Maradona would have songs of praise and adoration sung to him. Not by the English though, the cheating bastard.

World Cup Finals Mexico 1986

England v Poland

June 11th, 1986   Estadio Universitario, Monterrey

England, now managed by Bobby Robson, had qualified again without any problems and were placed in what seemed like a fairly easy group, with Portugal, Morocco and Poland being our opponents in the group stages.

We managed to make a fairly easy group look like a very difficult group, losing our opening match 1-0 against Portugal. Back then in the mid-eighties, after the great Eusebio, and before such iconic players as Figo and Cristiano Ronaldo, Portugal were not the force in world football they are today. England were expected to beat them relatively easily, but our campaign got off to the worst possible start, the complete opposite to Bryan Robson's 27 second goal in the last World Cup. This time Robson had only just recovered from the shoulder injury which had kept him out of the second half of Man United's season, and he looked out of form and frankly not fit enough to be playing.

In the next game, against Morocco, Robson's injury jinx returned, falling awkwardly and dislocating his shoulder, ending his World Cup. But at least we still had our other world-class midfielder, Ray Wilkins. Well, we should have had him, but just before half time he picked up a yellow card, and then stupidly threw the ball at the referee, which earned him a second yellow, meaning we would only have ten men for the whole of the second half.

We held on for a 0-0 draw, and so with only one point from two games, the third match against Poland was absolutely crucial. The English press had already been abusive towards Bobby Robson even before the tournament had started, having failed to qualify for the European Championships of 1984, and if we had got knocked out in the group stages, then I am sure that he would have been sacked. Thankfully, our old friend Gary Lineker helped us all out.

The match kicked off at 4pm local time, which meant that it was 10pm in England. I remember it being on a school night and mum gave me special dispensation to stay up until midnight to watch the outcome. It literally was now or never for England that night; we simply had to win.

Gary Lineker's first half hat-trick was a thing of wonder, typical of such a great goal scorer. If anyone was a great goal scorer, but not a scorer of great goals, it was Lineker. I don't think I can remember him ever scoring from fewer than twelve yards out, but he wasn't in the team to score great goals. He was there to poach, and I don't mean eggs.

His first goal, after only nine minutes, was a fairly simple finish from a cross by Gary Stevens, his then Everton right-back and team-mate. His second, only five minutes later, arguably the best of the lot, was a gorgeously crafted team goal, which started with our own keeper Peter Shilton. A beautiful ball down our left flank from Peter Beardsley, who was only in the team due to Robson and Wilkins' absence, found Steve Hodge in space. He delivered a pinpoint ball for Lineker to slot home.

We were 2-0 up in the first quarter of an hour and looked to be cruising. The third was swept home with his left foot after the Polish keeper had completely missed a corner. We were 3-0 up after only thirty-four minutes, and we could then shut up shop, and hold on for a comfortable victory to secure second place in the group behind the surprise package of Morocco.

Our next opponents were another surprise team. Paraguay, always living in the shadows of their bigger and more successful neighbours Uruguay, had qualified for their first World Cup since 1958, and had got through to the last sixteen by drawing not only with the fancied Belgians, but also the hosts Mexico. However, momentum was now with England after our stunning performance against Poland.

In the Azteca Stadium, Lineker bagged another couple with Beardsley slotting home the third, which meant that Lineker had now scored five times in effectively one and a half games, to take the lead in the race for the Golden Boot. Glenn Hoddle's through ball for Lineker's second is one of the most exquisite passes you could ever wish to see, and I urge you to have a look on YouTube. Bobby Robson seemed to have more faith in Hoddle than previous regimes, and he was repaying his manager's faith in him with the classiest of performances.

With two 3-0 wins in a row, we were full of confidence as we prepared to meet Argentina in the quarter-final, and we all know what happened next. The cheating bastard!

Argentina v England

June 22nd, 1986   **Estadio Azteca, Mexico City**

By now there was something else competing for my leisure time apart from football, and no I hadn't gone back to my Lego. By now I had my first proper girlfriend, one whom I was prepared to cycle the few miles to her house on frequent occasions for. I'd met her parents and everything, we walked her dog down the canal, we held hands, we even kissed occasionally, and quite a lot of the time we listened to her records and chatted in her bedroom.

Her favourite singer was Madonna, as her "True Blue" album had just come out, and I got to know that bloody album word for word. I'd been at my girlfriend's house all that Sunday afternoon, but after we'd had tea, I was not in the mood for any more holding hands, or even any more kissing, and certainly any more Madonna; I wanted to see Maradona now.

This was my first proper World Cup quarter-final, as at the previous World Cup there was a second-round group phase which didn't have the knockout element to it. Yes, our game against Spain in 1982 was effectively a knockout match in that if we didn't win then then we would be going home, but there was to be no extra time or the prospect of penalties as it was still in a mini-league basis. This game felt bigger, more important, and more dangerous, and not just in terms of football. I didn't realise just how huge this game was until after the event as I wasn't fully aware of the political situation between the two countries.

I knew that our two countries didn't like each other. From my World Cup book I'd read from cover to cover before the last World Cup, I knew that we'd beaten Argentina on the way to victory in 1966, and that it had been an extremely ill-tempered affair, with Alf Ramsay refusing to allow the players to swap shirts and calling the Argentinians "animals" afterwards. The game was called "the theft of the century" by the Argentinian press.

I also knew that the two countries had been at war during the last World Cup, although I was only nine then and didn't really understand the ramifications and the consequences. All I knew in 1986 was that it was more than just a football match, particularly for Argentina and their captain, Diego Armando Maradona.

To the Argentinians it was a chance to get revenge, not just in footballing terms after what had happened in 1966, as this was the first time the two countries had met since that game at Wembley, but also for their military humiliation; a chance to put us in our place, by whatever means necessary.

The game was on a Sunday evening, and my dad was preaching somewhere ("Papa does Preach!), my mum was busy with something, and my brother wasn't really interested, so I had the television and the living room all to myself. I didn't realise that I was about to watch what would become one of the most famous games in World Cup history.

A very cagey first half ended 0-0, with Maradona starting to dictate the play, but we all know what happened next. In the 51st minute, somehow the rather stocky and diminutive Maradona managed to beat the 8-inch taller Peter Shilton to a looping ball, apparently nodding it into the net to take a 1-0 lead. Nobody, apart from Shilton, a few other England defenders, and Maradona himself knew what had happened.

To me, at first glance, it seemed as though he had beaten Shilton's outstretched arm to the ball fairly, but as soon as the replays were shown, everyone knew that he had cheated and used his left hand above his head to reach the ball first. He knew exactly what he'd done, as he quickly got his teammates to hug him, which would somehow convince the Tunisian referee that it was a legitimate goal. It worked and the goal was given, despite the remonstrations from the England players.

Only four minutes later, Jimmy Hill was still rambling on in his rather pompous manner about the incident when Maradona picked up the ball in his own half, pirouetted past a couple of our midfielders before starting his now iconic 60-yard run towards our goal. Some pretty woeful defending it has to be said allowed him to just keep running until all he had to do was slide the ball past Shilton, triggering Barry Davies' "Oh, you have to say that's magnificent!" line.

It was magnificent, but I'm not sure it should be called the Goal of the Century, as it has become known. I've seen better individual goals, particularly from the player who would soon enter the game.

John Barnes, still playing for Watford then, had scored a goal of pure class and quality a couple of years earlier that in my humble and completely unbiased opinion, eclipsed Maradona's goal. After England had failed to qualify for Euro 84, they embarked on a tour of South America, playing Chile, Uruguay and the mighty Brazil in their own back yard. In the cauldron of the Maracana Stadium, Barnes scored the most sublime individual goal you could ever wish to see. The ball looked like it had been tied to his boots as he glided past and through the Brazilian team, before slotting the ball past the keeper. If it had been in a World Cup match, then surely it would have been voted as even greater than Maradona's. If only he'd scored that goal against Argentina. If only.

Even though he didn't score, Barnes did change the game completely. His trickery on the left-wing bamboozled the tiring Argentinians, and eventually it paid off. With only ten minutes remaining, he put a gorgeously weighted ball in for Gary Lineker to head home, his sixth of the tournament, to pull the score back to 2-1, although we all know that should have been an equaliser. If only he could do it again; he very nearly did.

Another tantalising cross from Barnes was this time just beyond the reach of Lineker, and instead of the ball landing in the net, Lineker landed in it after missing the ball by what must have been millimetres. Anyone watching, Argentinians included, couldn't quite believe how the ball did not go in. It was the most agonising moment of my footballing life so far. So near, and yet so far.

The Argentinians held on, to spark wild celebrations, both on the pitch, in the stadium, all over Argentina, and also in the Argentine dressing room, with the deflated and cheated England team able to hear the riotous singing and chanting, led by the hero and villain in one, Maradona himself.

Even though he was, and always will be, a cheating bastard, I kind of admired Maradona's cheeky facetiousness at the post-match press conference. He knew that the goal was not going to be taken away from him, and so, with more than a hint of glee, he said that the goal had been scored, "a little with the head of Maradona and a little with the hand of God." He did whatever was necessary to get revenge for his country, and as such, he kind of made his statement come true, as he became almost a deity in his own country.

His Godlike status was confirmed in the semi-final, scoring another magnificent goal against Belgium, jinking his way through their defence before putting it past the keeper. At least it wasn't just us he scored great goals against. He didn't actually score in the final as Argentina beat West Germany 3-2 in a thrilling match, but as he lifted the golden trophy aloft, his deification was complete.

To us English, cheating is wrong, and there are never any occasions when it should be deemed acceptable, unless of course you're Michael Owen, who blatantly dived to gain penalties for England in both the 1998 and 2002 tournaments.

To the Argentinians, Maradona's cheating was actually celebrated. They believed it to be better than scoring a legal goal. Cesar Menotti, the former manager of the national team, who had won his country's first ever World Cup in 1978 said, "Better, much better that the goal was so unjust, so cruel, because it hurt the English more." This summed up the intensity of the game and their hatred of us as a football team and as a nation.

Of course Maradona was not the first Argentine player to use his hand to influence a World Cup game. Back in 1978 when Argentina were the hosts, Mario Kempes basically saved a goal by becoming a second goal keeper against Poland. He flew to his right, stuck out his hand and performed what would have been classed as a great save if he were the actual goalkeeper. But he was the centre forward and would go on to win the Golden Boot in the tournament. His save resulted in a penalty which was then subsequently saved by the actual goalkeeper. He didn't even get sent off and was lauded for his piece of ingenuity by the Argentine dictatorship government. Argentina then went onto win the game quite comfortably.

This was very similar to another cheating bastard, Luis Suarez, when he saved a certain goal with his hand against Ghana in 2010, denying the Africans a place in the Semi-Final. He at least was sent off and watched the Ghanaian penalty being saved from the touchline. It would seem that it is not just Argentina which actively celebrates cheating. It is no wonder that the Argentinian players were almost encouraged to cheat, as their government and footballing powers staged the most obvious and cruel piece of cheating when they denied one of their South American neighbours a place in the Final of 1978.

That tournament did not have a knockout stage, but two group stages. For the second group phase, the two teams finishing top of their respective groups would go on to the Final. Argentina were in a group which included Poland, Peru and Brazil. Back then the final group matches were not played at the same time, and after Brazil had beaten Poland 3-1, Argentina would have to beat Peru by at least four goals to go through to the final on goal difference, and leave Brazil, a team which included Zico and Rivelino, to contest the Third Place play-off.

Many rumours and conspiracy theories have been put forward as to how Peru were somehow beaten 6-0 that night. Peru were not that bad, and Argentina were not that good for that scoreline to be legitimate. It has been alleged that the Argentine dictatorship offered a large shipment of grain to the country of Peru, as well as the unfreezing of a Peruvian bank account that was held by the Argentine central bank. Another alleged deal is that 13 Peruvian dissidents who had been exiled in Argentina were freed and allowed back to Peru.

Whatever the truth, if there is any truth to these rumours, it would seem that cheating is viewed very differently in Argentine culture. It is no wonder that Mr. Maradona thought that doing what he did against us was ok. He'd been brought up in a country where it was not only ok, but actively encouraged.

The course of footballing history could have been so different if only there was a system where the referee could check his decision by looking at a slow-motion replay. That would be a novel idea wouldn't it?

Season 86/87

Middlesbrough v Preston North End

January 10th, 1987   Ayresome Park

Maybe the price of going to watch two teams, one of which was a First Division team, had caught up with my dad, and either for this reason, or something else, we didn't go to any more games at Old Trafford. Neither did the United manager Ron Atkinson for that matter. After two FA Cups and nothing else in his reign as Manchester United manager, the fans and the board grew tired of waiting for success, particularly in the league, and so in November

1986 he was replaced with the manager of Aberdeen, Alex Ferguson. Maybe he would be able to bring them the title. We'd all just have to wait and see.

It may well have been the cost of going to watch United, but I'd prefer to think that it had something to do with Preston's remarkable turnaround in fortunes that we stopped going to watch them. Preston had such a good season that my dad did not feel the need to go and see a better standard of football elsewhere.

From finishing second to bottom the previous season, we would end up in the completely opposite position, second from top, a turnaround of twenty-one places. Very few teams, if any, can say that within the space of one season they have gone up the table by such a huge swing.

As the embarrassment of our lowest ever league position subsided, we needed to do something drastic if we were to avoid a repeat, with this season having the threat of automatic relegation hanging over those teams at the bottom. We certainly did not want to be in that position again, so for something drastic, we laid down the plastic.

Preston became the fourth and final club to lay an artificial pitch, after QPR, Luton and Oldham had all done the same thing, with varying results. The pitch would reduce the number of postponed games, generate income by allowing us to rent the pitch out to local teams, and also give us a frankly unfair advantage over our opponents, as we would be able to train on it and so be more used to its bounce and pace.

As well as our brand spanking new pitch, we also got another new manager, although that wasn't quite so drastic seeing as we had tried three managers the previous season. In came John McGrath, the former Port Vale and Chester City manager, who immediately brought in a big central defender called Sam Allardyce. He also

144

brought in a big central midfielder, Oshor Williams, who would become our version of Ray Wilkins, but without the same refined skills. In too came a little attacking midfielder called Ronnie Hildersley.

McGrath kept faith with quite a few of the players who had failed so badly the previous season, players such as Gary Brazil and John Thomas up front, and "Skilful" Bob Atkins at the back. Would our new manager be able to get more out of these players? And so, with a plastic pitch, Big Sam, Big Oshor and Little Ronnie we embarked on our attempt to not finish near the bottom of the league. We all hoped for an improvement in our fortunes, but none of us expected such a great season.

Whatever John McGrath did, it seemed to work. We got off to a great start, not losing until our eighth game of the season, but what a defeat it was. 4-0 away to Scunthorpe. Alan Latchley would have been proud. Things were certainly going in the right direction as we beat Burnley 4-1 at Turf Moor. We were by now fighting for top spot with Northampton, and our bubble was burst when they beat us 3-1 at their ground to stake their claim as potential champions of Division Four.

In the next few weeks we beat Bury 5-0 and Chorley 5-1 in the FA Cup to put us into the third round of the cup for the first time I could remember. I was used to being beaten by five goals, not winning by that margin, and we now had the chance of getting a big team in the next round of the cup.

It could have been Man United or Liverpool, but instead we got Middlesbrough away, hardly the most glamourous of fixtures. They were leading the division above us and I was deflated. If we were going to go out of the cup, at least we could go out to a huge team and get some money and the experience of playing against top players. Middlesbrough did have a very young Gary Pallister in their team before he moved to Man United a couple of years later and won multiple trophies, but back then nobody apart from the Boro fans had heard much of him.

I listened intently to the game on Radio Lancashire and was gaining confidence as we held Middlesbrough at bay as half time approached. Could we even nick a win? Little Ronnie Hildersley thought so, and after picking up the ball 25 yards out, he unleashed a rocket into the top corner of the Boro goal. To us Preston fans, there was a Rocket Ronnie years before snooker star Ronnie O'Sullivan gained that title.

We managed to hold on throughout the second half and Ronnie's rocket turned out to be the only goal to send us through to the fourth round. Maybe this time we'd get a big team from Division One. To get this far in the cup was already beyond my wildest dreams and when we were drawn against Newcastle at St. James' Park, I was not disappointed. I just wish it had been at Deepdale, but at least our players would get to play in front of a crowd of over 30,000 at one of the biggest stadiums in the country.

I didn't expect us to win. I didn't really care. I just wanted us to be able to compete and give the Magpies a game, and that is what we did. Again, I listened to the match avidly on Radio Lancashire, hoping that some sort of miracle could happen. It didn't, and we lost 2-0 but we did compete against a team three divisions above us.

The previous season we hadn't competed against teams that were only a few places above us, so I could handle a 2-0 defeat to Newcastle. But for the first time in ages, possibly the first time in my life, I hoped. All I'd known so far was disappointment and ultimately failure with Preston. Our trajectory had been nothing but downwards, and here we were, in a promotion spot, and playing Newcastle at St. James' Park. Things were looking up.

Preston North End v Northampton Town

April 3rd, 1987   Deepdale

By now we were firmly looking like promotion contenders, still in second place behind the leaders Northampton. We were due to play them for some reason on a Friday evening instead of the normal Saturday afternoon. This would cause a potential problem. It was a game we just had to see as we would not only reinforce our promotion chances, but also close the gap on the leaders. A real six-pointer.

The problem was that not only was my dad a lay preacher, but he had also started up the local Boys' Brigade company in my home town of Carnforth. We had our weekly meetings on Friday evenings and so would clash with the top of the table clash at Deepdale. My dad's solution was to take all the boys, probably about thirty lads ranging from the age of eleven to sixteen, to Deepdale. Not only would he and I not miss the game, but he would also be able to give lots of lads who never got the chance to watch a football game the opportunity to do so.

Each boy had to pay subs every week, probably a pound or so, and so he had some sort of fund to use, but I suspect that what he had available to him nowhere near covered the price of the thirty or so tickets. I wouldn't be surprised if he used his own money to fund these lads' chance to go to Deepdale. So, into the minibuses we all got, and on a balmy spring evening, me, my dad, and thirty mates all went to watch the footy.

Most, if not all of these lads had never been to a match before and were probably in awe as they stepped onto the Spion Kop at Deepdale. The crowd that night was a quite frankly staggering 16,456, remarkable really seeing as we were averaging around 3,500 the season before. For most of these lads it was their first ever game and were part of our biggest crowd for years. It was the biggest crowd I'd ever been in at Deepdale and it was brilliant. I did have to tell a few of them that it wasn't always like this.

The game was predictably very tight, but Gary Brazil grabbed a goal and we clung on for a hard-fought win, to edge closer to automatic promotion. This to me was the season that just kept on giving and I finally started to believe that we could actually do it. Another few points and we would be there; promotion out of Division Four.

Preston North End v Tranmere Rovers

April 28th, 1987   Deepdale

Six games after the fantastic Friday night football against Northampton, we secured promotion, the first I had ever been a part of. Preston went down to East London and beat Orient to secure the most remarkable of turnarounds and promotions. It was as if Preston knew it would be my birthday straight after and gave me the best birthday present I could have wished for. Three days later we were at home against Tranmere where the team would be welcomed by their ecstatic fans, many of whom would only just have recovered from the celebrations on the Saturday.

My dad came up with the goods again. I knew he was up to something as he said we were leaving earlier than normal; mum was coming with us, and I could bring a friend along too. The chosen one was my school teammate who I had been vying for a first team place with when we were in Year 7, the one who had scored the winner in our District Cup Final. His dad never went to watch football so I thought it might be nice for him to see what I got up to with my dad most Saturday afternoons and Tuesday nights.

I was now fourteen and my birthday presents had progressed from Lego to clothes and records, and so with my new deck shoes, pastel-coloured t-shirt and grey Farah trousers on (it was 1987 after all), we parked up near Deepdale much earlier than other games. Instead of going to the entrance to the West Stand, we went around the other side of the ground to where the players entered.

I don't know who dad had spoken to, whether he had paid them something, but in through the players' entrance we strolled, met one of the club officials and proceeded to meet some of the players. It brought back memories of the game I was mascot for, six years earlier, but thankfully we didn't see any full-frontal nudity from the players this time. And I didn't have to decipher an aggressive Scottish accent.

We had a mini tour of the inner sanctum of Deepdale, looked at our rather bare trophy cabinet, shook hands with and thanked the man who had been showing us around, and then walked back around to the West Stand to take our seats for the game. I did have to point out to my mate that it wasn't always like this and that I didn't get special treatment for every game.

Well over 12,000 were in the ground that beautiful spring night to welcome our heroes onto the pitch. They did a lap of honour before the game as they probably knew that there would be a pitch invasion at the end, particularly now that the club couldn't even use the excuse of fans ruining the grass as a deterrent from going on.

We had also recruited the now almost legendary Frank Worthington, who had made quite a few appearances for us, mostly as a substitute. He brought his rare brand of skill, flair and nonchalance to our team.

Even his warm up before the game showed all these traits, and he managed to make the pre-match kickabout entertaining too that evening. He would juggle the ball effortlessly before catching it on his neck, rolling it down his back, flicking it over his head with his heel before volleying the ball into the goal, delighting the hordes of fans who would watch, spellbound. I was certainly one of these, and I resolved to one day be able to do what I'd just seen Frank Worthington do.

I was almost disappointed when the game started as I wouldn't be able to watch Frank's skills any more, but there was a game to go and win for our fans, and we didn't disappoint. Gary Brazil scored in the first half, and then in the final minutes, our leading scorer for the season, John Thomas, finished the game off to spark wild celebrations.

The crowd were already lining the perimeter of the pitch, and when the referee blew for a free-kick they all thought that was the final whistle and ran on. It took a while for the last few seconds of the game to finally get played, and when eventually the final whistle blew, the players made a mad dash for the tunnel for their own safety. As me, my mate, my mum and dad watched from the West stand, the pitch was engulfed with supporters. We made our way down to have a stroll on the plastic pitch and waited for the team to come out into the Pavilion Stand to wave back at us all and join in the singsong.

I couldn't quite believe that we had actually done it. We'd got promoted; finally, my trajectory had an upturn in it. It had been a very special evening for me at the end of a very special season. But the entertainment hadn't finished yet.

As we pulled up outside my mate's house to see him home, he had opened the door and put his foot on the ground whilst the car was ever so slightly moving. It finally came to a stop but must have trapped the back of my mate's trainer as it rolled to a standstill. My mate got out of the car and then realised that he couldn't move. None of us knew what he was doing as he just stood there, looking a bit gormless.

We were just waiting for him to close the door and wave goodbye, but he literally couldn't move. After a few seconds of confusion, he quietly and very politely said to my dad, "Erm, excuse me, but the car's on my foot." My dad instantly panicked, thinking he had crippled my best mate by running over his leg or something. Dad immediately jumped out of the car to see what had happened and then realised that all he had to do was reverse the car a few inches to release his trapped trainer.

As he finally was released from the tyre's grip and went inside his front door, totally unscathed I might add, we all just burst out laughing. Even now, thirty-two years later, whenever I mention that I've caught up with the same mate, dad always does the impression which made us all crease up with laughter that surprising, wonderful and altogether glorious night when Preston celebrated promotion for the first time in my years of going to Deepdale.

***

As a footnote to our wonderful promotion season, I just want to say a few words about our local neighbours, and sometimes rivals, Burnley FC. Like us, The Dingles, as us North End fans call them, had been founder members of the Football League and had a long, proud history. Like us, they are a fairly small club from Lancashire with a fairly small fan base. Like us, they had won the FA Cup and also won the League twice, the last one as recently as 1960. Yet on the final day of the 1986/87 season, they very nearly dropped out of the league itself. This was the first season that automatic relegation was introduced for the very bottom club in the league, and Burnley had to go to Orient and win to ensure their survival.

Like us the previous season, they were second from bottom on the final day of the season, but unlike us, who knew that whatever happened we would not be relegated, they had to get a result away from home. They did win the game to give their fans a moment of what must have been a weird mix of massive ecstasy and utter relief, with fans still to this day referring to the match as "The Orient Game".

Survive they did, and eventually got themselves back on track, climbing the league over the following seasons to ensure they would never have to go through that trauma again.

They are now an established Premier League club and are an example for smaller clubs like us of how to sensibly and effectively manage a club. In 2010 they finally got back into the top division of English football, although only for one season. But they did not panic.

They consolidated, took the money they made from the Premiership, and added to their squad. Four seasons later they went back up to the Premier League, again only for one season. Most clubs by now would have sacked their manager, but not Burnley.

They remained steadfastly committed to their manager, Sean Dyche, the man with the gravelliest voice ever, and after only one season out of the Premiership, they regained their place and have now been there for the last three seasons, finishing as high as seventh and qualifying for Europe.

From near oblivion, they stood firm and reaped the rewards. They haven't splashed out on players who demand ridiculous wages. They haven't changed their manager for someone with great credentials but who knows nothing about the club and its fans. They've just got on with it and improved as a club and as a team.

I started this book writing about never having had the chance to watch my team in the Premier League. Burnley are the club Preston should aspire to be like. If we can manage ourselves similarly to Burnley, then we have a chance of achieving the same thing. Well, maybe not the Europa League, but a chance of getting ourselves into the Premier League and possibly even establishing ourselves. If they can do it, why not us?

Our fans always sung the tune from "Mary Poppins" to the Burnley fans; "Chim-chiminey, Chim-chiminey, chim chim cheroo, we hate those bastards in claret and blue!" We never get to sing it now as Burnley are a Premier League club. We don't mean it. We like you really. We're just jealous of you that's all.

Coventry City v Tottenham Hotspur

FA Cup Final May 16th, 1987

Wembley Stadium

With Preston's glorious promotion season occurring, you may have noticed that I haven't mentioned me actually playing football this season. I was still in the school team and playing in the Inter-House competition, but the truth is, I wasn't enjoying it very much this year.

I'd got bored of the Bible Basher piss-taking from my mates, and I was finding life quite hard as a teenager. I was, shall we say, a later developer in physical terms than most of my mates. As they were all getting bigger, stronger, more powerful, and more hairy, I remained a weedy little kid. During matches I was getting pushed off the ball and was losing my confidence. It didn't feel like a level playing field that year until my body, and my pubes, caught up by the end of it.

By the end of Year 9, my circle of friends had changed, and I gravitated to the mate whose foot my dad had parked his car on. He, like me, had had a difficult year too, and I think this brought us closer together. We are still great friends over thirty years later.

We travelled around Europe together the summer we left school. We attended each other's weddings. We watched each other's families grow. This was the year our friendship started. We had been rivals back in Year 7, but now were best mates. I'm also glad to say that I am much hairier now. In fact, far too hairy in all the wrong places, and not hairy enough in the place I would most like it; the top of my head. I haven't checked, but I'm guessing it's much the same scenario for him too.

Part of our friendship was based on us both playing on our Sinclair ZX Spectrum 48k computers, and we would swap games with each other. He lent me two football games, and anyone who ever owned a ZX Spectrum will probably remember "Match Day" and "Football Manager", the earliest versions of the huge games like Fifa, Pro-Evolution Soccer, and Championship Manager.

Looking at the games of today, those early games were truly crap, but that was all we had to sustain our love for the game. The graphics and gameplay were the most rudimentary, and each game became quite repetitive. On "Match Day" all you had to do was play it into the corner, cross it into the area and someone would always score. On "Football Manager", the stick men who re-enacted the game you'd been preparing for always seemed to score with every shot they had, usually from at least 40 yards out every time.

The truth is, I never really like playing football on a computer or a games console. It didn't seem right to me. Why would you play football on a computer when you could go outside and play the real thing? I much preferred a good shooter, like "Commando", or a classic platform game like "Chuckie Egg". Even when the much better football games came out, they just didn't appeal to me. I wanted the real thing, and the Cup Final during my Year 9 was a proper game of football.

***

There is a classic Monty Python sketch in which Eric Idle has invited four great leaders of Communism onto a forum. John Cleese plays Lenin, Terry Jones plays Karl Marx, Michael Palin is Che Guevara, and Terry Gilliam is Mau Tse Tung. Host Eric Idle then proceeds to ask them trivial questions about English football, leaving all these eminent thinkers on the merits of a Marxist philosophy and socialist principles of Communism all with blank and confused expressions. One of the questions which flummoxes these great minds is "What year did Coventry City last win the English FA Cup?" Of course they all look bemused, as at the time it was written, this was a trick question, as Coventry had indeed never won the Cup. 1987 was the year that sketch would become obsolete, although it remains very very funny.

This year felt like a welcome throwback to my first ever final, with Spurs being huge favourites to beat the underdogs. They just about managed it in 1981, needing a replay to eventually beat Man City, but this year would be the underdog's turn.

This would also prove to be Glenn Hoddle's last game for Spurs, before moving to Monaco. Chris Waddle was also in the team, along with Clive Allen up front, who had scored 48 goals in all competitions that season, a huge return in a remarkable season, and one that I think I am right in saying still has not been beaten in an English season. His 49th came only two minutes into the game at Wembley, heading home a Chris Waddle cross to put Spurs into the lead.

Coventry then got a surprise equaliser only six minutes later, when Dave Bennett finished coolly after taking it past Ray Clemence in the

155

Spurs goal. The now late, but great Cyrille Regis had a goal disallowed, before Spurs regained the lead just before half time, after their captain Gary Mabbutt bundled the ball over the line from a cross from Hoddle. We all expected Spurs to go on and score another, but Keith Houchen had other ideas.

After 62 minutes, Dave Bennett turned provider, putting in a tantalising cross into the area. The ball looked just out of reach of the oncoming Houchen, but he launched himself at the ball, connecting beautifully with a classic diving header to take the game into extra-time. The winner came in the cruellest of fashions only five minutes into the extra half an hour.

Gary Mabbutt, Mr. Spurs himself, inadvertently deflected a hopeful cross over his keeper and into the net, and Coventry held on to win their first and still only FA Cup. Maybe the Pythons should update their sketch now and ask the question "Who scored Coventry's winning goal in the 1987 Cup Final?" I suppose it would still be a trick question as it was an own goal, but it was Keith Houchen's diving header which will always be remembered.

The whole game was a proper old-fashioned end to end game of football, with both teams having the lead, some great players and personalities on show, and a great goal to try and recreate later that evening.

I cycled through to my mate's house and a load of us went onto the local school field and had a brilliant game of footie, just as I had with my other mates in previous years. After the game petered out, me and a few others spent ages, until it got dark, trying to deliver a similar cross for each other to copy Keith Houchen's diving header, but with only reasonable success at first.

At the start of the year, I had always been a bit nervous about sliding and diving around. I was, and always have been, a useless keeper due to my aversion to diving and landing on a cold hard pitch. But that night, with my newly found set of mates, I realised just how much fun you could have diving around, heading a ball past a keeper as you were horizontal in mid-air. My awkward year seemed to be coming to an end and I loved playing football again. Thanks Keith.

Season 1987/88

Wimbledon v Liverpool

FA Cup Final May 14th, 1988

Wembley Stadium

Not much happened for me this season after starting with so much promise. Preston found it quite difficult to make an impact in Division Three. We did ok and troubled neither the promotion places nor the relegation places, eventually finishing a respectable sixteenth in the table, just below halfway.

Alex Ferguson was now firmly in charge of Man United, and after their worst finishing position of eleventh since getting promoted back into Division One, he was beginning to make United into his team. But as usual in the 1980s, Liverpool pipped them to the title, infuriating Ferguson even more, and in this day and age would probably have threatened his job. Back then managers were given a bit more of a chance to succeed. I'm guessing that United were glad they gave him a few more seasons considering what happened in the 1990s.

Liverpool were obviously going to win the Double again after Wimbledon had miraculously got to Wembley to meet them in this year's FA Cup Final. Everyone remembers John Motson's famous line about it being a clash between the Culture Club and the Crazy Gang. It was a great line and very true too. Liverpool were a cultured team, oozing class in every position. They were definitely the best team in the country, and probably still the best team in Europe. I wonder how many more times they would have won the European Cup in the years they were banned.

Wimbledon, on the other hand, were certainly crazy. They had only been a league club for ten years before the start of this season and had rapidly risen through the divisions. They had got into the top-flight only the season before, actually being top of the whole league on September 1st, 1986 before eventually finishing sixth. It was an unbelievably meteoric rise for this small club who had been constantly overshadowed by some tennis tournament that was in their neck of the woods. They would remain in the top division for the next thirteen years.

Thinking about it now, it seems even more astounding what they managed to do. I suppose if Burnley have given me hope that Preston will one day get into the Premier League, then literally any club in any league can take heart from the fact that a club like Wimbledon had already done it. I seriously doubt it could ever happen again with the massive financial inequalities the Premier League has created, but it did happen once before.

Wimbledon's "Crazy Gang" nickname was well founded. They were bonkers, in a bad way. They played a certain style of football combined with a lethal malevolence. They scared and quite often scarred their opponents. They knew that if they couldn't outplay a team, which was frequently the case, then at least they would be able to outbarge, outkick and outhurt the other team.

The spine of their team made other teams look spineless. It started with their captain Dave Beasant in goal, two uncompromising centre backs in Lawrie Sanchez and Eric Young, who always seemed to have a bandage around his head, Dennis Wise and Vinnie Jones in midfield, with John Fashanu up front. They scared the living daylights out of me just looking at them, so I don't know what it must have felt like as their opponents prepared to try and play against them. The word "play" has many connotations, one being a certain childish innocence, which the best football should include. There was nothing childish or innocent about Wimbledon.

The most brutal and nasty of the lot was Vinnie Jones, the man who literally squeezed his opponents' bollocks to unsettle them. The famous picture where he has Paul Gascoigne in hand, so to speak, typifies his and his team's style of play. A snarling, scary, almost psychopathic style of play, and one which was often just downright illegal. After his playing career ended, it was very apt that he went into the film industry playing exactly the same sort of role. In fact, he would prove to be a far better actor than a footballer. At least on film his victims only had to pretend to be hurt, whereas his footballing opponents were very often actually hurt. Badly.

Jones' "tackle" on Steve McMahon in the 1988 Cup Final typified him. It was very high, very late, and very illegal. Credit goes to Steve McMahon for not reacting violently and not showing any fear. Less tough players would have crumpled and cringed. He wasn't going to be bullied by Jones, but many of the Liverpool team were.

On paper, Liverpool should have won the game easily. They were easily the better players and the better team, but Wimbledon just had the better of them that day. They managed to nick a goal shortly before half time from a free kick near the corner flag. Lawrie Sanchez got to the ball before the defender, and looped it into the far corner. They clung on for the whole of the second half, not budging an inch and not giving in.

Even when Liverpool got a harshly awarded penalty, they would not allow the ball to go into their net. Dave Beasant made history when he became the first keeper to save a penalty in a Wembley FA Cup Final when he thwarted John Aldridge. Nothing was going to stop

159

them from winning that game, not even a penalty. And so, they lifted the trophy after the most remarkable, if not exactly pretty win. Let's just say that football was not the winner that day. But did Wimbledon care? Bollocks to football; they couldn't give a toss.

England v France (Under 15s)

June 1988   Carnforth North Road Primary School

I had now completed a year of my GCSEs, and as part of my study of the French language, it was highly recommended that we take part in the French Exchange system. I had gone to stay with my exchange student, Frederic Boucher (or Fred Butcher as I worked out his anglicised name was), in his home somewhere just outside of Paris the previous November.

As part of the exchange experience, we had been paired up with students with similar interests. We both enjoyed playing football, and we both liked table tennis and would often play each other in his garage. Our battles over the table were more than just friendly games; there was national pride at stake.

He was also a member of his local football team and so on the evening he had training I went along and joined in. I performed ok but felt as though I didn't do myself justice. I was surrounded by French lads and could understand very little of their banter, if indeed it was banter. They may well have been full-on taking the piss for all I knew.

One drill we did was to play a one-two out wide and then cross it back in for our partner to finish it. After delivering a perfectly good cross, Fred fluffed his finish and I remember getting berated in French because I didn't deliver the cross onto his preferred and stronger left foot. My thinking was that it didn't matter what foot it fell to, if the cross was good enough then the striker had to be able to finish it with either foot.

I'd always been much weaker on my left foot and used it only for standing on really. From that point on I was determined to work on my left foot and build up confidence with it. Fred was due to stay with me later on that academic year, sometime in June, and I was not going to let My Left Foot let me down, as his right foot had done.

By the end of Year 10, I was now 15, and had come through my awkward patch bigger, stronger and most definitely braver. I now relished sliding challenges and diving around the pitch. Frederic arrived and he settled in well, having too much of an impact for my liking. The girls who I fancied at school, and thought I had a chance of getting off with, suddenly turned their attentions to my French friend.

He was different, almost exotic, despite his very unromantic sounding anglicised name, and his accent was definitely more appealing than my broad North Lancashire drawl. His accent made his name of Fred Butcher sound charming and delightful, and not like some character from Coronation Street, who's just moved to Manchester from Rochdale. I couldn't blame the English girls for fancying him, but I wasn't going to let him, and his slightly arrogant bunch of mates, beat me and my mates when we all met up one evening for a game of football on the primary school field that I had played on for so many years.

All the kids who had an exchange student had come to the field with their exchange partners. There were loads of us there, and it was a great chance for everyone to catch up with each other, and to basically talk about each other's students and discuss how annoying they were, or in the case of the girls, how handsome Fred Butcher was.

We got a game of footie organised, and this time we didn't have to pick teams, it was England v France, Us v Them. One of the French lads, Fred's best friend called Rolland if I remember rightly, particularly annoyed me. Not only did he seem more arrogant than the others, with an even more supercilious smile, but he was also going out with a goddess. Laetitia; ah! that name still makes me wistful. She was gorgeous, and she looked even more gorgeous when she wore her little cap with such French flair. *(The way you wear your hat.)*

I had met her back in November when we were in Paris. On our final night there had been a school dance/disco organised, and after having been fascinated by her earlier in the week when we had all been introduced to each other, I finally plucked up the courage to ask her if she would like to dance.

I'd learned my line and delivered it perfectly, and gobsmackingly, she said "oui". We had a slow dance to some awful late 80s power ballad, and then she was gone. *(The way we danced till three (well, 11.30 anyway)).*

I wouldn't see her again until the return visit in June. So, when I found out that the lovely and luscious Laetitia was now going out with my exchange student's best mate, I was tres displeased.

Our game of footie was going well. It was competitive and very well matched. There were loads of girls watching, both French and English, including Laetitia, which made me want to impress that bit more. My left foot was performing well and Fred and Rolland's gallic panache was getting beaten by our English grit and determination. Maybe in the back of my mind I was still trying to be Bryan Robson in that game against France in the 1982 World Cup. Rolland in particular didn't like this and he particularly didn't like me. The feeling was mutual.

Rolland decided to put his foot down, literally. I had the ball at my feet, and as he came in for a challenge, I managed to nick the ball past him. Unfortunately, my foot didn't get past him too, and he left his foot firmly on mine. It hurt, a lot, and my French rival would definitely have received a yellow card these days if it had happened in a real match, and not on a local primary school playing field. From the ensuing free kick, I received the ball and Rolland seemed intent on chasing me and getting it off me, right in front of the girls, and right in front of Laetitia. *(The memory of all that).*

I was running down the wing and he was tapping at my heels, trying to make me trip over and look stupid in front of the girls. He didn't manage it, but he finally lost patience and dived in, taking both me and the ball with him. This was deemed to have been a fair challenge by everyone else. He now had the ball and was running down the wing in the opposite direction to the one I had just been travelling in.

I couldn't believe what had just happened. I wasn't about to be humiliated and so like the Incredulous Hulk, I caught up to him, channelled my inner Vinnie Jones, and launched myself at him, two footed. I amazingly took the ball cleanly.

If his challenge on me deserved a yellow card, then mine would definitely have got a straight red in this day and age. It wasn't a challenge which was meant to injure or hurt in any way; I hadn't channelled my inner Vinnie that much, but it was definitely a dangerous challenge. He was left sprawling on the ground in front of the girls as I casually resumed my run towards their goal that he had so rudely interrupted.

I have no idea what the score was that night, it was probably about 22-21 to either team, but the important thing was that Rolland had not got the better of me, at least on the football field. He still had Laetitia, and for all I know he may have been happily married to her for many years now, but I won our little battle out on the right wing that night. *(No no they can't take that away from me!)*

USSR v Holland

European Championship Final

June 22nd, 1988   Neckarstadion, Stuttgart

You can tell how old I feel right now as games involving countries that no longer exist are being mentioned. The Iron Curtain was still drawn back then, although it was on its way to being opened, letting the light of the West in. Or at least that was the idea. The Soviet Union, or USSR, were one of the teams that had humiliated England in the group stages, progressing all the way to the final, but that tournament was one country's only; The Netherlands, that great team which included Ronald Koeman, Frank Rijkaard, Ruud Gullit, and the one and only Marco van Basten.

What was it with England and the Euros? After our thrilling performances at the last World Cup, we had finally managed to qualify for the European Championships, my first as an England fan. Surely we would be able to build on the relative success of our achievements in Mexico, despite our loss to Maradona's Argentina. But exactly the opposite happened.

We ended up bottom of our group, losing our first game 1-0 to the Republic of Ireland. Our second game was lost to the eventual winners Holland, with van Basten bagging a hat-trick in a 3-1 defeat. Then to seal our bottom place, we also lost 3-1 to the USSR.

We were awful, and the pressure started to pile up on Bobby Robson again. His namesake, Bryan, was starting to look past his best by now, the cumulative injuries starting to take their toll. The rest of the team were basically the same team that had eventually impressed so much in 86, so I don't know what happened to us that year.

Holland that year were superlative, apart from their first match which they lost to the USSR. They used the match against us to firmly get back on track and from then on it was obvious who was going to win the tournament. And there was one man who would basically win it for them. Marco van Basten.

There were only eight teams in the tournament back then, so after the group stages the four teams went straight into the semi-finals. After his hat-trick against us, van Basten would go onto score again in the semi-final against West Germany, setting up a final against the USSR, and a chance to get revenge for their defeat to them in the group stage. And revenge is what they got, beating them 2-0, but it could have been many more. Ruud Gullit, dreadlocks flying, put them in the lead with a bullet header (Gullit the Bullet) but it was van Basten's goal in the 54th minute that everyone remembers.

I'm still not sure how he did it actually. A diagonal looping ball was played over to him and he watched it from over his left shoulder. When it fell to him, he was level with the six-yard line and almost on the edge of the penalty area. I'm sure someone has worked out the angle he was at, but whatever it was, his finish was truly staggering. He struck the sweetest right foot volley which flew past the keeper into the far corner before he'd even seen it. The players' faces were incredulous. Even the Dutch manager could not believe what had just happened.

It was one of the best, if not the best volley ever. End of. It will take something truly extraordinary to beat that goal as an example of a perfectly executed volley. I bet if van Basten himself was delivered the same ball a hundred times I doubt he would be able to replicate it. Me and my mates certainly couldn't.

165

After we had spent ages trying to replicate the perfect diving header after last year's Cup Final, we tried to do the same with van Basten's perfect volley. Our attempts got nowhere near the target, flying high and wide for the ones we even managed to connect with, and usually ending up sprawling on the ground in a twisted mess after completely missing the ball. Let's just say that running in one direction whilst looking in another is not as easy as Marco van Basten made it look.

The Dutch had deservedly won their first, and incredibly, still their only ever tournament. A nation that has produced some of the greatest players that have ever graced a football field had been like England to some extent – a nearly team. They lost two consecutive World Cup Finals in 1974 and 1978; the team of Johan Cruyff invented the phrase "Total Football", and yet to this day the Dutch have never won another tournament since that day when van Basten scored the ultimate volley. They certainly were not a nearly team that day.

The next time England would meet them in the European Championships would be a different story though, and this time it would be on our own manor.

Season 1988/89

Preston North End v Chesterfield

February 25th, 1989   Deepdale

After what could only be called a season of consolidation, Preston were now ready to make a push for promotion again, and it nearly happened. There's that word "nearly" again. I'm getting sick of it.

We had some very topsy-turvy results this season. After a rather inconsistent start, we seemed to hit our stride in October, winning three matches in a row without conceding a goal, and scoring ten of our own. But only a month later we got absolutely obliterated 6-0 by Wolves at Molineux. I thought the days of getting pasted by teams had gone, but if nothing else, Preston are the team that keeps on giving if inconsistency is what you want.

We carried on either winning or losing, with very few draws, until the end of February. We were in contention for a play-off place by now, after the system we all are used to now had been introduced only two seasons before, in our glorious promotion campaign. We were never going to go up automatically, but if we could finish in the top six then we would have an extra chance.

We had already beaten Chesterfield 3-0 away earlier in the season, but no one expected us to beat them by such a margin in the return fixture at Deepdale. We won 6-0 and it was the start of a run of four straight victories, scoring seventeen goals. A 5-3 thriller against Brentford was the highlight of this little run, but impressive victories away to Gillingham and Mansfield gave us the firm belief that we could go and secure a top six spot, which is exactly what we did, finishing sixth, and so starting what would become a long and painful relationship with the play-offs..

We would need to beat Port Vale over two legs to give ourselves a chance of promotion, but our inconsistency came back to haunt us, losing 5-2 on aggregate. This would be the start of our frankly abysmal experiences of the play-offs. It would take us ten attempts, over the next sixteen seasons to eventually succeed, but more of that later.

***

I had now entered my final year of high school and would take my GCSEs at the end of the season. As Preston were being consigned to remain in Division Three, I had more important things to think about; or less important things depending on whether you agree with Bill

Shankly's affirmation that even life and death is not as important as football.

I had always loved school, and this was my chance to show that I was quite bright. I was determined not to let myself down and so, around the time Preston were thumping Chesterfield 6-0, I worked out a carefully constructed revision timetable which I would follow almost religiously. Maybe it is due to my dad's strict Methodist work ethic, but I would stick to my revision plan through thick and thin.

Our teachers had told us all about how doing smaller chunks of revision was the best option, with breaks in between. I would split my subjects into half hour blocks and make sure I gave my brain a complete break from quotations, formulae, equations and vocab lists. My plan was to use footie as a break in between each half hour block.

After my grandma, my dad's mum, had died the previous year, dad seemed ok with me playing for the local Sunday league team. I joined up and performed well, quickly gaining a starting place each week. I was now a much more mature footballer. I'd worked on improving my left foot, my sliding tackles, my diving headers, and my van Basten volleys, but there was still one thing that I was rather embarrassed about. I was still awful at keepy-uppies.

Ever since I had embarrassed myself at the Bobby Charlton Soccer School when I was nine, I had always been in awe of any of my peers who could juggle a ball. I was determined to teach myself how to do it and now seemed like the perfect opportunity to do so. A fifteen-minute break in between half hour revision slots didn't give me enough time to go and actually play footie, but I would be able to go onto our front driveway and practise keepy-uppies, as well as smashing the ball into our garage door to see how much I could dent it. I was trying to relive the time I had broken our front gate when I was eight, but this time it was a metal up-and-over garage door as my target.

My revision was going to plan, and so were the footie skills. A few little practice sessions a day would see me not just be able to keep the ball up using my feet and my knees, but I also started using my shoulders and my head. I also remembered the little promise I made a couple of seasons before when I had seen Frank Worthington's tricks as he warmed up at Deepdale on my fourteenth birthday.

If ever I was going to fulfil that promise of being able to catch the ball on my neck, roll it down my back, flick it over my head and volley it, then now was the time. Another few practice sessions and I had almost mastered it. This Methodist work ethic was paying dividends, although I'm not sure Frank Worthington ever had much of a work ethic, and definitely not a Methodist one.

I also taught myself how to spin a ball on my finger, as The Harlem Globetrotters used to do with a basketball. I would spin it on my index finger, and then tap the ball to keep up the momentum. I started to show off properly when I was able to spin it on my little finger, flick it into the air and perform the neck catching manoeuvre with it still spinning. Down the back, over the head, smash it into the garage door again.

In my twenty-five years as a teacher, I may, on only a few occasions of course, have shown my classes this skill of mine. If ever one of the students in my class brought a football in, I just couldn't resist seeing whether I could still perform like a seal in front of them. I would always use it as an opportunity to tell them that if they wanted to be the best, and if they wanted to beat the rest, then dedication was what they needed.

But really it was just a chance to show off, which is one of the reasons why I became a teacher in the first place.

Preston North End v Notts County

April 15th, 1989   Deepdale

This was a truly pivotal game in not just my life, but anyone who has ever watched and loved the game of football's life. Not because Preston won 3-0 and moved closer to a play-off place, but because that famous phrase mentioned in the last chapter by Preston's Cup winning captain in 1938, Bill Shankly, took on a horrifyingly macabre meaning.

As Preston were scoring their first goal that afternoon, I can assure you that thousands of football fans were finding out that football certainly was not more important than life or death. For 96 of those thousands, it would be the last match they would ever go to.

Back then, both FA Cup semi-finals were played at exactly the same time as all the other matches around the country; 3pm on a Saturday afternoon. Without such wonders as the internet and smart phones, we all waited eagerly on the West Stand Paddock at Deepdale for the scores to be announced during the half-time break. When the score between Liverpool and Nottingham Forest was not given, me and my dad started asking people with transistor radios if they knew what had happened. Nobody did.

It was only once we got into the car and turned the radio on that we heard the still very sketchy details. There had been deaths, that was for certain, but no one was sure of how many. On our drive home the death toll kept rising. Once home, I watched the news to find out the full scale of this needless waste of so many lives, and I cried. I was almost sixteen by now, and crying was for kids, but I don't mind admitting that I cried.

I don't know why I cried. Maybe it was the fact that I had been to Hillsborough a few seasons before and had watched a game of football there with my dad. I had returned home, but there were plenty of lads my age who had done the same thing that day and not come home. If he'd have been a Liverpool fan, my dad may well have taken me and we both could have been killed. Or maybe I cried just because of how senseless it all was.

I watched the events unfold all evening until Match of the Day came on. Des Lynam informed us all that 93 supporters had been killed in "the most tragic accident". It was certainly tragic, but it was certainly no accident.

Many, in fact, countless people were to blame for what happened at Hillsborough. I hopefully will never understand the loss that the victims' families have gone through since then, but I can understand their need for someone to blame, someone to take their grief and anger out on; someone to hate.

The desire to bring those people who made mistakes on that fateful day to justice must be so powerful and so strong. But those people, namely Chief Superintendent David Duckenfield, the match commander on that day, were only one factor in a whole series of factors. Yes, they may have been more significant than others, but they were still only one part. Their crime was not criminal negligence, although negligence played its part, but human error. And the clue is in the title there, "human" error.

All of us make mistakes. "To err is human" as Alexander Pope wrote, but the second part of the phrase is often ignored: "to forgive, divine." I'm not saying something so trite and so glib as to suggest that the families should just forgive and move on; that is impossible, but many humans erred not only that day, but also in the years building up to the tragedy.

Any so-called fan who caused trouble at a game, which ultimately caused all fans to be shut in cages when watching their team, cages which would then trap those fans who died at Hillsborough, they made an error.

The government, and the way they treated football fans like animals, as if they were a stain on society, which would create hatred between fans and those whose job it was to control them, leading to uncontrollable pressure between the two which would spill over into mistrust and violence that day, they made an error.

The FA, whose organisation of match schedules and timings, ticket allocations and travel arrangements, which caused too many fans, both with and without tickets to try and get into the ground at once, they made an error.

Many, many people, some who were at huge fault, some with very little fault, and many more through no fault of their own, made errors which caused the tragedy, but as I said, it was all human error. No part of that tragedy was not caused by anything other than human error. There was no natural disaster that day, nothing which would have made it easier to accept. It was all down to many errors by many humans.

Even in the aftermath, the human errors continued. The editor of The Sun, Kelvin Mackenzie, made a huge error printing the most disgracefully ironic of newspaper headlines ever with "The Truth".

The initial inquest into the disaster made huge errors. The police and the way they behaved towards the victims' families, they again made huge errors. Many more people made errors. The whole thing was one huge human error, but I repeat, to err is human, to forgive, divine, and if we can't forgive, then at least we can learn from these errors. Thankfully I think we have learned many lessons.

Many positives have come out of that disaster, and each and every one of these positives honours those fans who died that day. We no longer just want safer stadiums; we demand them and even expect them now. Every time we go to a football game and come back safely, knowing that there were enough stewards, enough police officers, enough members of the emergency services on hand to keep us safe, we honour the victims.

Every time a game involving huge numbers of fans passes off without any trouble, without any injuries, without anything other than what we went to the game in the first place for happening, we honour the victims.

Hillsborough changed the game for the better, and though that will never ease the pain and loss for the victims' families, their sons, their daughters, their dads, their mums, all those who died, did not die in vain.

We now take our safety for granted, and that must be a positive. Such a tragedy has never happened since. Such errors have not been repeated since. Such a needless waste of life has never been close to happening since. That is most definitely a positive. As I said at the start of this chapter, Hillsborough was a turning point for all fans.

Liverpool v Arsenal

May 26th, 1989 Anfield

Football stopped mattering for the next few weeks after what happened at Hillsborough. The Liverpool players and staff attended funerals day in, day out, sometimes two or three a day. Kenny Dalglish, who attended four funerals in one horrendous day, had made a point of standing beside those fans' families and honouring the fans who had died by making sure that someone from the club was at every single funeral.

The toll this must have taken not only mentally and emotionally, but also physically, is beyond anyone's imagination. Dalglish would also play a huge part in the quest for justice for the families and was honoured with a knighthood in 2018, not only for his services to football, but most proudly for him I'm sure, for his services to charity and the victims of the Hillsborough disaster.

Due to the funerals, Liverpool did not play another game until early May, appropriately enough against their Merseyside neighbours, their once rivals, Everton. A city came together to do what had played such a huge part in making it into such a great city; they watched football together. There must have been a feeling of a strange normality returning for those fans, although it would forever be a different kind of normality from now on, as indeed it would be for all football fans.

The game would be repeated a few weeks later as the rearranged Cup semi-final was won by Liverpool, so producing the second Merseyside FA Cup Final in the space of four seasons. This would be a nice break from my GCSE revision, watching the Cup Final with my mum and dad. Little did I know then that it would be the last final I would watch at home with them.

I realise that sounds a bit ominous, but don't worry, nothing happened to them, they're still alive and well. Well, they're still alive, although not as well as they used to be. Circumstances over the following few years would mean that this year's game would be the last time we would settle down together and watch the Cup Final.

This year's final felt different to other finals. This was the first time that fans had not been segregated, the fans of both clubs wishing to show solidarity rather than any sort of division, and the terraces were a vibrant mix of blue and red, rather than the two colours juxtaposed at either end.

It was also the first final I'd ever experienced where the league had not been decided yet. Liverpool's backlog of games meant that the season had to be extended beyond the traditional last game of the season at Wembley, but first they had to win the Cup.

It was a great game, and Liverpool managed to win it for their fans, eventually winning 3-2 after extra time, with Ian Rush scoring the final goal, just as he had done three years before. With one trophy safely won for those fans, they still had the League to go and win. If they could do the Double and win the League, then it would be the first time any club had won a double Double. But a double Double would bring toil and trouble for Liverpool on a balmy evening in late May.

But I didn't see any of it. I was drunk. The most drunk I had ever been in fact.

***

The final game of the 1988/89 season is the climax to Nick Hornby's "Fever Pitch", subtitled in the book as "The Greatest Moment Ever". I'm absolutely certain that, for Mr. Hornby, it was the greatest footballing moment ever. In fact, we can probably dispense with the word "footballing". But for me that night, I was drunk, in a tent, in a field, with my mates.

We'd got a bit tipsy, or even very tipsy before then at various parties we'd been to, but tonight was the night we would get absolutely hammered. The match fell on a Friday night, the Friday night that me and my mates would all officially leave school. We had already had a few of our exams by now, but this Friday was the last day before the half-term break, the start of our official study leave, before the rest of our exams would be taken in June.

175

We had all actually sat an exam that morning and we all now had nine whole days before our next exam. "Study" leave was not part of our thinking, at least not for a few days. We'd left school, we had a few days' breather, and some of us looked old enough to get served alcohol, if you knew which off-licences were dodgy and didn't bother to check any sort of ID.

Let's just say that I wasn't one of the older looking ones in our group. I definitely looked as though I'd just turned sweet sixteen, but some easily looked at least seventeen and a bit, which would just about convince the man behind the counter at the offy to sell as many cans of lager to us as he could. We obliged him and came out with about ten cans of very strong and very cheap lager each.

But where were we to consume these delights? We couldn't stay at home with our parents in as that would be rather restrictive. We couldn't yet get into pubs, and we didn't want to just hand around the local park and look like a bunch of scallies. It was a gorgeously hot day, more like midsummer than late spring, and we all wanted a night in the fresh air. So, the plan was to find somewhere to camp, get a fire going, and just get hammered.

A couple of mates lived in the beautiful town of Kirkby Lonsdale, just inside the border of Cumbria, about twelve miles away from where the rest of us lived. The plan was to find a nice field away from everyone, pitch our tents, drink ridiculous amounts of strong lager, and go jumping off a bridge fifty feet above a cold and fast flowing river to put ourselves in mortal danger. What could go wrong with such an awesome plan?

For anyone who has ever been to Kirkby Lonsdale, they will know of Devil's Bridge, an ancient old structure dating from 1370, which spans the River Lune about fifty feet below and provides an ideal opportunity for idiots like us to jump from it. We had seen others do it and it had become almost a rite of passage for teenagers to jump from the bridge into an area of water of about fifteen square feet. Anything outside of this small area would mean a rather less euphoric landing on very hard, and very sharp rocks. We were determined to fulfil our destiny.

We got the bus up there, furtively drinking at the back of the top deck, and found an ideal spot to camp. We would be on the riverbank about half a mile away from the bridge. We were already half-cut as we pitched the tents and with Dutch courage (or Kestrel Super Strength at least) running through our veins, off we went to perform feats of thrilling stupidity.

I was determined not to bottle it, and after watching some other lads do it and seeing exactly where to land, I climbed up on the side of the bridge and contemplated my future, trying not to display my nerves to the spectators. I realised that contemplating my future was not the best idea, as at some point you start imagining what it might feel like to die a horrible death. The best way to deal with this situation was not to think about it, and just do it, as Nike used to tell us.

I leaned forward and dropped from the side of the bridge, landing just where I wanted. I was now a man! I enjoyed it so much that I did it another couple of times just to prove to myself that it wasn't a one off. One of my mates though, he of the parked car on his foot, had taken ages to psyche himself up, but had eventually launched himself off too, landing awkwardly in the water, but perfectly safely. He wasn't about to go and do it again though. At least not yet anyway.

We went back to our tents and got a fire going, making a woeful attempt at cooking sausages. If the bridge didn't get us, then maybe food poisoning would. The lagers kept flowing and, as planned, we got steadily more drunk. At least our evening was going to plan, which is exactly the opposite to how Liverpool's evening was panning out.

We all know what happened in that game. If you don't then please read Nick Hornby's brilliant account. All Liverpool had to do was to avoid defeat by more than one goal. A win, a draw, even a 1-0 defeat would have been enough for them to win the league and complete the double Double. But Michael Thomas had other ideas.

Just as he was scoring the goal which provided the most unbelievable finish to literally the most unbelievable of seasons, and won the title for Arsenal, I was staggering, swaying and slurring around, with my mates all doing the same thing. At some point we all puked violently that night, on many occasions. The piles of vomit around our tents resembled something like the scene in "Family Guy" when Peter Griffin and his whole family cover each other with the contents of their stomachs. It was disgusting, but what fun we had.

Later on, after we had all thrown our guts up, my mate wanted to prove to us all that he could do the jumping off the bridge feat again. With all of us being completely inebriated, at no point did we think this would be a bad idea. In fact, we all encouraged it as at least it would be entertainment for us at 1.30 am.

We got back to the now deserted and moonlit bridge, and he rather clumsily climbed onto the side of it. But just as he was about to stand up and take aim at the water, he lost his footing and fell off. No surprises there really, and as we all peered over the parapet, we all envisaged our mate lying squashed on the rocks, but luckily, he had managed to correct his fall enough to land just inside the safe zone.

He climbed back out, rather less shakily now and contemplated his past. Falling into very cold water from a height of fifty feet has a knack of sobering you up and I think at that point we all realised that that was enough jumping off bridges and putting our lives at risk for one night thank you very much.

We retreated back to the tents for a night of restless and yet more vomit inducing sleep, before packing up our stuff, catching the bus, and thinking why the hell we'd done what we'd just done. But at least we lived to tell the tale. Just.

The following morning I got a newspaper to read on the bus journey back to our comfortable, safe, and definitely not stinking of puke beds. It was at this point, reading the back page, that I found out that I had missed one of the most incredible results in the history of the league. I had been completely oblivious to what had happened at Anfield the night before. Even at 10 am the following morning, no doubt the Arsenal fans were still much more drunk than I had got. They may have won the league in the final minute of the final game of the season, but they hadn't jumped off Devil's Bridge.

I'm guessing what they went through that night was much more euphoric than my experience though. They could call themselves Champions of England, whereas I had to wait for my immense hangover to fade and get back to the revision and the keepy-uppy practice. At least there wouldn't be a World Cup to try and fit in with my rather OCD approach to my revision. My GCSEs and A Levels both fell in years when there was no summer tournament to distract me. I don't know how I would have fared if I had been a year younger and had to try and prepare for my exams with Italia 90 to contend with too.

That would be another year off, and none of us knew then how much of a distraction to everyone it would be. But for now, I had another three weeks of exams ahead of me in what felt like a never-ending cycle of quotations and facts, starting with an English Literature exam on Macbeth. "Tomorrow and tomorrow and tomorrow, creeps in this petty pace from day to day" felt like my reality back then. Oh well, after the shenanigans of Devil's Bridge and Anfield, I had to get back to it.

Is this a York Notes Study Guide I see before me? Unfortunately, it most definitely was.

Season 1989/90

Walney Island U18s v Carnforth Rangers U18s

September 1989   **Walney Island, Barrow in Furness**

All that revision I had done must have sunk in, as just after the new footy season had started, I received my GCSE results which were pretty good, if I do say so myself. I got top grades for every subject, reinforcing my status as a bit of a swot, being the only boy in the school to get those grades. One girl did the same, but not being competitive or anything, I could say that I'd got better grades than any of my mates.

Some of the subjects I knew I was capable of doing well in, but not all of them. Now I just had to decide what I was going to do with these grades. The obvious route was to carry on and do A Levels, but my school did not have a sixth form, so the question now was where would I go?

My dad had come from the generation of the Grammar school system. In the 1950s if you passed the 11+ and got into a Grammar school then you were destined for a white-collar job and were set for life. If you failed it, you were destined for a blue-collar job and would learn a trade. He didn't pass and so became an apprentice joiner at the age of 15. He so wanted me to take a different route, but even though I passed my 11+, we lived outside the catchment area for Lancaster Royal Grammar School, and the school only accepted a few boys from outside the area. My score was not good enough to be one of those selected, so I had ended up going to the local comprehensive.

Now, with a great set of GCSE grades, I would easily be able to get into the Grammar to do my A Levels. All my mates had decided to go and do their A Levels at another comprehensive, but I knew how much it would mean to my dad if he could say that his boy was at the Boys' Grammar, so I obliged and enrolled in the sixth form at LRGS.

The only problem with this was that the school was an old school rugby and cricket school. They seemed to view football as a sport for ruffians and plebs and did not provide any way for me to continue playing football.

On my first Wednesday afternoon timetabled PE session, all the boys who were involved with the rugby teams went off to smash their heads into each other and chase a weird shaped ball. Those of us who were left were asked what we wanted to do. Those who said football, me included, were simply tossed a ball and told to have a game over in the corner of the playing fields. We had no staff assigned to us, no pitch, no goals. It was like being a young kid again using jumpers for goalposts.

Some of the lads who were much more academically minded had no option but to join in with the football plebs like me, and to be honest, some of them had no idea what football was. They just kicked the ball as hard as they could whenever it came near them with no attempt to actually play. This was not what I had been used to. It was rubbish.

For the last couple of years, I had been used to playing organised football both for school on Saturdays, and for the local Sunday league team on Sunday afternoons. Neither of these were available to me now, with football not an option at school, and as I was now classed as over 16, I was too old for the Sunday league team. My only option for any sort of decent, organised footy was to join my local non-league team, Carnforth Rangers. This would mean joining the Under 18s side, which had lads my age, but also many who were one or two years older than me. They also played on Saturday afternoons, which would prevent me from going to Deepdale with my dad.

Me and my mate decided to join up and see if we could get into the team. I knew most of the lads, a lot of them being the same bunch of lads I'd played with on the school playing field every evening; the same bunch of lads who'd taken the piss when I had to walk past them to church. My mate and I had a successful training session and were told that we'd be in the team for our first game of the season, a trip up to Barrow, round the other side of Morecambe Bay, about fifty miles from where I lived.

I was only used to travelling to play against other much more local teams, the furthest journey being only about eight miles away. This meant that an away fixture for the Under 16s did not take up that much time. I now had a serious amount of homework to do with my A Levels, and realised that an away fixture now could easily take up a whole day, such as this one to Walney Island. We were to meet at the local pub sometime in the morning, drive up in the minibus, play the game, then drive back. We were due to get home by around six or seven in the evening.

I had chosen to do English Literature at A Level, and I had an essay on Hamlet to do that weekend, as well as other work for my other subjects. I needed to crack on with discussing whether Hamlet's apparent insanity was feigned, whether there indeed was method in his madness, or whether he was actually going slightly potty, along with his girlfriend Ophelia. I'd still be able to get the essay done later that evening. I was wrong.

A lot of the lads who were older than me had now got proper full-time jobs and were used to having a beer before the game, and certainly having a few after the game. I was an innocent sixth-form student, who had only ever got drunk at parties, or next to rivers, and had never really been into a pub before. My parents certainly never went into such dens of iniquity, so when we all met up to start our journey around the Bay, I was expected to join in with the drinking, which would then make the minibus journey more enjoyable. That was the theory anyway.

For a start, I didn't have much money. Most of the lads were earning a wage now and had spare cash, but I was an A Level student still relying on pocket money from my parents. I couldn't afford to get the beers in, and frankly I'd rather not get slightly drunk before I had to play a game of football.

I had enough money for one pint and tried to join in with the banter but felt increasingly out of place with these lads now. When we were all at school together, we had something in common. We could talk about which teachers were best to wind up, and who had had a fight with whom. But now, me and my mate had nothing in common with the rest of them. We were now both studying the greatest works of Literature ever written and writing essays about the most enduring of literary characters. The other lads' idea of culture was to put on a tape of Roy Chubby Brown on the way to the game.

All the way up to Barrow, I had to listen to the most vile misogyny and racism, and try to join in with the ensuing chat which these so called jokes created. I was trying to think about the essay I had to do, and of how I would argue that Hamlet was indeed going mad due to the pressure put on him by his now dead father to avenge his most foul murder. In fact it was me going slightly mad as I listened to the mellifluous tones of Roy Chubby Brown, or Royston Vasey to use his real name, as he enthusiastically and repeatedly told us of how he'd taken some girl up the bum by accident, or how a man of Pakistani origin had annoyed him in some way. I don't want to come across as a snob, but this just wasn't my idea of a good day out.

After being surrounded by Royston Vasey for the whole journey, we arrived in Barrow and realised that we had actually gone somewhere resembling the town of Royston Vasey from "The League of Gentlemen".

Barrow is an odd place. It is stuck out on the far edge of the Lake District, cut off from other civilised places. I certainly did not feel like one of the local people as we went into a local shop for some refreshments before the game. I'm just glad we didn't have to get a cab or go to the local butchers or joke shop. I just wanted to play the game and get the hell out of there before I was ceremonially sacrificed by someone resembling Papa Lazarou.

I think we got a draw and after a freezing cold shower, we all got back on the minibus for the second act of Roy Chubby Brown's soliloquy. By this time I was actually starting to think like Hamlet himself. "To be or not to be" was becoming a very relevant question to me, and I wasn't sure whether I could suffer the slings and arrows of outrageous fortune for much longer. I just wanted to get home and away from Royston Vasey. Both of them. However, all the lads were of the consensus that stopping off at another pub for something to eat and more beers was the best idea, and who was I to argue?

More drinks which I couldn't afford, more casual racism and misogyny, and more time being taken away from my essay. We eventually got back around 9pm and the lads were going out to the pub to get absolutely hammered. Me and my mate made our excuses and slinked away. No doubt the others were all talking about what dicks we were and how much better off they were to be learning to be a plasterer or a mechanic rather than studying some poncey book and still going to school.

It's safe to say that I didn't get my essay done that evening. It would have to wait until the next day. I was still recovering from a rather surreal day with, and in, Royston Vasey. "To play or not to play" was now the most apposite question in my mind. If this was what I would have to endure every game, then I could do without it. I had too much homework, and I simply didn't want to play with these lads anymore. It would also mean that I would not be able to go to Deepdale with my dad and watch our team, apart from on Tuesday evenings, depending on how many essays I had to write that evening. Missing out on watching Preston with my dad was something I was not yet prepared to sacrifice.

Whatever my dad was, he was thankfully nothing like Chubby Brown, and instead of playing football on Saturdays, I would continue to watch football with him. But Preston's outrageous fortune would take a turn for the worse this season. Maybe I should have stuck with Chubby.

Whitley Bay v Preston North End

FA Cup Second Round

December 9th, 1989   Hillheads Park

The new season had started awfully for Preston, losing our first five games. We picked up a draw at home against Huddersfield before getting tonked 3-0 away to Bristol Rovers. Our old friends Chester City gave us hope when we thrashed them 5-0 the following week, but this hope was only short-lived. The hope and tentative optimism we had sort of got used to over the last three seasons was definitely waning, and we were back to our default mindset of wondering whether we would be able to avoid relegation.

We got through the first round of the cup and were "rewarded" with what looked like a tricky tie away to non-league Whitley Bay. Surely, we would not perform as badly as we had done against Telford United a few seasons before. The match was to be the featured game on that evening's Match of the Day, with John Motson providing commentary. I'd never seen my team on the television before, and definitely not with Motty doing the honours.

That morning I couldn't wait for the day to be over so that I could watch my team being praised and lauded by the BBC pundits, as obviously we were bound to beat such a lowly team now that we had got promoted and got through that darkest period of the early and mid-80s. We'd beaten Middlesbrough away only three seasons ago, so another trip to the North East did not frighten the now mighty PNE.

Well, we didn't do as badly as we had done against Telford United a few years previously. This time we would only concede two goals, rather than the four we had let in against the team from Shropshire. But that time we had scored one, whereas we were clueless up front against the part-timers from Whitley Bay. This 2-0 loss meant we were again unceremoniously dumped out of the Cup by another non-league side. The 1980s seemed to be ending as they had started for us; rather desperately and despairingly.

Instead of watching Match of the Day to see my team cast aside a little minnow of a club and reach the third round again, where they would surely this time get Man United in the draw for the third round, I had to endure the commentary of John Motson describing the greatest day in Whitley Bay's history.

I still masochistically taped the programme, expecting to keep it as a memento of "When Preston Were On The Television", but for some reason I must have accidentally on purpose taped over it. Helpfully though, the YouTube footage is still in pride of place on Whitley Bay's club website, so please feel free to watch how bad we were that day. I've just watched it again, and I found myself actually being really pleased for the plucky non-leaguers from Whitley Bay. Every team deserves their day, and that day was theirs. I just wish it hadn't been against us.

That day signalled the start of the end for our manager, John McGrath, who had been our messiah only three seasons before. In January we went on a run of six straight losses, conceding fourteen goals and only scoring twice, and would be the death knell for McGrath. He left after we had been beaten 3-0 at home to Leyton Orient. He was no longer the Messiah; he was now a very naughty boy, and so left the club by mutual agreement, which is of course a slightly less embarrassing way of saying that he'd been sacked.

His replacement was one of McGrath's stalwart players, Les Chapman who took over as player/manager for the next two seasons. His first game in charge seemed to pave the way for what would happen over his reign as manager of PNE, getting hammered 6-0 away to Reading, and we eventually finished the season clinging on for our lives, ending up just two places above the relegation zone. The rot had sunk back in and we were back to where we used to be. But at least we weren't fighting for our existence in the whole league by now, just our existence in Division Three. It almost felt quite comforting.

Lads v Dads

May 12th, 1990 Deepdale

In the past year, my parents had moved churches, and now attended the Free Methodist church in Lancaster. What they were now free from was still a bit of a mystery to me, but I dutifully went along with them. I certainly felt more free, as I no longer had to walk past the lads playing footie on the school field and have the piss taken out of me anymore.

At the new church, not only were there more lads my age, but there were also quite a few girls. Very attractive girls too. I would actually look forward to going with mum and dad every Sunday morning, and some Sunday evenings too if it meant that I could meet up with other teenagers in similar circumstances, and especially get to know the girls better.

Apart from the female company, the lads who attended were also decent footballers and we occasionally had games against other churches in the area. As school was not giving me the opportunity to play, and as I had decided against persevering with the Roy Chubby Brown laced journeys with Carnforth Rangers, this was my only chance to have a decent game of footie.

Around about Easter time, we decided to organise a Lads v Dads game on a local playing field. This would not only give me a chance to play another proper game of footie, but it would also mean I would play against my dad. I'd only ever played against him when we had a kickabout when I was a little kid, but I'd never seen him play a proper game. He'd been a no-nonsense full-back in his youth. He was strong and fit, and was renowned for his tackling, albeit not always the most legal. He was now well into his forties and the tables had turned. I was almost seventeen now and strong and fit myself. I couldn't wait to nutmeg him and put him on his backside.

The evening of the game was a lovely spring Friday night. The Dads' team had some good players, but you could tell it was a shock to most of them and at first, they struggled to keep up with us Lads and our quicker pace. I could beat my dad quite easily by knocking it past him and simply sprinting round him. I got some decent crosses into the area, one of which was finished by our centre forward. I don't think I ever did nutmeg him though; he was much too wily for that.

Although we were 1-0 up, we did have quite a few much younger lads playing, lads of around twelve or thirteen, and they proved to be the weak links. The dads could easily knock them off the ball (good job we didn't have to fill in any Health and Safety forms) and exploit our weaknesses. They pulled a goal back and then just after half time they took the lead.

I wasn't about to let my dad get the better of me and so tried to rally our team. I certainly didn't want to lose to my old man, especially as those very attractive girls had come along to watch us males lock horns.

I poked in an equaliser from a corner after some rather pinball machine style defending, and then with about ten minutes to go, I received the ball on the edge of the area with my dad breathing down my neck. I tried to turn him, but he stood firm. I was determined not to lay it off as that would mean that he'd won that little encounter, so with my back to goal, I flicked the ball up over both our heads, turned, and with my dad still wondering where the ball was, volleyed it into the bottom corner to win us the game 3-2. Dad was very magnanimous about the goal, but I'm sure he squeezed my hand much harder than any of the other lads' hands when we all shook hands after the final whistle.

The dads suggested a rematch. Us lads had organised the first match, so we left it in the dads' capable hands to sort out when and where we would get the chance to beat them again. The answer to these questions would not be any sort of playing field. It wouldn't even be on grass. It would be on the hallowed turf, or rather the plastic pitch, of Deepdale.

Deepdale's pitch was available to rent out and the dads came up trumps. Me and my dad would now be able to go into combat again, but this time at the ground where we had spent so much time together watching proper footballers play. It was our turn now. The only problem was that the only Saturday afternoon when we were all available to play, and crucially when the pitch was not being used or already booked, was Saturday, May 12th; Cup Final Day.

That year I was really looking forward to the final as Man United would be in it again, the first time they'd been back at Wembley for the Cup Final since 1985, when me and dad had been. United would be playing against Crystal Palace after the two craziest of semi-finals, in which Palace had beaten the mighty Liverpool 4-3 after extra time, only a few months after losing 9-0 to them in the league. Only an hour later United would be taken to a replay by Second Division Oldham after the first game had finished 3-3 after extra time. The two semi-finals had provided thirteen goals in one crazy Sunday afternoon.

United managed to squeeze through the replay with Oldham, again needing extra time to do so, to set up a final which they were definite favourites to win. Alex Ferguson had almost got the sack earlier in the season, and this cup run to Wembley provided him with a chance to hold onto his job and win his first silverware as United manager. It was a game none of us wanted to miss, but with the chance of playing at our own version of Wembley, at Deepdale, then we all opted to play, rather than watch football that particular Cup Final day. Cup Finals happened every year; playing at Deepdale against my dad did not.

So, as Ian Wright was coming on as a substitute for Palace, scoring twice in a thrilling 3-3 draw at Wembley, and providing one of the greatest Cup Finals ever, I did not see a single moment of it. Instead I was involved in just as tight a game, but with far fewer goals, only one in fact, and it was scored by my dad.

The dads this time had brought in some reinforcements and they were a much stronger team. I just remember how big Deepdale's pitch seemed, and how much it hurt when you slid in for a challenge or ended up on the ground after being tackled. My knees were cut to shreds after that game and I understood why so many players played in leggings when they played at Deepdale in that era of the plastic and very painful pitch.

The game was much tighter this time and the only chance I had was something out of nothing really. I picked the ball up in midfield, dropped my shoulder and cut inside my marker, before curling a lovely shot from the corner of the penalty area, only to see it hit the angle of the post and crossbar. My postage stamp shot was just off target by a foot or so.

The only goal came when one of our defenders made a clumsy challenge in the penalty box and gave away a spot kick. The other dads all knew how much of a Preston fan my dad was, so with a certain amount of sentimentality, a little bit of romance, and quite a lot of doubt as to whether he would actually convert the penalty, they unanimously gave the ball to him. He placed the ball on the spot in front of the Spion Kop, where he had seen countless goals go in, more often than not by the opposition rather than by Preston.

Even though it meant we would probably lose the game, I was willing my dad not to mess up and to slot the ball home, which he thankfully did. The crowd didn't exactly roar, as there was no crowd there to do any roaring. My dad had actually scored at Deepdale to win the game for his team. He would just have to imagine the euphoria instead.

The game ended, and this time I squeezed my dad's hand as hard as I possibly could when we all shook hands. As soon as we got back to the car, we turned the radio on to find out the Cup Final result and were rather pleased that United and Palace had obliged us with a draw. We would all have the opportunity of watching the replay the following Thursday evening. We still didn't know who had won the Cup, and whether Alex Ferguson still had a job next season.

As for the replay, the only things anyone remembers about the game are that Jim Leighton, the United keeper, got ruthlessly dropped by Alex Ferguson in his desperation to win a trophy, replacing him with Les Sealey, and how well United's left back Lee Martin swept in the goal which would win Ferguson his first trophy for Man United. We all know what happened to United after that game and how many trophies United would go onto win under Ferguson, but that night was the start of it all. I'm sure he felt a sense of pride that night at Wembley, but I'm not sure it matched the pride my dad felt after scoring at Deepdale only a few days before.

World Cup Finals Italy 1990

Cameroon v England

World Cup Quarter-Final

July 1st, 1990   Stadio San Paulo, Naples

And so the World Cup rolled around again, but this time England had a secret weapon; an actual good song which would inspire them and their fans. Unlike the songs from 1982 and 1986 which tried to jauntily recapture the spirit of 1970's "Back Home" which would go onto be the tune for Fantasy Football League, we had entered the 90s now and music was just better. We had a proper song, written by proper musicians, performed by a proper band, although I can't say that John Barnes was a proper rapper on New Order's "World in Motion".

Not only was that song permeating the airwaves, but the BBC came up trumps by using Pavarotti's version of "Nessun Dorma" for their coverage of the World Cup. Both songs got us all well in the mood to hopefully get our revenge on Diego Maradona, the cheating bastard, after he had put us out of the last World Cup.

The tournament opened with Maradona's Argentina getting beaten by Cameroon, Roger Miller and all, as well as some of the most lethal and illegal tackling I'd ever seen on a football pitch. Some of the tackles that went in on the Argentinians that opening match put Vinnie Jones to shame. But seeing as they were being inflicted on Maradona's mob, then nobody actually cared whether they were illegal. The more illegal the better actually.

England had been drawn in a group that contained both Holland and the Republic of Ireland, two teams we had lost to in our last tournament. If the rest of us weren't shitting ourselves at the prospect of facing the European champions, then Gary Lineker certainly was. After suffering from a dodgy belly, Lineker actually shat himself on the pitch during our opening draw against Ireland, but still managed to score his first goal in his quest to win a second Golden Boot in successive tournaments.

Along with our proper song, our second game against Holland was where we would all realise what a proper player Paul Gascoigne was. The players had persuaded Bobby Robson to experiment with a sweeper system, which gave Gascoigne more freedom to run the middle of the park. Even though we only got a 0-0 draw, we looked far better than the European champions, and Gascoigne showed the whole world what a special talent he was.

With two draws under our belt, we only needed to beat Egypt to qualify for the second round, which we duly did 1-0 with a headed goal from Mark Wright. Compared to the tension of the last World Cup group, we almost breezed into the knockout stage this time, where we would be facing Belgium.

No one remembers anything about the game against Belgium apart from the final few seconds of extra time. With the threat of our first ever World Cup penalty shootout looming, Gascoigne lofted a free kick into the area, for another emerging star, David Platt, to swivel and volley us into the quarter finals. But this time we would not be facing Argentina, but ironically the team who had already beaten Maradona et al, Cameroon.

The semi-finals were within our grasp. Anyone of my generation had never seen England get to the last four of a tournament before and here we were, only ninety minutes away. All we had to do was beat a team who had only ever been in one World Cup before now, and had never got through to the knockout stages before now. It should have been a doddle.

In between the Belgium and Cameroon games, we as a family were due to move house. My dad was, and still is, a man who would rather just get on with a job on his own rather than have me attempting to help. So when the opportunity to escape for a few days arose, my parents had no objections.

One of my mates who had already started university in Nottingham had invited me and another mate to go and stay with him at the end of his first year. As I was considering going to university myself in just over a year's time, I thought it would be a good way of experiencing student life and help me in my choice of which Higher Education establishment I would grace my presence with.

I would also be able to watch the quarter-final game, and if we won, the semi-final too. My parents were all for the idea and could get moved into our new house with one less bedroom to have to sort out as quickly as possible. Dad has always lived by the tenet "Don't delay what you can do today." In fact, he would rather have a job done the day before he actually did it, if that was possible. He wanted to get moved in and sort everything out, assembling new bedroom units and all the other jobs he would have to do. Me being away meant that he didn't have to do my bedroom until just before I returned from Nottingham.

They, like me, also thought that I would be able to immerse myself in student life and give me an idea of what to expect from university, helping me make up my mind as to whether I wanted to actually go. Amazingly, I managed to blag my teachers into letting me have a week off school, particularly as we were meant to be preparing for our end of year exams. My argument was that seeing as we were only going to be revising in lessons, I could do that in a university library where I had access to so many more resources to hone my intellectual skills, and fully prepare for my exams. I also used the same argument I had used on my parents; that I could also immerse myself in student life and experience what study at a university meant.

For me though, immersing oneself in student life would mean basically one thing; getting drunk, which, to be honest, is what student life is for most students. I was now seventeen and could happily pass for eighteen. It was frankly easy to get served alcohol underage back then, particularly if you were at a Student Union bar where everyone else was over eighteen. So, the plan was to kip on my mate's floor, get drunk for a week either at the Union bar or experience the Nottingham nightlife. Studying or research had nothing to do with my trip, but then again, neither of these things are particularly high on most students' agenda anyway. Drinking was though.

Both my school and parents bought my argument and they wished me well in my newly found sense of adventure and thirst for life experiences. I packed a few textbooks with my clothes and proceeded to never look at them once for the whole time I was there. I had a different kind of thirst.

As I left to catch the train to Nottingham, I realised that I would never walk into that house again. This was the house where I'd got through my GCSEs and more importantly, taught myself keepy-uppy skills on the driveway. When I returned to a different home, I would be in a new house, with a new bedroom, and maybe England would be in the World Cup Final.

My first night in Nottingham, the day before the quarter-final, went according to plan; we got absolutely hammered in the Union bar. The next day was spent nursing a major hangover and instead of going out to watch the game, we decided to stay in and watch it, to give our livers a break if nothing else. I've never been a fan of watching big games in a rowdy pub where the view is restricted and it's just full of rowdy drunk people who aren't even watching the game. I was very happy to watch the biggest game for England since the Maradona handball game in the Hall TV lounge with a random mix of students of varying nationalities. This felt truly like a World Cup game as I settled down next to a group of Japanese, a group of Spaniards, and a few other random nationalities ranging from American to Malaysian. I'd never felt so worldly before.

The game itself proved anything but a doddle for England, even though we went 1-0 up after 26 minutes to a David Platt header. However, the Cameroon team certainly did not lie down and be beaten. They played out of their skins and in four minutes just after the hour mark scored twice to take the lead, the first being a penalty. Little did Peter Shilton know then that this would certainly not be the only penalty he would face before England came home.

Yet again England looked like they would be knocked out just before the semi-finals, as they had done at every World Cup they had taken part in after they had won it in 1966. But good old Gary Lineker had other ideas. With only eight minutes of normal time remaining, he won us a penalty and placed the ball on the spot to equalise and give us some time to regroup before extra time. If he had shat himself in the first game of the tournament, I wouldn't have blamed him if he had done it again just before he ran up to take the penalty. Luckily, he controlled his bowels, and side footed the ball to the keeper's left. We now had an extra half an hour to get a winner.

We only needed until the end of the first period of extra time to find that winner, and it was all down again to Gary Lineker, who won us another penalty after a sumptuous through ball from Paul Gascoigne. Still keeping his bowels at bay, Lineker smashed the ball as hard as he could down the middle to put us in the lead; a lead we would this time hold on to, to reach our first semi-final since 1966.

The multi-national members of the audience did not seem quite as enthusiastic as me and my English mates did about our victory, so we decided to get out of there and celebrate properly. Unsurprisingly, my hangover had now completely gone, so we went out into Nottingham to revel with all the other somewhat disbelieving fans. We were in the last four of the World Cup, and we would have to beat our old enemy, the West Germans, if we were to exact our revenge on Maradona in the final.

The next few days of my stay in Nottingham were spent exactly as I expected them to be spent. We drank a lot in the Union bar and went out to the various nightclubs of Nottingham, as well as looking around the campus and even visiting the library once to see what it was like, although as far as doing any actual study, that just wasn't happening. The exams didn't mean that much really. They were only school exams and didn't count towards my A Levels. Or so I thought.

My mate who was already at university told me the night before the semi-final, on our fifth consecutive night of getting drunk, that my teachers would be using the grades I got for these exams as a way of predicting my actual A Level grades. These predictions would then be used by prospective universities to either offer me a conditional place, or decide to give my place to someone who hadn't been getting drunk when he should have been doing some actual revision.

This information had a somewhat sobering effect on me, and I felt the need to get back home and do some work. I would also be able to watch this historic match with my mum and dad in our new home. After sleeping on the floor for five nights and eating very unhealthy and always disappointing food, I was ready to get home and be fed properly by my mum, even if it meant I would have to go back into school and do some proper revision. Well, any sort of revision actually. But mostly, and much more pressingly, I wanted to be fed by my mum.

West Germany v England

World Cup Semi-Final

July 4th, 1990   Stadio delle Alpi, Turin

I didn't bother ringing my mum or dad to tell them I would be returning home earlier than expected. My dad still thought he had three days to get the house sorted and put my bedroom together, but I thought my early return would be a lovely surprise for them. My parents would welcome their prodigal son back into their bosoms, feed me profusely, and settle down to watch us beat the Germans. My dad isn't the biggest fan of surprises though, so when I turned up at our new house, I didn't exactly receive the warmest of welcomes from him.

He greeted me with "What are you doing here?" and proceeded to rant about how it would have been best if he'd known I was going to swan in and expect a functional bedroom. I politely told him not to worry about it and as long as I had a bed then I would be fine. I'd been sleeping on the floor for the last five nights, so any sort of comfort would suit me. As long as mum made my tea for me was all I was bothered about.

But as I said earlier, my dad is a man who like things done as soon as possible, if not before, and he still grumbled about not being able to watch the game as he now had my bedroom to sort out. He was just being stubborn now. I repeated that there was no need for him to do it that night, I would be glad to sleep on an unmade bed in my sleeping bag, and I'd rather he sat down with me to watch the game.

All throughout my deeply appreciated tea which mum was all too happy to cook for me, me and my mum gave each other knowing looks as dad continued to grumble. When he was like this there was no point in arguing with him, so it was best to just let him be a martyr. I told him I would gladly help him as soon as I got back from school the following day, but he was having none of it. It had to be done that night.

So instead of settling down with mum and dad to watch the game, just me and mum sat down in our new front room to watch what would be, and probably still is, the most intense game of football I've ever experienced, certainly as an England fan. Dad would listen to it upstairs on the radio whilst putting shelves up and assembling my new desk and chest of drawers. He was actually in his element up there, and he could always rush down if there was any sort of incident in the game which required the television to be watched.

It's fair to say that he was up and down the stairs quite a lot that night, that night in Turin, which would be remembered by so many England fans for so many different reasons.

Dad remained pretty much undisturbed for the first half, apart from Chris Waddle almost scoring from near the halfway line, but once we went behind to the cruellest of deflections off Paul Parker's foot from a free kick, then he listened more intently. The tension was building. Were we again going to go out due to sheer bad luck? Again Mr. Lineker thought otherwise. A hopeful ball into the box from Paul

Parker, a little flick with his left knee, "And Lineker!" Gary had saved the game yet again to take it into extra time.

At this point I just told my dad to stop and come and watch the rest of the game. He yielded and sat down with us to endure the rest of the drama as it unfolded. Gascoigne's stupid and immature challenge which brought him his second yellow card of the tournament put a complete dampener on proceedings. I remember feeling that even if we won and got through to the final, that game would be spoiled because of his absence. He certainly felt that too as his tears welled up and Gary looked to the bench for Bobby Robson to have a word. From then on, the intensity increased.

Both sides hit the post, with Waddle's shot bouncing agonisingly wide of the oncoming Lineker, who would have surely put the rebound in. Shilton made a brilliant point blank save from Jurgen Klinsmann, but unfortunately that would be the last save he would make due to the quality of the West German penalties.

We are all so used to penalty shootouts now, but you have to realise that before Italia 90, there had only ever been three, and West Germany had been involved in two of them. They had cruelly beaten France in the 1982 semi-final, and also beaten the hosts Mexico in 1986. Out of the ten penalties they had taken in World Cup penalty shootouts, they had only missed one. And they would not miss another one that night in Turin.

On the other hand, it was all new territory for England. We had never been involved in any sort of penalty shootout before, but I still believed it was our destiny to beat the Germans and go onto to claim revenge against Maradona, the cheating bastard. We had matched them for the first three penalties, Lineker, Beardsley and Platt all slotting their spot kicks away with German-like efficiency, and when Stuart Pearce stepped forward, we were all confident he would slam his home too.

Well, he certainly slammed it, right down the middle, but it was low, and the keeper didn't have to do much to save it. If you're going to put a penalty down the middle, it has to be high as most keepers will dive. If it's low, then the keeper's legs still have a chance.

Chris Waddle wasn't going to make the same mistake; he was definitely going high with his penalty. High, wide and definitely not handsome, as the ball flew into orbit, causing not just Gascoigne to sob, but it brought a tear to Bobby Robson's eye too, along with millions of us around the country. It was the ultimate in being so near yet so far. Once again, we were a nearly team; much nearer than before, but that just made it so much worse somehow.

The only consolation was that we all watched Maradona shed his own tears after his Argentina team lost the final, with yet another ruthless German penalty winning it. We would have won that final, even without Paul Gascoigne. He knew it, we all knew it, and Bobby Robson certainly knew it.

He left his job as England Manager with the ultimate "If only" hanging over his head. With "Nessun Dorma" reverberating in our ears, and our spines poignantly tingling, no longer with anticipation, but now with the sadness of what could, and even should have been, we would all have to wait another four years for another chance. It turned out to be eight years actually, but we all knew we would not get another chance quite like that one.

Season 1990/1991

Nottingham Forest v Tottenham Hotspur

FA Cup Final

May 18th, 1991 Wembley Stadium

You may have noticed that the only game I'm including this season is the final game of the whole season. The truth is, I didn't go to many games this season, and I didn't even watch this game either. Now that I was in the Upper Sixth, my studies were cranked up even more, and I was regularly doing three or four essays a week. I had started the previous year not knowing what I wanted to do with my A Levels, but now I definitely knew. I wanted to go to university to study for a degree in English Literature.

I had fallen under the spell of my A Level English teacher. It was around the time that "Dead Poets' Society" came out, and although he didn't make us rip pages out of textbooks or encourage us to read poetry in a cave in the middle of the night, he did make me realise how much fun you could have being an English teacher. I certainly would have stood on my desk for him, and my other subjects paled away into insignificance. I still took them seriously and did all that was required of me, but there was no passion there, unlike for English Literature.

I now had to decide which universities would go on my entry form. After that week in Nottingham, I immediately put that as my first choice, and I also put Sheffield, Birmingham and Bristol down. My rather leftfield choice was the University of Reading. I wanted to see what life Down South was like, and wanted to be near to London, without making the huge step of moving from a small town in North Lancashire, to one of the biggest cities in the world. Not yet anyway. I had already been to the open day at Reading. I loved the campus and liked the course I would be studying. So, onto the form it went, almost as a backup if nothing else. I didn't realise that it would become my only choice.

Apart from my studies, the real reason I saw very little football was that I had now discovered the joys of drinking in the pubs of Lancaster and even being able to get into clubs. This required money, and so the point came that a Saturday job was needed. I managed to get myself a job working in the second-hand department of Carnforth Bookshop, surrounding myself with literature and books all day every Saturday. It was easy work, if slightly boring at times, but it helped me gain a pretty good knowledge of writers and what they had written. I also got discount on any of the books, which would obviously help me if I was to become a Literature undergraduate.

This job obviously meant that I could no longer go to Deepdale with my dad, apart from a few evening games. I didn't miss much that season frankly. Preston struggled again in Division Three, and eventually ended up in 17th place, slightly better than the year before, but still nearer the relegation zone than the play-off places. Dad was obviously still persevering, and was able to watch us get knocked out of the cup by Mansfield this year. At least they were a league club this time. He'd found a group of similarly curmudgeonly blokes to stand and suffer with, so at least he wasn't missing my youthful company.

This was also the year I fell by the wayside in terms of attending church with my parents. One of the reasons for going in the first place was the girls, but I soon realised that there were many more girls in the bars of town and were more fun when they were drunk too. I also soon realised that getting up with a hangover on a Sunday morning and going to church was not much fun at all. I had been tempted by the Devil and had succumbed to the delights of wine and women, except it was very rarely wine that I drank.

My year carried on, working hard at school, earning enough to pay for a night out on Saturday, and starting the whole process again, week after week. But I suppose that's what life is like for most people. My university entry form had been sent off and I now just had to wait for the offers to come rolling in, so I could decide where my future would lie.

My future was kind of made up for me as my lack of work and revision for the exams during the World Cup resulted in me getting an awful set of results. My teachers used these grades to predict my A Levels and as a result, every university deemed me not worthy to attend their academic institution. The rejection letters kept coming in, except for one. Reading University must have taken pity and offered me a place, on condition that I got at least three grade Bs. I knew I could do this but was still in two minds as to whether I wanted to go there.

The possibility of taking a year out and re-applying came up, once I had got my actual results. I thought this sounded viable as I would then have some definite proof of my abilities, not just what my teachers had predicted for me based on a set of exams I had prepared for by drinking and watching football.

My parents however weren't too happy about this, especially dad, as he did not like uncertainty. He wanted to know what was happening, and what I would be doing. I think he probably thought that if I took a year out, I would just end up in a dead-end job and not use the talents I had. I sympathised with him to an extent and was also rather sceptical about taking a year out. I'd rather just get on with it and escape from Carnforth. The only option I had was Reading though.

The crunch time came around May, as I was preparing for my A Level exams. Dad came up with a plan to try and help me make my mind up; if we went down to Reading to have another look around the campus, the town, and the surrounding areas, then maybe that would focus me on going there the following September. The only problem was that the only free day we could go was Cup Final day. I had by now given up my Saturday job to focus on my revision (I wasn't about to make the same mistake twice) and so was able to go down to Berkshire for the day. If we set off early enough, we would be able to listen to the Cup Final on the radio on the way home.

So, only two weeks after I had turned eighteen, I was awoken at an ungodly hour and bundled into the back of our car for a day trip to Reading. I managed to get some more sleep and do a bit of revision on the way down and was pleasantly surprised by what I saw of the areas around Reading. The campus was still great, the countryside was lovely, but the town was rather uninspiring. I defy anyone to tell me that Reading is a beautiful town, but if it was good enough for Oscar Wilde, then it was good enough for me.

Dad was also keen as he would be able to come down and visit me when Preston were playing Reading at Elm Park, as both teams were in the same division back then. That must have clinched it for me.

We had a drive back through Windsor, Eton and Henley-on-Thames and fell in love with just how different they were to anywhere I had experienced Up North. My mind was made up. It was now full steam ahead for Reading, and also full steam ahead for home up the M42. I could now concentrate on the Cup Final on the radio.

Brian Clough had finally got to Wembley and had the chance of winning the only trophy that had eluded him. But first we listened to how Paul Gascoigne basically wrecked his career with one of the most ridiculous challenges ever, with Stuart Pearce smashing the ball in from the resulting free kick. If only he'd done the same with his penalty against West Germany.

Everyone remembers how Forest's most dependable of defenders, Des Walker, scored the winner for Spurs, heading into his own net after Spurs had equalised in the second half, but no one remembers the fact that Gary Lineker missed a penalty. Yes, even Gary could miss chances, even from the penalty spot. This made Walker's own goal even more cruel, as had Lineker scored his penalty, then Spurs would have won without the need for extra time. And so, Brian Clough, the man who had won the league with Derby, the League again, the Charity Shield, four League Cups, a UEFA Super Cup and two European Cups with Nottingham Forest, remained destined to never win the FA Cup. His was one of the most remarkable records ever, but I'm sure he would have loved to have completed the full set.

Once we arrived home, I watched the highlights on Match of the Day to see Gazza's tackle in all its awful glory. My last Cup Final at home before I would hopefully move Down South, and I didn't even watch it. It was now full steam ahead with revision. To revise or not to revise was definitely not the question this year. I had to get at least three Bs.

Season 1991/92

Manchester United v Notts County

August 17th, 1991   Old Trafford

After finishing my exams, me and my three best mates, the two who have already been mentioned, and another who I would end up sharing a flat with in London, went Inter-Railing around Europe. We all either had savings, generous parents, or in my case, some inherited money from my late Grandma which would be able to provide a rucksack, a tent, a ticket and some spending money to travel around Europe and broaden our so far rather limited horizons. Our goal was to get as far East as possible, and that meant getting to Istanbul.

We eventually got to our destination, by way of Paris, Munich, Venice and Athens, with a little stop off on a couple of the Greek islands. Istanbul was vast and exciting, sprawling and exotic. Forget Liverpool's comeback from 3-0 down at half-time to win the European Cup in 2005, the summer of 91 was when the real Miracle of Istanbul occurred.

Whoever we met in Istanbul, they would always ask us where us English boys were from. We told them Lancaster, but this small city on didn't register with the locals. So, we told anyone who asked that we were from near Manchester, which technically we kind of were. As soon as we mentioned Manchester, the locals would all light up in recognition and say the same thing: "Ah, Manchester United!" It was then that I realised just how huge a club United were. It seemed that everyone in the whole world knew that name, and it gave us some sort of cache with our Turkish hosts.

One bloke though took our new found spirit of comradely solidarity to a new level. He was a street shoe shiner and was kindly and rather constantly offering his skills to polish our trainers. After the usual response once we told him that we were from near Manchester, he started to roll off some names of United players he knew. As I had some knowledge of the subject too, I joined in with him and eventually agreed to let him at least try and polish my battered, old, but oh so comfy white Nike trainers for a nominal fee.

He daubed some white polish all over them, gave them a bit of a rub, before holding his hand out for his hard-earned fee. I didn't realise that the etiquette was just to give the smallest note available, which back then was worth about 20p. I stupidly asked how much he would like, and he looked in my wallet and pointed at a particular note.

I was still yet to understand fully the rate of exchange and blunderingly got the note out. In a blink of an eye, the note was gone, and he had vanished, blending into the Istanbul sprawl. It was only then that I realised that instead of paying 20p, I had just paid a hundred times more. The note I had confusedly proffered was actually worth around £20. I probably still hold the record for the most expensive shoeshine in the whole of the Ottoman Empire. And my trainers looked worse than before.

We arrived back home after a month of travelling, our horizons suitably broadened, and in my case, my wallet suitably emptied, just in time to get my A Level results. Joy of joys, I had got the required grades, even getting a couple of A's to prove to my teachers that their predictions were very far off the mark. I was accepted onto my course at Reading University and had a few weeks to get ready before I would head off into the great unknown. It most definitely was the great unknown for my family, as no one had ever been to university before. None of us knew what it would be like, and the realisation dawned on my parents that once I left in September, I would basically be flying the nest, only returning during my holidays for a few weeks at a time.

I think my dad wanted to get in as many games of football with me as possible. So, on his twenty third wedding anniversary, instead of treating my mum to a romantic day out, he took me back to Old Trafford one last time. This was United's opening match of the season, the last season they would not win the league, before they kept on winning it for most of the next twenty seasons. Old Trafford itself had had some improvements done since the last time we'd been, and it was now an even better stadium, although still a long way off the arena it is today.

Whilst I had been galivanting around Europe, so it seemed had Alex Ferguson, signing up two of the best players he would ever buy. The lightning quick Russian winger Andrei Kanchelskis had been recruited and this was to be his home debut. Another home debut was to be given to some new goalkeeper called Peter Schmeichel. I wonder what became of him.

Also on the pitch that day, for Notts County, was Don O'Riordan, the player who, as captain for Preston in 1981, had held my hand and led me out onto the pitch as mascot for my eighth birthday. Apart from Preston, he played more games for Notts County than any other club, and here he was, playing at Old Trafford in front of over 46,000 fans. He, like me had come a long way since 1981. We had both played at Deepdale, but alas, I'd yet to feature in a game at Old Trafford.

My old hero, Bryan Robson, who by now was being used as a sub, came on and scored the second of United's goals in a 2-0 win that day, so it was nice to have two very different players on the pitch at the same time, both of whom had given me very significant and very happy memories in my childhood.

***

Me and dad also fitted in as many games at our beloved Deepdale as we could before I left. I saw Preston draw with Bournemouth and Bradford, but the only win I would see was a quite extraordinary game in the first round of the League cup, in which we beat Scarborough 6-4. The return leg finished 3-1 to the Yorkshire side, meaning that it was 7-7 on aggregate. You don't get many ties like that anymore. Our season would be very similar to the previous year, ending up 17th again, but my attentions were now firmly fixed on going to university and saying farewell to the North, but never a farewell to North End.

At the end of September, me and my tight-knit group of mates, one by one, went our separate ways, on our different adventures. One would take a gap year, work in London, before trekking the Himalayas, one would go to study in Newcastle, another to Aberdeen, and I was off to Reading. As mum and dad drove away after leaving me at my new Hall of Residence, I thought maybe that was it, maybe I would never return properly Up North, apart from to visit them both.

Little did I know that seven years later I would return with a wife and daughter to settle down only a few miles from where I grew up. Little did my mum know that either, as the tears welled up in her eyes, leaving her eighteen-year-old little boy standing there with his future all before him.

Windsor Hall v Greek Students' Team

November 1992   **University of Reading**

During Freshers' Week I met a gorgeous girl who happened to be doing the same course as me. She was on the next floor up from me in my new Hall of Residence, Windsor Hall, a big concrete block where we were all packed into our individual rooms. Amazingly she seemed to not mind my company and we got closer over the next few weeks. We went to lectures together, helped each other navigate around the campus, and crucially she had a love of films and cinema that I shared, and so we would often go to the cinema together or get closer in my room watching a video.

She also was not a football aficionado, which I was rather glad about. I would have found it disconcerting if she could have told me who had scored West Ham's goals in the 1975 Cup Final and which school he had attended. (Alan Taylor, Carnforth High School, my old school, if you were wondering). I didn't want to go out with a girl who had a geeky knowledge about obscure footballing facts. That would have been so dull. I wanted someone vastly different to me and she was definitely that.

I was falling in love, or whatever love is, in Prince Charles' famous words. I was still a kid, even though I was eighteen, and I had no idea what real love was back then. All I knew was that I loved being with my new girl friend and wanted so much for her to be my actual girlfriend.

As I was now over two hundred miles from Deepdale, there was no way I could watch my team regularly, and quite frankly, I didn't really care. I was now an undergraduate, apparently an intellectual studying Chaucer, Marlowe, Modernist Literature and Virginia Woolf's Stream of Consciousness narrative style. That was the idea anyway. My Methodist work ethic which had served me so well up to now was slipping somewhat. Yes, I attended all my lectures, even contributed to seminars, and diligently wrote my essays, but the intensity of study that I had experienced during my A Levels was no longer required. I now had more time to watch films with my girlfriend and get drunk with some of the other freshers.

With no way of watching football, I was desperate to play football again. I went along to the stall during Freshers' Fair where the university football team were recruiting, but they all seemed like a bunch of idiots. They all looked much better footballers than me, and I didn't want to commit all my time to travelling around with a bunch of dicks, playing drinking games to prove my worth to them. It just wasn't my thing, but at least they probably didn't listen to Chubby Brown, although I wouldn't have put it past some of them.

I hadn't really played much organised football in the last two years, so when I saw that my Hall was having a trial session to recruit new players for the Hall footy team, I jumped at the chance. One Wednesday afternoon early in my first term, all those who wanted to be considered for the Hall team were required to turn up and have a game of football. I could do that.

I must have impressed the captain, a third-year student, as he asked me and a few others to join the team. We would play a league system against all the other halls as well as a cup competition which would take place every few weeks. I couldn't wait to get started. I could play football on campus every Saturday morning and still be able to do all the other things I was getting used to doing as a student.

Myself and another fresher slotted into the midfield, and I soon realised that we had quite a good side. We had a solid keeper, our captain as centre back who was tall and quite classy on the ball, a bit like Alan Hansen in his day, and a quick, powerful striker. All these lads were in their final year and would be leaving at the end of the season. I knew it would be difficult to replace them, so we had to make the most of our team this season.

The league consisted of fourteen teams; the twelve Halls of Residence along with two other teams made up of International students; the Greeks and the Japanese. The season would be spread out over the first two terms, up until Easter, and we would all play each other once. The cup competition was slightly different as we only had fourteen teams. There would be four rounds, with two teams getting a bye into the second round, which were actually the quarter-finals. Just like the FA Cup, our cup competition wouldn't start until after Christmas, so we concentrated on the league for my first term.

It soon became apparent that we were one of the better teams in the league, but had no chance of winning as Childs Hall, the biggest Hall in the whole university, had the widest choice of players, and had many of the university players available to them. We got easily beaten by them early on but managed to win or draw all our other games. Some teams were fairly rubbish and only had a few players who were any good, their numbers being made up from enthusiastic if rather uncoordinated individuals. Some, like us, had decent players throughout the team and we had some great games against these teams.

I remember finding it hard to beat the Japanese as they were tough and resilient, and jabbered on constantly in their angry sounding voices. Their grasp of English was not the best, so it was hard to verbally wind them up. They had no idea what I was saying to them. However, they had much more idea of what I was saying to them than I had of what they were saying to me as it was safe to say that my grasp of Japanese was significantly worse than their command of the English language.

The Greeks were much easier to wind up, and in our match against them I nearly got my head kicked in by one of them. I'd been out for a few pints with some mates, one of whom had Greek heritage. He told me that saying the word "Malaka" would do the trick if I wanted to wind them up a bit. He was not wrong.

I found out that the word was the Greek word for someone who has masturbated so much that his brain has gone soft. On a football pitch, everyone gets called a wanker at some point. I had been called it many times before, and in turn had called others it frequently. But it seemed that the Greek connotation was much worse than the English version.

I'd been tackled rather painfully by one of the larger Greek players, so I decided to try out my new linguistic skills. I shouted "malaka" at him and he just stopped and glared at me with menace. He had a word with some of his teammates, and the game carried on. To use cricketing parlance, it was obvious that my sledging was doing the trick. My new found worst enemy was getting so wound up every time I referred to him as a malaka that his play was being affected. He made a mistake which led to our first goal, so obviously I kept on doing it. The half time whistle went with us 1-0 up and as we were jogging back to have a little team talk, I whispered the seemingly innocent expletive in his ear as I passed him.

This was the final straw for him, and the red mist descended. I felt like a matador in a bull ring, with no cape and no sword, with the most incensed and enraged bull of a man staring at me, with almost cartoon like steam coming from his nostrils. He charged at me, and like any sensible matador with no way of protecting himself, my only option was to run away. Luckily, I was quicker than him and instead of having a team talk, I spent half time being chased around by a big Greek bloke with severe anger issues, whilst both teams just watched and laughed.

I eventually apologised profusely, and he calmed down, no doubt with the intention of getting me back for my misdemeanours on the pitch. He duly did after only a few minutes of the second half, crashing into me and sending me flying into the air, a little like a matador being gored funnily enough. No damage was done, and we now had a new sense of respect for each other. He'd made his point and we shook hands. We still won the game without me referring to anyone as a malaka again. It was a top Saturday morning's entertainment all round.

Windsor Hall v Whiteknights Hall

Inter-Hall Cup Semi-Final

February 8th, 1992   University of Reading

Windsor Hall were second in the league by the end of my first term, and we all went back home for our first Christmas break full of confidence. My girl friend was now officially my girlfriend and as she lived in Derbyshire, it wasn't too far to travel to stay with her, and vice versa. We met each other's parents, and everything went well. I could not believe how far above my weight I was punching but I wasn't about to start questioning it. I could've gone to a couple of matches at Deepdale with my dad over the Christmas period, but the truth was, my passion for watching Preston had been substituted for another. I just wanted to get back down to university so I could see her every day. And get back to playing football. We had a cup to win.

Our first cup game was won easily, and we were through to the quarter-finals without much effort. As long as we avoided drawing the favourites Childs Hall then we had a chance of progressing. We did avoid them and won our next game quite convincingly again, but even better was the fact that Childs got beaten somehow in their quarter-final game. Most of their players must have had a university fixture to fulfil, leaving what was in effect their second team to play their quarter-final. They should still have won, but incredibly lost to the team who would be our opponents in the semi-final, Whiteknights Hall. We were now the favourites to win the Cup, but our semi-final match would not be easy. Our opponents had just beaten the best team in the league, albeit a weakened team.

We knew that if we could get through this match then the other semi-final was being contested by two teams who we had already beaten in the league. It was ours to lose now. I had an added incentive to win as the final was due to be played at the end of February, the same day as Preston's league game at Reading. Dad had already planned to come down to visit so we could both go to Elm Park, Reading's old ground. If we got to the final, then he could come down earlier to see me hopefully lift another cup, just as he had done when I was eleven.

The morning of the semi-final match was a cold, blustery one. Even though we were favourites to win, this somehow made me more nervous. This was more like the final, as whoever won would be able to beat either of the teams from the other semi-final. We got off to a good start, scoring fairly early on, but were pegged back soon afterwards with our opponents getting an equaliser.

With about ten minutes to go before half-time, our centre forward poached one, Gary Lineker style, to give us a 2-1 lead at the break. We had our team talk and it was agreed that the next goal would be crucial. Whichever team got it would probably then go on and win the game. Whoever scored it would give their team a huge boost. That someone happened to be me.

If you remember me describing the best goal I ever scored, at the age of nine in my primary school playground, then this goal a very different one but still almost as good, if I do say so myself. Ten minutes into the second half, we were pressing for that third goal when I received the ball on the halfway line. I had no idea what to do with it, so I just pushed on towards their penalty box. No challenges came in, so I just carried on, head down, now oblivious of my teammates. I was finally closed down but managed to skip and weave past three defenders before hitting it into the bottom corner, just eluding their keeper's outstretched hand. I didn't exactly fire it in, but it had enough power to sneak inside the post.

I couldn't quite believe it had gone in until I saw my teammates charging towards me. I didn't want to be bundled over into a heap by them, so I just turned and had my own Marco Tardelli moment, screaming with outstretched arms as I ran towards our half. Professional footballers always say that there is no better feeling than scoring a goal, and they are often embarrassed by their antics when they celebrate. I understood that for the first time that day. I'd never felt so euphoric on a football pitch, and even better, my girlfriend had promised to come and watch that morning, so she got to see my bulging eyes in all their glory. How attractive that must have been for her.

We did indeed go onto win the game, 4-2 if I remember rightly, and were through to the final. As soon as I could, I rang dad and told him that he'd have to set off earlier than he was expecting to in three weeks' time as he had another final to watch.

When the day of the final arrived, dad set off even earlier than I thought he would, getting up at 5am to make sure he didn't get stuck in traffic. With only minimal traffic at 6am, it only took him two and a half hours, whereas normally it would take at least four. He must have arrived at least two hours before the game was due to start but waited patiently in the car, no doubt having a little kip after his mad dash down the M6 and M42.

As many students from the Hall as possible had been encouraged to come out and watch us, and all those who could be bothered to get up after the previous evening's drinking or other means of relaxation were on the side-lines waiting for the game to start. So, in front of a crowd of about ten people, my dad and girlfriend included, we won the Cup, easily beating our opponents 3-0, although I wasn't able to repeat my goal scoring exploits of the previous round. Dad took pictures again of me holding a trophy aloft and sent me off to have a quick shower so we could get some lunch, before heading to Elm Park for the second biggest match of the day.

This was the first time I'd ever been to Elm Park, Reading's quaint little ground, surrounded by terraced housing, which was their home before they moved to the splendid new Madejski Stadium in 1998. Me and my dad spent a cold but pleasant afternoon watching two half-decent teams draw 2-2. It was nice to be sat with him again watching our team, and at least we didn't lose. It was also another ground we could tick off on our way to the 92 club. We must have been well into double figures by now.

He must have been knackered after the game and he still had a drive of over 250 miles to endure, so he dropped me back and we said our goodbyes, knowing that I would be back home in a few weeks. It had been a great day, but not so great for dad. In his haste to get home, he got a speeding ticket. He was obviously a bit too keen to get away from Reading.

***

The only other football matches I watched that year were quite lonely experiences. My girlfriend was prepared to watch me play in important games, but as for watching proper players on the television, she did not deem the Cup Final between Liverpool and Sunderland to be worthy of her time.

I didn't blame her; it was the most predictable and uneventful Cup Final I'd ever seen, with the possible exception of Spurs/QPR in 1982. But it was still the Cup Final, and having missed it the previous two seasons, I wanted to settle down for the afternoon and watch some live footy on the television. I never really missed my parents that year, but that afternoon I did. I knew they would be watching it, as we had done so many times before, and as all my other mates were not really into football, I simply sat in my room all by myself. Liverpool won easily, 2-0, though it must have been dull, as I can't remember anything about the game at all, not even the goals. What a top afternoon that was.

Sweden v England

June 17th, 1992 Rasunda Stadium, Solna

All that was left of this season was to watch England perform dismally yet again in a European Championships, this time in Sweden. After our heroics in Italy, we had high hopes, but again, we were awful. We were now managed by Graham Taylor and some of his decisions were bizarre to say the least.

218

After two mind-numbingly boring 0-0 draws against Denmark and France, we had the chance to go through if we could beat the hosts. David Platt got us off to a great start, scoring after only four minutes, but our steel and resilience had gone from the team. Without Bobby Robson, the players looked clueless, but then again so did our manager.

Sweden equalised early in the second half to set up what should have been a thrilling finale. Gary Lineker, our saviour so often before, would surely come up with the goods. He needed only one more goal to equal Bobby Charlton's tally of 49 England goals and this was his chance. But, with just under half an hour to go, Graham Taylor, in whatever wisdom he thought he had, thought it best to take off our tried and tested goal scorer, our best chance of getting a winner, and replace him with Alan Smith of Arsenal. No disrespect to Smith, but he had scored the princely sum of two goals for England, neither of which had been at a tournament, which made Taylor's decision even more baffling.

Lineker himself could not understand the decision, but being the gentleman he is, did not kick up a fuss as he left the pitch. If Lineker was not kicking off about this ridiculous and frankly insulting decision, then I, and millions of other England fans certainly were. I was screaming at my little TV screen, but to no avail. Sweden's Tomas Brolin went on to score a winner with eight minutes to go, sending us crashing out again, after failing to win a game for the second European Championships in a row, causing The Sun to print their famous picture of Graham Taylor as a turnip under the headline "Swedes 2 Turnips 1". However cruel it may have been, at that moment it seemed justified.

Gary Lineker may have suspected that this may well have been his final England appearance, but none of us did. It was the most absurd end to an illustrious international career, and he was left hanging on

48 goals. Bobby Charlton may have scored one more goal, but Lineker was the best goal scorer for England that I had ever seen, and this was no way for him to be treated. It was appalling.

If none of us realised that this would be Lineker's final game (it would also be Alan Smith's last game coincidentally), then certainly none of us realised this would be the last time we would see England play in a major tournament on foreign soil for another six years. The next Euros would be in England so at least we wouldn't have to try and qualify next time. And as for the World Cup in two years' time, Graham Taylor would have yet more pearls of wisdom to show us all in that disastrous qualifying campaign.

Euro 92 felt very strange. For me it didn't have the intensity of other tournaments I'd watched. This sense of strangeness was compounded by the fact that the eventual winners had not even qualified for the tournament in the first place. With Yugoslavia ripping itself to bits militarily, their football team was disqualified, and their place was instead allocated to Denmark, who had finished runners-up in Yugoslavia's qualification group.

They scraped through from England's group into the semi-finals where they would beat the holders Holland on penalties, before miraculously beating the hot favourites Germany 2-0, to win their first and only piece of silverware. It was a weird end to a weird tournament. Perhaps the best way to prepare for a tournament was not to prepare for it at all. Maybe that was the key to success.

Season 1992/93

Manchester United v Blackburn Rovers

May 3rd, 1993 Old Trafford

After finishing my first year as an undergraduate student, I spent the summer working various jobs, including being a fruit picker where I got the worst sunburn ever, a packer in a biscuit factory, which wasn't so Nice at all, and a labourer for my dad's joinery and building firm. Although it was nice to be back at home for the summer, I couldn't wait to get back down to university. I had a new house to move into. After a year in Halls, I had the option of staying on with all the new Freshers, or finding a shared house to live in. I chose the latter.

My girlfriend had got a lovely little house with some of her friends, and me and my mates had found a less than lovely house about ten minutes' walk from campus. It was complete hovel and reminded me of something like The Young Ones' accommodation, rats and all. I should have known how bad it was going to be, as when we turned up to sign our contracts, the witness to the signatures our landlord had brought out was his uncle, who just happened to be blind. A blind witness says it all about that place. It had mould growing in every room, broken guttering, sticky carpets, and worst of all, rats.

Some nights I would get out of bed to go to the toilet and see rats in the kitchen and worst of all, in our bathroom where the hole in the wall near the toilet gave them easy access into the house. Having a rat scurry over your feet as you stand there over the toilet is not the most pleasant of experiences.

But we were prepared to put up with our new rodent flatmates as we all had much bigger rooms now and a shared living room, which is where I spent many hours that year. However, I was not discussing politics or the finer points of James Joyce's "Ulysses", but playing

Sonic the Hedgehog on the Sega Megadrive which one of my human flatmates had brought with him. Many inebriated evenings were spent collecting rings and killing Dr. Robotnik. I should have been reading Dickens, Keats and Joyce, which I did to an extent, but I had now realised that you could get away with doing very little studying and still be able to get decent grades. That Methodist work ethic was being severely tested and was found wanting on many occasions that year.

My girlfriend and I were hardly ever apart that year, with me staying at her place occasionally, and more often than not, her staying at mine. Maybe she liked the rats' company. Her knowledge of films was much wider than mine and we had found an excellent video shop near to her flat which had all the old films available to rent. I was introduced to all of Hitchcock's films, screwball comedies of the 1930s, most of Cary Grant's films, and most significantly, the films of Frank Capra, with "Mr Deeds Goes to Town" instantly becoming my favourite film, and still is to this day. If only my degree had been in Film Studies.

As for football, I watched very little, despite the sparkling new formation of The Premier League, with more football being shown than ever before, on Sunday afternoons and even Monday nights now. As poor students, we could hardly afford to pay our bills, let alone a subscription to Sky TV, so this new wonderful world of glossy televised football passed me by for the first few years of its existence. I still watched Match of the Day religiously, but that was about it.

I was still affiliated to Windsor Hall and continued playing in the Inter-Hall league and cup, but with the spine of our team having graduated, we became one of those teams we would easily have beaten the previous year and ended up somewhere around mid-table. Our defence of the cup was rather pitiful too and we got knocked out at the quarter-final stage this year, so when dad came down again to watch Preston, he only had one game to watch this time.

Preston's fortunes were now worse than my own team's and that day at Elm Park we got hammered 4-0. Les Chapman, our manager at the start of the season had left by the end of September, before my second year of study had even started. Big Sam Allardyce took over as manager for a month, but even he could do nothing. He had not yet gained his reputation for being able to save clubs from relegation.

His replacement was John Beck, who had taken Cambridge United to two successive promotions, and had almost got into the First Division. He played an uncompromising long ball game, which was criticised by many other managers, including Glenn Hoddle who was now manager of Swindon Town. Beck would never have needed a player like Glenn Hoddle, the ultimate in footballing skill, and now my team was playing football that was the antithesis of what Glenn Hoddle was all about. There was no room for finesse, skill, vision, or even passing. Beck's philosophy was to play long balls up and hope for the best. As my dad said, "You got a constant crick in your neck watching his team play football."

He couldn't save us this season and that 4-0 defeat away to Reading was one of many losses on our way to relegation, and we would fall back down into the bottom division, or Division Three as it had now become known as due to the Premier League's formation and breakaway from the rest of the league.

Whether it was Division Three or Division Four, it was still the basement division of the whole league. We were back to where we had struggled to get out from six years before. So much for long ball tactics. But I was so far removed from it all by now that I didn't really care that much anymore. Watching Preston seemed now to be something that I used to do. I had a new life Down South.

Preston's demise coincided with Man United's rise to become the first ever Premier League Champions. They had been battling for top spot with Aston Villa, who ironically were managed by Ron Atkinson now, United's former manager who had been sacked for not winning them the league. By April they were clinging on to the lead but were in serious danger of losing it, especially as they were 1-0 down at home to Sheffield Wednesday, with only five minutes left. Everyone remembers the scenes at Old Trafford after Steve Bruce got two headers in the final few minutes to win the game, with Ferguson and his assistant Brian Kidd, the one-time manager of Preston, leaping onto the pitch in celebration. I think it's safe to say he chose the better option of being Ferguson's assistant rather than the manager of Preston.

United now had one hand on the trophy, and after Villa lost at home to Oldham in early May, Alex Ferguson had finally fulfilled his promise of knocking Liverpool off their perch and won United's first league title since 1967. The following day, on the Monday Night Football, United would be presented with the sparkling new trophy after their match against Blackburn. A special Match of the Day was even put on television to allow us ordinary, non-Sky subscribing fans to watch what happened.

It was a night of celebration at Old Trafford, not only in the stands but also on the pitch. United won 3-1 with the teenage Ryan Giggs opening the scoring, and even Gary Pallister getting on the scoresheet to score his one and only goal that season. Steve Bruce and Bryan Robson lifted the trophy and I still felt a certain pride. Even though I could not class myself as a Man United fan anymore, I still had a huge affection for them after my few seasons watching them regularly in the mid -80s. They had given me one of the best days of my life that day at Wembley in 1985, and now they were officially the best team in the country. With Preston's relegation having already been confirmed by then, at least I had something to be happy about in footballing terms.

There was only one more game to watch (which would become two actually) as Arsenal and Sheffield Wednesday contested that year's FA Cup Final. So, my housemates and I turned off Sonic the Hedgehog and all settled down in our shared living room to watch a dull game at Wembley. I think even the rats were bored by that game and sodded off for the afternoon, missing out on a tedious 1-1 draw. But this would mean that there would be a replay, the last FA Cup Final replay ever.

Those Thursday night replay games of 1981, 82, 83 and 1990 had been such a huge part of my early footballing life, providing so much drama and entertainment, but after goals from Ian Wright and Chris Waddle, this one fizzled out, and was rather appropriately won by possibly the least famous winning goal scorer in an FA Cup Final ever.

As the game was creeping towards a penalty shootout, Andy Linighan rose highest from a corner to head home the winner. Perhaps Chris Waddle was secretly pleased that he wouldn't have to take another penalty in a shootout after his effort in the 1990 World Cup semi-final. His penalty in Turin was probably still in orbit as Tony Adams lifted his second cup that season, Arsenal having already won the League Cup by beating Sheffield Wednesday again by the same score line.

If that season will not be remembered for the FA Cup Final, it is certainly remembered for how the Premier League changed the game forever. None of us realised back then just how much of an impact it would have on our game, but it has transformed the game beyond belief, in both good and bad ways. Post Hillsborough, maybe it needed to happen, allowing such tragedies to never happen again. All-seater stadiums have transformed the way we watch the game, as has the constant TV coverage. The game has become more accessible to more people than ever before, but it has created huge divides. The astronomical amount of money now dominating the game has inevitably created a league that is hugely entertaining, but also hugely predictable in many ways.

Apart from Blackburn winning in 1995, which without Jack Walker's millions would undeniably not have happened, and Leicester's miracle of 2016 (more on that later) the Premier League has been won by only four clubs; Manchester United, Arsenal, Chelsea and Manchester City, who have taken over their Manchester rivals' mantle. Every season starts now with only a few clubs having realistic expectations of even have a chance of winning the Premier League. I know Liverpool dominated the league in the decade or so before the Premier League was formed, but in the 60s, 70s and 80s, teams like Burnley, Ipswich, Everton, Leeds, Nottingham Forest, Aston Villa and even Derby County won the league. Derby even won it twice, in 1972 and 1975.

The prospect of any of these teams winning again is laughable in today's climate. But then again, we all said that about Leicester. The Premier League is a juggernaut which smashes any smaller teams like Preston not just off the road, but through the barrier and down the cliff. The rest of us have little chance of getting into the Premier League, and even if we did, we would constantly be choking from these massive clubs' fumes as the juggernaut continues on its destructive but thrilling course, as in Steven Spielberg's first film "Duel". Teams like us are trying desperately to evade being smashed into oblivion, and some are failing quite frankly.

Smaller teams, even ones that used to be in the Premiership are constantly under financial threat, and their existence is a tightrope walk every season. It is only a matter of time before they finally lose their balance and fall into the abyss. But as long as the Premier

League players get their millions every season, and in some cases, every week, then who cares about teams like Bury and Bolton going bust? It is now the survival of the fittest, and inevitably in that situation, there will be clubs who will not survive.

Bolton Wanderers, a founder member of the league, finished sixth in the Premier league in 2005, and yet fourteen years later they are on the brink of survival, not as a Premier League club, but as an actual football club. I wonder how long they will be able to walk that tightrope, as they are seriously wobbling. If a club like Bolton can just cease to exist, then it could happen to any team in the lower leagues. I wonder how many of the league's 92 clubs are still alive within the next ten, twenty or thirty years. I suspect that some will endure a slow and painful death, and some will be obliterated quickly and ruthlessly. But it will certainly not be painless for the fans. I just hope my team will be able to stay on the road and not become a victim of this marauding and menacing juggernaut.

The irony of it all is that teams like mine long to be a part of the Premier League so we can have a chance of smashing others off the road. It truly has become a dog eat dog world now. But as Samuel L. Jackson's character in "Pulp Fiction" says, "dogs ain't got enough sense to disregard their own faeces." Do we really want to be eating our own shit? I hope not.

But then again, a dog's got personality, and personality goes a long way!

Season 1993/94

Reading v Blackpool

November 6th, 1993 Elm Park

Another year, and another house. We could stand the ratfest no longer and found a better, if smaller house for my third and final year at university. We each had a bedroom, but the spare room was too small to use as a living room. You could just about get a Subbuteo pitch in there, which of course we did, and spent many hours playing tournaments with our index fingers rather than our feet. The communal room, the Sonic the Hedgehog room, was one of my housemates' bedrooms, and we spent our days and evenings in there until he kicked us out when he eventually wanted to go to sleep. Fortunately, his work ethic was the worst of all of us and he rarely did kick us out, which seemed to suit us all.

I had to do more work this year if I was going to get a decent degree. I did do more reading and actually went to the library on campus quite a few times. My knowledge of obscure black and white films was coming on strongly though, despite not seeing as much of my girlfriend as I had done last year. Maybe she just missed the rats.

I was now one of the senior players in the Hall team, which I still turned out for regularly. I was now classed as a veteran, even though I was still only twenty years old, and when our regular captain was unavailable, I stepped in, more by default than design. I was a useless captain and gave cliched team talks about it being a game of two halves etc. when we were 3-0 down at the break. The Freshers who had come into the team were not that good, and we performed even worse than the year before. The glory days of my Freshers' year were now a distant memory. My heart was no longer in it and I had more to think about, like what the hell I was going to do with my degree and what I wanted to do for the rest of my life.

I knew that I would make a good teacher and wondered whether I would be able to do the same for students as my own A Level teacher had done for me. But I was also toying with the idea of journalism. I decided to join up with the student newspaper and wrote a few articles which were probably read by a handful of people. But my main role was as chief football reporter, which meant that I would get free entry to Elm Park to cover Reading's games, a seat in the press box, and even access to some of the players after the match. All I had to do was write a report of the match. I could do that.

One of my first games was Blackpool's visit to Elm Park, and I was so hoping to see the Seasiders get blown away by Reading, who had a very good side that year, including Shaka Hislop before he moved to Newcastle, Jimmy Quinn and Stuart Lovell up front, and were managed by Mark McGhee, who was cutting his teeth as a manager after a successful playing career, winning the European Cup Winners' Cup with Alex Ferguson's Aberdeen side, and then going onto win two league titles and two Scottish cups with Celtic. Reading would eventually end up as Champions of Division Three, and I was there to see most of their home games, for free.

Unfortunately, Blackpool held Reading to a 1-1 draw, but during the game I got chatting to a proper, real-life journalist who wrote for The Daily Express. He got me into the players' lounge after the game, where I interviewed Hislop and McGhee (well, I asked them both a question). My new found journo friend must have liked my enthusiasm as after the match he gave me his card and told me to get in touch so we could organise a day with him at The Express's headquarters in central London. This was unbelievably exciting, if rather daunting for a callow twenty-year-old from Up North.

It took me a while to pluck up the courage to make the call, but I eventually did, and sometime in the new year I met him at the reception of The Daily Express building, which back then was near to Blackfriars Bridge. I had a great day and learned loads about the inner workings of a newspaper, and I even got to write a small piece about any injuries that the Premier League teams had. It was even printed as part of the back page of the paper the following day. I felt like a proper journo now and applied for journalism courses, being accepted onto a couple.

I was not completely decided though. I was still contemplating becoming a teacher. The prospect of getting paid a full month's salary in August, even though I didn't have to do any work that month, was still very appealing to me. I had the rest of the year to make up my mind, as well as get a degree in the first place.

San Marino v England

World Cup Qualifier

November 17th, 1993   Renato Dall'Ara, Bologna

England matches were still being shown on terrestrial television, and we would all pile into my mate's bedroom to watch the games. In the room was the obligatory student accessory, the lava lamp, and he also had the most amazing hamster cage I'd ever seen. He'd got himself a hamster at the start of the year and had housed it in one of those plastic contraptions which could be added to with various adornments. Over the next few weeks, he kept adding to his hamster house, with long tubes going around the room, with other spaces for the hamster to show off his acrobatic skills connecting the tubes. A huge wheel and a house consisting of mini tubes and ramps made watching football in my mate's room a quite surreal experience. If the game ever got dull, then we could always watch the hamster race around the room and perform for us to liven up proceedings.

England, still under Graham Taylor, had had a stuttering World Cup qualification campaign so far. They had drawn with Holland, drawn and got beaten by Norway, drawn with and beaten Poland, beaten Turkey twice, and hammered San Marino 6-0. With two games to go, against Holland and San Marino again, qualification was still possible but very tight.

The Holland game would prove to be our downfall, losing 2-0, meaning that we needed a miracle against San Marino. We would need to beat them by seven clear goals and rely on Poland to at least get a draw against the Dutch. The most likely result was us winning 7-0 as the Dutch were a great team back then and would surely be able to draw with Poland.

With the hamster joining us for the game, going round and round in his wheel, almost spurring the England team on, our hopes were dashed after just eight seconds. A poor back pass from Stuart Pearce allowed the San Marino striker to nip in front of our keeper and slot the ball home to take the most unlikely of leads. At that point I think I just watched the hamster for the rest of the match as at least he provided some entertainment.

We eventually went on to win 7-1 and that early goal would have stopped us from qualifying had Poland done their bit and got a draw. They inevitably didn't, Holland beating them convincingly 3-1 to take the second qualifying place behind the surprise package of Norway. Our fate was sealed. We would not be playing in the World Cup the following summer. I couldn't quite believe it; this was the first time in my footballing life that England would not be at the World Cup.

I awoke the next morning and for a few seconds I'd forgotten about the nightmare of the previous evening, but then my radio confirmed what I already knew but had been pretending hadn't happened. Not only would England not be at the World Cup, but as the next

European Championship was to be held in England, we would not be playing a competitive international game for over two and a half years. All I would have to survive on in terms of England games were endless and meaningless friendlies. A little bit like a hamster running round and round in a wheel.

The fact was that England just weren't good enough that year. Graham Taylor had been horribly vilified in the press after his failure at Euro 92 with the Turnip Head picture, and now the headline writers had a field day, justifiably so to an extent. There was no point in even trying to continue as manager of England, so he resigned a week later. The Sun used the same picture to wish him farewell, but this time under the headline of "That's Yer Allotment". Genius.

Chelsea v Manchester United

FA Cup Final

May 14th, 1994 Wembley Stadium

The only other match available for us and the hamster to watch was the FA Cup Final, in which Man United would prove their almost complete dominance in England. After winning the Premier League for the first time the previous year, they had kicked on and won it again, this time at a canter, eventually gaining 92 points, 8 more than their nearest rivals Blackburn, and 21 more than Arsenal in fourth place. They'd had an off day in the League Cup Final, losing to Aston Villa, but they still had the chance to complete their first ever Double against Chelsea.

In the league campaign, they had either drawn with or beaten every other team apart from one. Chelsea somehow had done the double over United, beating them home and away, and so United wanted to put that right at Wembley. They certainly did that.

Me and my mates took a break from revising for our finals and spent the whole day drinking a certain brand of American beer. This company shall remain nameless but as it would be the World Cup in America for the first time, they were putting on a special promotional offer. For every pack of six beers bought, you would get a peel-off sticker with the name of a player from one of the squads that would be competing in the tournament. Obviously, there would be no English players' names as we had failed dismally to qualify, but that certainly did not put us off. The deal was that if the player whose name you peeled off scored at the World Cup, you could get another six-pack for free, and I don't mean nicely toned abs.

We all entered into this deal with enthusiasm and bought many packs of beer, collecting our stickers in readiness for the feast of football which would start in just less than a month's time. So, from around lunchtime of Cup Final day we started drinking. We were all nicely merry by the time the game kicked off and we just continued in the same way for the rest of the day. We collected a fine stash of stickers by the end of the day and saw Man United annihilate the one team they had failed to get any points from all season.

Cup Final days are always sunny, at least that's my memory of the majority of them, but this day was horrible. It was heaving it down at Wembley and also in Reading, but that somehow made the game more entertaining. Well, the second half at least. It was goalless at half-time, but United then decided to start playing properly. The wet surface meant that tackles were flying in all over the place, and one of these led to United's first goal on the hour mark. Denis Irwin was upended rather spectacularly by Eddie Newton and Eric Cantona, collar upturned as usual, stepped up and nonchalantly slotted the ball into the net.

Only eight minutes later, United had won it, with Cantona converting another penalty after Andrei Kanchelskis had been barged over. He put the ball in exactly the same spot as the first one and the Chelsea keeper just kept diving the other way.

Mark Hughes fired home a third and it was only then that Chelsea started to put any pressure on, giving Schmeichel a few saves to make. He was not going to be beaten that day though and as the game was petering out, United went on to score their fourth goal. Paul Ince had the chance to get himself a Cup Final goal, but he unselfishly squared it for Brian McClair to tap home and complete the rout.

United hadn't just won, they had demolished, obliterated, thrashed Glenn Hoddle's Chelsea team. It was like men against boys actually. I had never seen a team so dominant in a Cup Final before. With the Double achieved, they could take their place as one of the truly great sides of English football. We all know that in fact they were only just starting their dominance. Liverpool had been well and truly knocked off their perch and the United fans were loving it.

The drinking continued for the rest of the evening before we would all (maybe not all actually) continue with our revision. Our finals would start later that week, but all I was bothered about were the other types of Finals, the footballing ones which frankly were much more important than some stupid exams.

Preston North End v Wycombe Wanderers

League Division Three Play-Off Final

May 28th, 1994 Wembley Stadium

As for Preston, we made a determined attempt to get promoted straight back into Division Three, or Division Two as it now was. John Beck's style of play seemed to be working. With my dad's crick in his neck getting ever worse, we managed to end up fifth in the league and so get into the play-offs for our second attempt to get promoted this way, already having lost in 1989 before even getting to Wembley. This time would be different, but ultimately still with the same result.

We had to beat Torquay in order to get to Wembley. After losing 2-0 in Devon, our prospects were not too hopeful, although we did have our plastic pitch as our not so secret weapon. The night of the second leg at Deepdale was the night before I would take my first ever final exam, and instead of revising, I spent the evening desperately checking Ceefax on my television or trying somehow to find any sort of commentary. This proved very difficult, as unsurprisingly Radio Lancashire was not available in Berkshire. I eventually found some radio station that would give me updates and it was worth the perseverance.

As I had found out when I had played on the plastic pitch and had my legs cut to shreds, all the players who played at Deepdale had now learned that wearing leggings was essential. This would also prove to be the last game on the plastic as we would rip it up and go back to good old grass the following season.

With all twenty-two players sporting tights or leggings, Preston got off to the best of starts, getting a goal back after only eight minutes. But shortly after, Torquay got a crucial away goal even though the ball had been clearly handled in the build-up. We would now need to score three more goals if we were to get to Wembley.

Torquay gave us a bit of a helping hand, or more like a helping fist, as Darren Moore, their big striker, got sent off for basically assaulting one of our players. David Moyes, who would go onto become our manager, headed in our second before half time, before we snatched a third, to make it 3-3 on aggregate.

235

Away goals only came into play after extra-time, so we still needed another, and with only four minutes left of the game, our constant pressure paid off, grabbing a winner to take us to Wembley. The crowd streamed onto the pitch to celebrate and to say goodbye to the plastic pitch, which that night had proved to be our plastic fantastic.

The Final, ten days later, was on the same day as my final final exam. A case of too many finals. For some reason I had an exam on the Saturday morning and dad had a plan to come and pick me up as soon as I finished the exam so we could get to Wembley in time for the 3pm kick-off. The exam was on Romantic and Victorian poetry, and for some reason, maybe it was nerves about the exam or the game, I could not sleep very well. I was up around 5am and crammed in as much revision as possible. I just wanted to get to Wembley, the first time Preston had been there since dad had been to watch them in the Cup Final of 1964.

I duly answered questions on Keats, Shelley, Gerard Manley Hopkins and Tennyson, and went to meet dad. He'd done the now all too familiar journey down to Reading again, and we set off to Wembley. Surely, we could beat Wycombe, a team who had only been a league club for one season, getting promoted into the league for the first time in their history only the previous May.

As so often with Preston, my expectations were unfounded, and we lost the game 4-2 despite being 2-1 up at half time. Our second half performance was woeful, conceding three goals with no reply. There would be no repeat of me and my dad's glorious day at Wembley in 1985.

As dad drove me back to Reading, I couldn't help thinking of lines from Shelley's poem "Ozymandias" which I had been writing about only a few hours before.

236

"My name is Ozymandias, King of Kings;
Look on my Works, ye Mighty, and despair!
Nothing beside remains. Round the decay
Of that colossal Wreck, boundless and bare
The lone and level sands stretch far away."

Preston, albeit it many many years before, had been the King of Kings in footballing terms, and yet we were now a shadow of what we once were, a team that couldn't even beat a team with literally no experience of being a league club. I was so tired after my frantic revision that it was me feeling like a colossal wreck. No doubt the Preston players were feeling the same despair after they had worked so hard to get to Wembley, only to be toppled by the mighty Wycombe.

At least they wouldn't have to wear tights next season.

South Korea v Bolivia

World Cup Finals, USA

June 23rd, 1994   Foxboro Stadium, Foxborough

Just after I finished my finals, my wisdom teeth decided that they were no longer needed. It was as though I had used up all the wisdom I would need, and they were on a mission to give me as much pain as possible on their way out. I was still enrolled at my dentist at home and so I thought I would kill two birds with one stone and go back home to visit my parents, and get my wisdom teeth taken out.

As I was now very skint at the end of the academic year, the option of a comfortable and quick train journey home was actually not an option, so I had to take the cheaper, but far less comfortable option of a National Express coach all the way back Up North.

It was the worst journey of my life. My teeth were killing me, and I had to endure a sweaty and cramped eight-hour journey up the motorway with what seemed like endless stops on the way. The World Cup was about to start and so I bought a paper with a special guide to all the teams and venues included. This would at least make the journey more bearable.

Over the eight hours of torture, I would get to know every team, every player, and every venue they would be playing at in the good old US of A. Despite England's absence, I was really looking forward to the tournament. For the first time I would be able to watch the football for its own sake, without having to put up with the rampant nationalism and at times quite sickening jingoism that always occurs when England are involved in a tournament. I was going to be looked after by my mum as I recovered from my extractions and the World Cup would provide the perfect distraction from the pain.

The tournament started the day after I arrived home, and a few days later I went to meet my fate, or at least my wisdom teeth did. Surprise, surprise, my wisdom teeth did not want to play ball. Instead of coming up at the normal angle, they were coming up diagonally, pushing my other teeth into each other. The dentist numbed me up and prepared for battle.

It was the worst experience I had ever had at a dentist, not that there had been many good ones actually. My teeth just would not come out and he had to cut into my gums to eventually prise them free. When your dentist has to have his sweat wiped away from his forehead to stop it going into his eyes, you know you're in trouble.

After what seemed like hours, he finally got the little bastards out so I could say good riddance to them. Well, I could only mumble it really as I could not talk properly. Once the anaesthetic wore off, the pain really began. My whole face was bruised, and mum could only feed me food through a straw. I lived off soup for the next few days, but at least I could watch as much footy as I could fit in. I had no studies to think about, just football and pain, which so often are the same thing for us football fans.

Since the FA Cup Final, me and my housemates had continued to collect stickers from the packs of beer and I had a healthy collection by now, or rather an unhealthy collection as this meant that I had drunk far too many beers than was necessary. It resembled the pile of stickers I had at primary school when I finished my Panini sticker album.

The beer company were not stupid. They very rarely put the names of players who would actually score on their packs. Instead of a Klinsmann, a Bebeto, or a Baggio, I think I had the goalkeepers for Bulgaria and Sweden, along with players who wouldn't actually be playing in any of the games.

I seemed to also have amassed many players from the Bolivian and South Korean teams, players I had never heard of. From the South Korean squad, I must have had at least three Kims, a couple of Hongs, three Songs but only one Shin, along with a few others from the Bolivian squad. The two teams were about to meet in the group stage and this was where I could fill my boots in terms of goal scoring names in my pile of stickers. If there were four goals in the match, then it was more than likely that I would at least get a couple of goal scorers and so a couple of free packs of beer.

Due to the time difference between America and the UK, games were either played in the early evening, late evening, or in the early hours depending on where the game was being played. This game was one of the ones that kicked off around 11.30 at night over here, but I had nothing to get up for so I could watch any game at any time. It was brilliant, apart from the constant pain I was still in.

It was one of the most frustrating matches I have ever watched. I couldn't care less who won, or even if anyone won at all. A high scoring draw would have been the best outcome as then I would have more chance of free beer. I think all the names I had in my sticker pile all had chances, but could any of them put the ball in the net? Resoundingly no.

Some of the chances my select bunch of names had seemed harder to miss than to score and yet at every opportunity, my beer stash was being thwarted. I think I woke my parents up at one point at about 1am with my shouts of frustration. The finishing was shocking and even though they were well over 3000 miles away, I tried my best to let those South Korean and Bolivian players know of my displeasure.

Incredibly, the game finished 0-0 and my stash of stickers would not be depleted in any way whatsoever. Over the course of that first week, I think I had only one player who had found the net and so provide me with free beer. I was beginning to suspect that this was a carefully worked out marketing ploy from the beer company, and not a sure-fire way of getting lots of free alcohol. It was almost as if they paid people lots of money to work out the ratio of beer to goals scored, to ensure their profits went up and my money went down. How dare they.

My mouth was just about back to normal by now, so I endured the return journey back down to Reading to collect my solitary six-pack and rejoin my housemates. They too had done the exact same thing during the South Korea/Bolivia match, although at least they hadn't had their parents telling them to shut up and stop screaming at the television. For the rest of the tournament, our lives became a bit of a blur.

With nothing apart from football to structure our lives, we probably watched every single game of that tournament. We all cheered when Germany went out to Bulgaria, when the Republic of Ireland, who most English fans were begrudgingly supporting, beat Norway, but booed when they lost to Holland.

We also felt very smug when Diego Maradona was finally found out to be the cheating bastard we all knew him to be anyway. When he ran to the camera after scoring a fantastic goal against Greece, the whole world could see his mad, bulging cocaine fueled eyes. His eyes were similar to Marco Tardelli's of twelve years earlier, but I can safely say that Tardelli was not a cheating coke-fueled narco fiend. Unlike Maradona.

It was a great tournament actually, much better than Italia 90 in footballing terms, but the final itself was one of the worst games ever. I challenge any football fan out there to recall any incident in that game apart from Roberto Baggio's penalty miss. It was the biggest let down ever.

With the World Cup over with, our contract for our house would expire at the end of July. There was only one thing to do for the next couple of weeks, and that was to keep drinking beer, which we succeeded in doing. The end of the month came and after two messy, smelly, sometimes hungry, but never dull years together, we all went our separate ways.

One went back to his parents before he would start his new career, another went to live with his girlfriend somewhere on the south coast, and another like me, would find a place with his girlfriend somewhere else in Reading. My girlfriend's contract was up too, so we were due to sub-let a room throughout August until we decided what we were both going to do with the rest of our lives. I still had the option of journalism courses, but the long summer holidays of a teacher were still nagging at me and tempting me. I still had a few weeks to make up my mind. I now just needed to get any sort of work to see me through the summer until that decision became a necessity. I was a Bachelor of the Arts with a 2:1 degree in English Literature. Surely there would be someone who would employ me. Surely.

Charlton Athletic v Reading

October 8th, 1994   The Valley

I managed to gain employment for the summer at a residential home for young adults with severe emotional, mental and physical learning difficulties. For the whole of August, I would go and help care for this group of people who needed full time care and supervision. I got the privilege of looking after Hugh, Barry, Nicola and Simon along with others whose names I have forgotten. We would sometimes take them into Reading town centre on the bus, or we would take them to a local stables so they could interact with and ride the horses, with us carers guiding them around the trotting area. We would often take them swimming or just sit and watch television with them. We would also sometimes have to restrain them if they became violent towards us, themselves, or each other.

Over the course of the month I gradually realised that I wanted to work with and help young people in whatever capacity I could. The journalism courses were rather daunting for me and I didn't fancy spending the next few years writing for a local newspaper reporting on whose cat had got stuck up a tree, or which houses had been egged by local youths. I knew I would make a good teacher and so by the end of August I enquired to the Education Department at Reading University to see if there were any places left for their teacher training course, a PGCE, which would start in the middle of September. I wanted to be an English teacher in Secondary schools. I wanted students to stand on their desks for me.

I had to write a little piece about which books had played a part in my life. To this day I will admit to being one of the least well-read English teachers ever. I wrote about how my childhood was spent either reading Bible stories from all the books my parents had made available to me, or superhero comics. My would-be tutor on the course seemed to like my honesty and how I was an expert on Jesus and Spiderman, but not much else.

Reading "proper" books has always seemed like work to me but work that I always found fascinating. I still rarely read fiction, apart from books I have to teach, preferring non-fiction texts much more for my own reading pleasure. None of this seemed to matter. Just because I wasn't particularly well-read did not mean that I could not be a great teacher. I have worked with plenty of teachers who claimed to have read vast libraries of books, but who have not been the best teachers. My talents were being able to interact with young people and make language fun. Or at least that's what I told my tutor-to-be. He must have bought it as he gladly enrolled me on the course.

My girlfriend amazingly was happy to find whatever work she could for a year whilst I trained and hopefully qualified as a teacher, on the proviso that we would both then move to London. I could get my first job in a school whilst she could look for proper work and hopefully a proper career once we got to London. That suited me fine.

We got a little flat together about fifteen minutes' walk from the Education department's campus, and we settled into our new lives as graduates. I still wonder what my life would have been like if I had taken the journalism course. Maybe I would have actually got paid to watch and write about football. It was one of those sliding doors moments that everyone has at certain points in their life. What if, and even at times, if only…

A few weeks after my course started, mum and dad came down to visit us for the day. Dad needed his fix of football with me, so we all went into London for the day. It was probably the first time I had been into central London with my parents since they had taken me as a kid, when I had had the tour of Wembley Stadium. My mum and girlfriend went off to see a show or a play at one of the West End theatres, but me and dad would go East. Reading, who I sort of supported now after my coverage of their glorious promotion season for the student newspaper, were away at Charlton that day, so off to The Valley we went. Another ground could be ticked off the list, and it also meant my girlfriend and I did not have to spend another boring Saturday afternoon together.

The truth was that we were no longer in love with each other. After the initial flurry of romance during our first two years of our degrees, we had grown apart in our third year and stayed with each other because we didn't really know what else to do. We were with each other more for the sake of it, rather than because of any sort of devotion we felt for each other. As undergraduates, we had our own set of housemates and our own separate lives to an extent. Now it was just us two with different lives and different ambitions.

But I will be forever grateful to her for working and helping me financially, as I progressed throughout my PGCE course. We became more like two friends who happened to live with each other and who shared a bedroom. We were not unhappy, but secretly we both suspected that our relationship would not last. Whereas there had been talk of marriage at one point during our degrees, that particular subject was certainly never mentioned anymore.

Me and dad had a very enjoyable trip to Charlton's ground and saw Reading get a very good 2-1 win. They were in what is now The Championship and would eventually end up getting into the play-offs. They even got to Wembley that year and were only 90 minutes away from the Premier League but were beaten 4-3 by Bolton after extra time. This would not be the first time that Bolton would thwart a team who I cared about in what has become known as the most financially lucrative game of football in the world, the Championship Play-Off Final. Reading, after finishing as champions of the division below the previous year, had a remarkable season. To get within 90 minutes of the riches of the Premiership was a huge achievement for this small, friendly club from Berkshire, not traditionally known as a footballing hotbed. I still to this day have an affection for the club and was really pleased for them when they eventually got promoted into the Premier League.

If only Preston could do something similar. We were still languishing in Division Three, still trying to get out of the bottom division. After our loss in the play-off final in May, we had another good season. The supporters, my dad included, could take the crick in their necks no longer with John Beck's long-ball game, and he left in December.

He was replaced by his assistant, Gary Peters, who had started his senior playing career at Reading, playing for the Royals 156 times in the latter part of the 1970s, and would play another 100 games for them in the late 80s. But this was his first management position. His style was much more attractive to watch and all the fans at Deepdale were grateful for this change of style. We ended up fifth and so reached the play-offs again, but it was not third time lucky for us. This time we could not get to Wembley and provide another day out for me and my dad, losing to Bury instead. But at least my dad's neck was better now.

Crystal Palace v Manchester United

January 25th, 1995   **Selhurst Park**

After most of my first term as a trainee teacher had been spent either at university, or in my first placement school, observing other teachers and researching student behaviour and methods of correcting, or at least trying to correct, their errant ways. I'd also made my own very tentative foray into actual teaching, taking small groups of children for certain parts of lessons. Two weeks before Christmas I was sent to what would be my main placement school, a lovely school just outside Reading, where I would gain further experience before taking over a few classes as their main teacher for a ten week block in which I would be observed frequently and have to produce detailed lesson plans and produce my own resources.

It was here that I met my professional mentor, the Head of the English Department, who I liked and admired very much. He, like me, was a northerner Down South, but unlike me was an avid

Sheffield Wednesday fan. Despite him being from the darker side of The Pennines, we instantly had an affinity with each other through our northernness and our love of supporting not very good football teams.

I watched him teach some brilliant lessons. His lessons were always fun, creative and very often, inspiring, if not always for the students, but definitely for me as a young teacher just starting life in a classroom. Along with my GCSE and A Level English teachers, he was one of the biggest influences on me and my teaching style and ethos.

He also played a bit of football and coached the Year 8 football team. He asked if I'd like to get involved and I jumped at the chance. It was a great way of getting to know the kids outside the classroom and gave me a chance to play a bit of footy too. I was so busy this year that playing football for anyone had not even entered my head. My mentor also turned out occasionally for a Sunday league team in one of the Berkshire leagues, and asked if I'd like to come down to a training session, which I eagerly did. I needed my own football fix.

I trained with a great bunch of lads and quickly became a key member of the team, moving from my usual midfield role into a more attacking full back kind of role; more of a Gary Neville type of player. I was twenty-one years old now and in my prime. Ah the sweet memories of being in one's prime.

I played really well for those games in the second part of that season, though I could not add to my goal scoring tally. I was now better at stopping the opposition from scoring and had become what my own dad used to be, a hard-tackling defender who had a bit of skill going forward too.

As far as the coaching of the Year 8s went, I loved it. I would help out with all aspects of the sessions, running 5-a-side sessions and preparing them for the games they would play on Wednesday afternoons after school had finished. I also made my first foray into refereeing which was interesting and something else I could add to my CV. It could come in handy as I tried to find a school to start my career properly, if I passed my PGCE of course. However, one of the tactical moves I did not teach to the students was how to launch themselves feet first at members of the crowd. Eric Cantona did that job for me.

I turned on Sportsnight that evening in January to be greeted by Des Lynam promising "some of the most extraordinary scenes witnessed at a football ground in this country." This sounded promising and frankly very exciting. I didn't realise that it wasn't anything to do with football, apart from the kicking aspect involved in Cantona's reaction to being verbally abused by a moron in the crowd as he walked along the touchline, after having already been sent off for misdemeanours on the pitch. He obviously was not content to restrict his bad behaviour to on the pitch, and his now infamous kung-fu style attack on the fan was exactly as Des Lynam had described it; extraordinary.

Gary Lineker, who had now started his television career as a pundit, called it one of the most amazing things he'd ever seen at a football match. He'd obviously never seen my goal when I was in Year 5 at primary school. All the great and the good of the game condemned Cantona, but he didn't care less, ridiculing the whole affair with his famous, or rather infamous, press conference in which he told everyone how seagulls follow the trawler if they think food might be thrown out for them.

I wasn't that bothered about what he did. Yes, I know it was wrong, and I also know that fans pay a lot of money to watch football and consequently have the right to express their opinions about the players. But if you want to abuse people, then at some point you will get beaten up. Cantona was actually a pioneer in this regard.

I was more concerned about how it would affect United's chances of winning three Premiership titles in a row, and being able to do the Double again, a proper double Double, in consecutive years. He would be banned from playing for the rest of the season, and even his own club went onto extend the ban until October of the following season. This would prove to be crucial in United's defence of the Premier League and the FA Cup.

It certainly gave me and my classes something to talk about in the classroom the next day. I wanted to encourage spontaneity in my students, but I'm not sure that Eric Cantona was the best role model in this regard. It was still great entertainment though.

West Ham United v Manchester United - Upton Park

Liverpool v Blackburn Rovers - Anfield

May 14th, 1995

I was due to start my 10-week block teaching placement after the February half term break. This is when I would prove myself as a teacher and would ultimately decide whether or not I was competent. I had to get ready.

I used the whole of the half term break to plan lessons, prepare resources and generally get ready for the biggest challenge of my life so far in terms of education. Taking GCSEs, A Levels, and a degree was a doddle compared to standing regularly in front of twenty-five or more teenagers who were not about to make my job any easier.

By the Thursday afternoon of the half-term week I still had a few lesson resources and schemes of work to sort out but I needed a break from it all. I needed to do something football orientated.

The Premier League was finely poised by this point in the season, maybe a point or two separating Man United and Blackburn for top spot. It was obvious that it would be one of these two teams who would eventually win the title. This was when Rovers were at their finest, with Alan Shearer in his pomp, banging in goals every game. They had finished second to United the previous season and were not in the mood to finish second again.

I decided to spend the afternoon predicting how the title would be won and who by. You have to remember that this was pre-internet and to do what I was about to do took effort and determination, something I wanted to instill into the students I would be teaching the following week. These days we can all get fixtures up on our smart phones instantly or use an app which can do what it took me three hours to do in a couple of minutes. Frankly it was more fun my way.

I found an old newspaper that hadn't been thrown away yet and turned towards the back pages. I knew there would be a fixture list for the whole season somewhere in the paper, except it wasn't an individual fixture list for each club, but one of those old fashioned graph type affairs with each home team's fixtures being displayed on the vertical axis, and the away fixtures on the horizontal axis. I can't remember which way round the x and y axes are; I was training to be an English teacher after all, not Maths.

To find out which team would be playing who and when, you would have to go through quite a laborious process of going along with your finger from the bottom axis and, with your other finger, going across from the side. Where your fingers met, the corresponding square on the grid would give you the date of the future match, or the score, if that fixture had already been played. I had to work out what the schedules were for both Man United and Blackburn, what order the games would be, and then, and only then, could I start predicting the scores and the eventual league positions. I admit, this was a very convoluted way of doing this ultimately pointless exercise, but it passed the time of day on a dreary February afternoon with my girlfriend out at work.

I finally got each fixture for each club in order and proceeded to predict whether each game would result in a win, draw or defeat. I even went so far as to predict each individual score line, as it was so tight that goal difference may well have played a part in deciding the title. A win here, a draw there, another win, and the occasional defeat for each club was duly predicted.

My inexact and inexpert method resulted in a prediction of United winning the title on goal difference on the final day of the season. I had Rovers to be on 89 points before their final game of the season, with United only two points behind, but with a superior goal difference. This would mean United would have to win their final game of the season, away at West Ham, and rely on Liverpool getting at least a draw with Blackburn at Anfield.

After having wasted an afternoon of planning, I got back on with it the following day and put my little predicted table to one side. I would keep checking it as the season progressed to see how close I was to the actual results. But for the moment I had a career to qualify for and I was determined not to let myself or the students I would teach down.

***

Two and a half months later I had finished my teaching block and had done what I set out to do. I had got through the teaching part of my course, passing with flying colours. It was now early May and I would be leaving my main placement school to do some final observations at my first school. But at that point I was more concerned with how accurate my predictions were as the final day of the Premier league season loomed.

I'm not trying to show off here, but my predictions were almost exactly the same as the actual results. Each predicted score line may not have been exactly correct, but the number of points and the corresponding position of United and Rovers in the table were, quite amazingly, unerringly accurate. On the final day of the season, if United beat West Ham and Rovers did not win, then United would win the league title on goal difference, just as I had predicted. My forecast for the final games were for United to win, and for Blackburn to draw. It almost, very nearly, and possibly even should have happened.

My professional tutor had organised a game of footy on the afternoon of the final day of the season, with beers afterwards in a local pub so we could watch the Premier League finale. He kindly invited me and a couple of other students to join in as a way of saying goodbye. The teams would consist of many of the staff I'd been working with and anyone else they could rope in. I was really looking forward to playing, and the beers of course, as I would then be able to see just how good my predictive powers were.

We had a great game, and I was on the opposite team from my tutor. I'm sure he wanted to test my Lancashire nerve against his obviously much stronger Yorkshire one. It was a bit of a War of the Roses that day. There were a few tasty challenges flying in from both of us, but all done in good humour of course. I think we had a mutual respect for each other, not only on the football pitch, but also in the classroom. He knew that I would be a good teacher, and by impressing him, I knew I had done well.

The beers were well appreciated by us that afternoon and my predictions were very nearly spot on. Rovers ended up not even drawing, but losing, Kenny Dalglish's dreams of Premier League glory as Blackburn's manager almost being shattered by, ironically, the team he had achieved so much glory with as a player.

Liverpool had done all they could to help their archest rivals, Man United to win the league but United could not do their own bit. An agonising 1-1 draw in East London meant that they ended up only one point behind Rovers. They may have become the best team in the country, but in my eyes they were still only Lancashire's second-best team.

United's failure to win also meant that my predictions did not match up exactly. If Brian McClair or Paul Ince, or any of the other players

251

who had chances for United that day had scored just once, then my predictions I had worked out three months and fourteen games ago would have been near perfect.

This failure completely deflated United's team, and even though they still had the FA Cup Final in only six days' time, you could see that they were reeling. They were to meet Everton, in a repeat of the Cup Final I went to exactly ten years previously, but this time the score would be reversed. Everton won with a Paul Rideout header which, even as he was nodding it home, at least two United players should have been able to clear. They looked tired and weary, like a piece of popped bubble wrap. Instead of being bouncy and lively, they looked limp and flat, and Everton hung on for the 1-0 win.

My nonchalance about Eric Cantona's kung-fu antics now turned into frustration. He cost United the Double that season. If Cantona had played in some of those fourteen games, then my prediction would have come true. In fact, no it wouldn't; United would have won much more easily than on the fine margins of a having a better goal difference.

No one could argue that United were as good a team without Cantona in it. He had proved to be massively influential in his three Premier League titles he had won in the last three seasons, two with United, and his first with Leeds to prevent United winning. His absence for the second part of this season proved to be just as influential. He was that kind of player; he influenced things, even when he wasn't on the pitch it would seem.

And so the season ended in frustration for both Manchester United and Preston North End. Both clubs came so close, although I grant that United were miles closer than us. But maybe the narrowest of margins would spur both clubs onto greater things the following season. Cantona would be returning for United, and as for Preston, Gary Peters would buy a bald guy called Andy Saville who also knew a thing or two about scoring goals.

All I had to do now was get two jobs, one for the summer, and one for the rest of my life.

Season 1995/96

Wimbledon v Newcastle United

December 3rd, 1995 Selhurst Park

I spent most of June of 1995 attending interviews at various schools in London. My girlfriend and I had agreed to move to London so that she could look for a way of starting a career there. I basically had the whole of London to choose from and there was no shortage of vacancies. As long as I found a school somewhere, we would then be able to find a place to live near enough to where I would be working, and also give her access to central London.

After applying to schools in East, West and North London and either being rejected, or me rejecting them (one school near Heathrow was a proper dump) a vacancy came up at a school in Enfield. If I could get this one, then we would be able to find a place to live in North London, near to a train station which would enable both me and my girlfriend to go our separate ways, me going to the outskirts, and her heading into central London. Little did I know then that it would also allow us to go our separate ways for the rest of our lives too, but more of that in a little while.

After yet another bus into Reading, a train to Paddington, a tube around the Circle Line to Liverpool Street, and finally another train up to Enfield Town, I arrived for my interview at Enfield Grammar School. The school was right in the centre of Enfield Town and even though it had retained its name, it was one of many ex-Grammar schools around the country that had become a comprehensive school in the early 1970s.

As soon as I walked in it felt right. It had lovely buildings and grounds, and was also relatively easy to get to. Thankfully, the Head of the English Department seemed to like me and offered me a job, which I gratefully accepted.

With a job now secured, we would now have to look for somewhere suitable to live. This would prove more difficult than getting a job in the first place. By this point, my other mate, another of the lads I had been Inter-Railing with, had finished his degree in Newcastle, and like me, wanted to experience life Down South. He had come to stay with us in Reading, sleeping on our living room floor.

My girlfriend and I by this point had drifted apart even further. The proximity to each other in purely geographical terms had ironically caused us to feel further away from each other emotionally, and we were both glad for the extra company my mate provided. It meant that we did not have to endure our rather awkward relationship alone, and gave us both an excuse not to have to try and pretend to be still in love.

We suggested that he should look for a flat with us in London so that he too could find work there. He jumped at the chance. Maybe my girlfriend and I knew sub-consciously that our relationship was, in Woody Allen's phrase from "Annie Hall", a dead shark. If my mate was with us, it would mean that neither of us would be left on our own if our relationship petered out, which it most definitely had been doing.

My mate had always been a big cricket fan, and we decided to go to Lords and watch a one-day match between Middlesex and Surrey. My girlfriend agreed to come as we would all be able to make some tentative reconnaissance as to potential places to live. As we wandered around St. John's Wood and Maida Vale, we all agreed that somewhere like this would be ideal, but then we realised just how expensive living in London would prove to be. We were never going to be able to afford anywhere like this.

Another reccy mission into London was needed, but this time we had to find somewhere affordable and also somewhere convenient for both central and outer London. After perusing the A-Z map, we decided to look around the Hackney area. If we could find somewhere which had a train into Liverpool Street and also a train up to Enfield, then this would be ideal. It certainly would not have the grandeur of St. John's Wood though.

We found a dodgy letting agency in Stamford Hill which had a flat available. For some reason the landlord had not been able to fill it as yet. We soon found out why. Our expectations of where we would hopefully live, and the reality of where we would actually be able to live, were hugely different.

We were shown a two bedroomed, partly furnished flat above a newsagents and next to a Dixy Fried Chicken shop on the Upper Clapton Road, and quite frankly it was a bit of a hovel, similar to my first shared house in my second year at university. We would have to buy a cheap sofa and put up with the wallpaper hanging off the wall and the constant noise coming from the road. But essentially, it was within our meagre budget. In fact it was the only one within our budget.

We couldn't afford to keep coming into London looking for the perfect flat, whatever the perfect flat was, so we accepted the landlord's offer and signed a contract. The landlord I'm sure had a little grin on his face as we naively put pen to paper. We felt like Nemo and Dory as they are confronted by Bruce the shark. We had no idea how big London's ocean was and how many dangers there would be. My girlfriend and I already had a dead shark on our hands, and we were now tiny little fish in a vast, ruthless ocean full of landlords who would gladly gobble us up. Our thinking was that once we were in London then we would be better placed to then find more salubrious accommodation. Or that was my girlfriend's thinking anyway.

Our contract would start in the middle of August. This would give us time to earn a bit of money before moving in, and also a week or so to buy a few bits of furniture before I would start my job in September. I'd already got one job, now I just had to find another to give me some cash to get through until my first pay slip at the end of September.

The temping agency in Reading found me a job in a double-glazing factory where I would essentially be a dogsbody. I spent the whole of my first week there sweeping up glass, both inside the factory and also in the huge area outside where the lorries would drop off and pick up their deliveries. It was mind-numbing, but not unenjoyable. I was outside in the sunshine, sweeping away, planning my career.

After a month or so of sweeping up, we all went to our respective parental homes to get anything else we would need for our flat in London, before hiring a van, loading up, and diving into the unforgiving ocean of London. The drive from Reading to London was one of the scariest things I'd ever done. With no sat-nav back then, I had to rely on my mate with our trusty A-Z to find our way around the maze of roads, and had to endure the wrath of many of the London drivers who I seemed to upset on that journey.

We unloaded what stuff we had, and spent our first night in our new flat sitting on the floor of our living room, before sleeping on a smelly mattress. This was not what we had expected from London, and certainly was not the gleaming urban lifestyle my girlfriend aspired to.

Another fraught drive back to Reading to return the van, leaving my girlfriend to do some unpacking, and then, as me and my mate got the train back into London, I said goodbye to Reading. It had provided me with a degree, a PGCE, and many happy memories. I will always have a fond affection for Reading, but there was no time for sentimentality; we had to find some furniture and get our bearings before my new job started and my mate and girlfriend could start looking for their own employment.

***

I settled into my new career and they found work in Central London quite easily. My girlfriend and I were now even further apart than ever. We both had new jobs, new friends, and new ambitions. We were spending less and less time together. She had got a job which was much better paid than mine. I still remember how little my first ever pay slip was, even with an outer London allowance added to it. The bright lights of London seemed further away than ever, despite living there now. For me and my mate anyway.

My evenings would be taken up with planning lessons and marking work whereas my girlfriend had met some friends at her work who lived in the kind of places we had seen on our trip to Lords, and she would go out with them and often stay over at their plush flats. I, on the other hand, would often go to the pub after work with my new colleagues. The pub was handily located right next to my school, and was affectionately known as The Staff Room. Most Fridays, I would relax with my fellow teachers at the end of a hard week's work by having a few, and quite often, a lot of beers, before heading back to what was essentially becoming a bachelor pad.

Occasionally, if my mate and I could afford it, we would all go into London and be tourists, or explore the bars around Camden. But this was becoming less frequent as we all settled into new routines. Mostly my mate and I would spend our Saturday nights watching the television as we could not afford any of the delights London's night life had to offer. My girlfriend though would often be with her new friends, and I started to wonder whether one of these new friends was male. I wasn't bothered by her absence though. It was more of a relief really as our charade of a relationship was on its last legs.

Me and my mate realised that there were more sporting opportunities available to us in London, and we decided to start making the most of these. With my girlfriend being mostly absent, we could do blokey things together, which obviously would include watching football.

After his time spent at Newcastle University, he had developed a bond with The Magpies and so when they were due to play against Wimbledon in a Sky Sports Super Sunday match, we decided we would go and watch. Wimbledon by then were playing at Selhurst

Park, and as their fanbase was still smaller than the ground's capacity, it was still possible to just turn up at the ground and buy tickets. On the first Sunday in December, we watched a brilliant game which ended up 3-3.

Newcastle were now being managed by Kevin Keegan, and this was the first half of their brilliant but ultimately not brilliant enough season, where they could and possibly should have won the Premier League. They had only lost one game so far and had already beaten Wimbledon 6-1 at St. James' Park, along with victories over Liverpool, and the champions Blackburn. This was the first Premier League game I had ever been to and it did not disappoint. Both teams held the lead during the game and a draw was a fair result in the end.

The following week we would also go to Wembley to watch one of England's countless friendly games in the run up to next summer's Euro 96. This would be the first time I would go to Wembley without my dad and I saw England, with Shearer, Gascoigne et al, draw 1-1 against Portugal, with Luis Figo featuring for the Portuguese.

My first term as a teacher ended, and so finally did my relationship with my girlfriend of the previous four years. It was obvious that she had a new life, with probably a new man in it too, and so after an awful night out in Camden on New Year's Eve, we decided to officially end our relationship.

A room in one of her new friend's flats had become available and we agreed to go our separate ways. She could now go and live the life she had dreamed of when we first moved to London, whereas me and my mate would stay in clapped out Clapton. Although I sulked for a few days, it was the best decision for both of us. I realised that I was young, free, and single, living in London with my best mate, and was about to have the best year of my life so far as 1996 dawned.

1996 would truly be a memorable year in footballing terms for all the teams I cared about, England, Man United, and especially for my true love, Preston North End. If I had been let down by my girlfriend, then Preston would come to my rescue. At least I could rely on them. For once.

Gillingham v Preston North End

March 9th, 1996   Priestfield Stadium

I returned to school for my second term without a girlfriend for the first time in over four years, but now with a new found sense of freedom. I realised that life had more possibilities opening up to me. I was living in London, a vibrant and throbbing city, with my best mate. We were both in our early twenties and even though we had lived geographically in London for over four months now, we hadn't really lived London life. Yes, our flat was awful, but it was cheap, and best of all, it was next door to a Dixy Fried Chicken shop, which we seemed to visit on a far too frequent basis.

My school had a decent staff football team, and I slotted in well in my new role as an attacking right back, playing in all the games we organised against other local schools from North London and Hertfordshire. We had some great games on Friday nights after school and would always finish off in "The Staff Room" for a few drinks. I no longer had to concern myself with getting back for my girlfriend and so would drink happily with my colleagues, who were also becoming good friends.

I was enjoying playing regularly again, but I was missing watching football regularly. I'd only watched two football matches since arriving in the capital and I was determined to go and see as many games as I could. Preston would regularly be playing in the South East and there were a few games I would be able to get to. My mate was only too happy to come along.

As we were the only ones of our group of friends who lived in London, it provided a perfect base for people to come and stay with us and experience London. Mates would very often come down and stay over, and we would go out into Camden, or go into the West End. We would also go and stay with them in various cities around the country. We stayed in Leeds, Newcastle, Manchester, Brighton, but there was one place I needed to make a pilgrimage to; Canterbury.

My mate Pete, who lived there, was a big West Ham fan, and when he came up to stay with us he would time it for when the Hammers had a home game at Upton Park. He took me to see West Ham beat Leicester, Derby and also Newcastle, the second time we had now been a part of the Toon Army on tour. I needed to return the favour, so when Preston were playing at Gillingham, just a few stops away on the train from Canterbury, this was the perfect opportunity to enlighten my Premier League supporting mates into the delights of fourth division football.

My flatmate and I had already "treated" ourselves to a match at Underhill in Barnet just after we'd started back at work in January. It was easy to get to from where we were living and so when Preston were due to visit, then so were we. Preston were unbeaten since the opening game of the season and were looking like genuine promotion contenders, but a dismal 1-0 defeat at Barnet made us realise that we still had a lot of work to do. We were now in third place in the table and could not afford to drop many more points if we wanted automatic promotion, which we obviously did considering our record in the play-offs.

By March we were in second place, only three points behind the league leaders, who just so happened to be Gillingham. My pilgrimage to Canterbury via Gillingham now had a top of the table six-pointer at stake too.

The town of Gillingham is nothing like I expected it to be. Kent is known as "The Garden of England" but Gillingham seemed more like the patch of weeds that needed eradicating. It was grim, and their fans were not too welcoming to us Dirty Northern Bastards either, as they frequently sang at us from the terraces.

Gillingham had always been a bit of a bogey team for us. We rarely ever beat them, and frequently lost, but this time we would at least get a hard fought 1-1 draw. The crucial thing was that we did not lose and allow them to go six points clear of us at the top. We were still well in touch for the final push towards the end of the season. Promotion was a definite possibility, but to go up as Champions would be much better.

I'd never seen my club win anything. In our last promotion season, nine years before, we had finished second, but now we had a real chance of actually winning something. It was all very exciting.

Liverpool v Newcastle United

April 3rd, 1996   Anfield

With Preston lying in second place in Division Three/Four, Man United were also in second place in The Premier League on the weekend I went on my pilgrimage to Gillingham via Canterbury. Famously, Newcastle had held a twelve-point lead over United in January, but cracks were starting to open in their title charge, which caused a certain amount of friction between me and my flatmate. He was very much wanting Newcastle to go on and win, whereas I still had strong affections for Man United.

Whilst in Newcastle as a student, he'd seen them getting stronger under Kevin Keegan, but never being able to make a real push for the title. This was the year that he, and basically anyone else who had no connections with Manchester United, would have loved it if Keegan's team could go on and beat the team who had won the Premier League twice already and had missed out on the last game of the previous season. I kept winding my mate up about how Newcastle would bottle it and let their seemingly insurmountable lead slip.

United had started the season by being heavily beaten by Aston Villa, causing the now infamous quote from Alan Hansen on Match of the Day about never winning anything with kids. Maybe he would have been right if United had stuck with those young players, the players who would become the legendary Class of 92. But on the opening day of the season, they did not have Eric Cantona available, as he was still banned until October. Once he returned, the team of kids now had a man as their focal point.

Cantona inevitably scored on his return game against Liverpool, and although United were still way behind Newcastle in the early new year, Cantona was building up a head of steam. By the time the top two teams met at St. James' Park in early March, the Red Devils were only four points behind, and it was now that Cantona would basically go on and win the title almost single-handedly.

A 1-0 win at Newcastle, the goal of course scored by Cantona, caused my flatmate to not talk to me for a few days after the match. Maybe he now realised that Newcastle's dreams were going to be crushed by the Cantona-inspired United, and he was certainly in no mood to be wound up by me anymore.

This game would be the start of Cantona's one-man mission to show everyone what we'd all missed in United's ultimately failed attempt the previous season to win three Premier League titles in a row. He got the only goal of the game against not just Newcastle, but also Arsenal, Spurs and Coventry, along with a goal in a Manchester derby win, and a crucial last-minute equaliser against QPR. By the time Newcastle travelled to Anfield in early April, they were now three points behind United. A defeat by Liverpool would surely end their hopes.

For some reason my school broke up for the Easter holidays on the day of the game at Anfield. We'd had our final staff game of the season after school and were then planning on having a bit of a pub crawl around Enfield. The game turned out to be one of the most extraordinary that the Premier League had seen. The score seemed to change every time we went into a different pub. After starting the crawl in one pub to see Robbie Fowler open the scoring for Liverpool, by the time we got to the next pub, Newcastle were leading 2-1.

The next pub saw Liverpool's first equaliser, but then Newcastle would regain the lead only two minutes later. By the time we got to our fourth and final pub, Liverpool had equalised again and the game seemed to be ending 3-3. But Stan Collymore would pop up at the far post to score Liverpool's winner and almost put the final nail in Newcastle's coffin.

I think we all knew that night that Newcastle had lost their chance of winning the League. Five games later we definitely knew they had lost it after Kevin Keegan lost whatever "it" was in his post-match interview. "It" may have been common sense, or rationale, or dignity, but whatever "it" was, Keegan had definitely lost it after being wound up by Alex Ferguson and famously exploding into a rant about how he would love it if his team could beat Man United to the title.

We all knew, Keegan included I suspect, that it was all over for Newcastle by then. United would go on and claim their third Premier League title in four years, and still had the chance of the Double. All they had to do was beat Liverpool at Wembley.

But first Liverpool had to get some lovely new suits fitted for the big day.

Leyton Orient v Preston North End

April 20th, 1996   Brisbane Road

Since our draw at Gillingham, Preston had remained unbeaten for the next eight games. We had overtaken Gillingham at the top of the table and were huge favourites to go on and win the title. A freak 3-0 defeat at home to the team who had prevented us from being champions in 1987, Northampton Town, meant that we were now only top on goal difference. We were due to play away at Cambridge United on a Tuesday evening, and as I was on my Easter holidays, and Cambridge was only a short train journey away from Liverpool Street, then me and my flatmate decided that another away game was in order, a trip to the great city of colleges and academia.

As an A-Level student I had dreamed of going to Cambridge as an undergraduate, before I realised that I would not be good enough to get there, so this visit to Cambridge would have to do. Instead of studying great works of Literature at somewhere like Jesus College, I would be studying Andy Saville, Preston's own saviour of a centre forward who had already scored twenty-five goals this season.

He would score another one that night, but it would not be enough, Preston losing 2-1. Every away game I had been to this season had not produced a win for me to savour on my journey home, and we were at risk of throwing the title away, being one point behind Gillingham now. But first we had the chance of at least securing promotion in the next game, which would be against Leyton Orient at Brisbane Road, just a short walk for me across the many football pitches of Hackney Marshes. This time Preston would not let me down.

After our walk across the seemingly never ending pitches, those famously used in the Nike advert, we were in need of a pre-match drink, but we decided to go into the wrong pub. I was wearing my Baxi sponsored PNE top and as we entered the pub, I felt like I had walked into The Slaughtered Lamb from "An American Werewolf in London". The whole pub stopped chatting and stared at us. I think maybe even one of them missed the dart board with his throw.

One of the scary Leyton Orient fans approached us and said that we were going to get "cut up". You have to remember that we were just two naïve young blokes from North Lancashire, and we were not used to such an aggressive welcoming party. We assumed that he meant that our team was going to get cut up on the pitch by our new friend from East London's team. We were mistaken.

Thankfully, my flatmate is six foot seven tall, and that day he looked a bit scary. A few days before, in a particularly competitive game of squash, I had smacked him in the face with my racquet and he had a black eye. He looked like someone you wouldn't want to mess with actually, even though I knew he wasn't at all scary, apart from after hitting him in the face with a squash racquet. I definitely knew that I wasn't in the slightest bit scary, and so before we discovered what the clientele of the pub meant about being cut up, we decided on balance that it was probably worth relocating to a different drinking establishment, or just forgetting about a drink altogether actually, and just get inside the ground where there would at least be wire fences to keep the locals at bay and stop them from ripping us to pieces.

We did exactly that, and it was definitely the best decision as I assume the Orient fans would not have been too pleased with what happened on the pitch. Andy Saville scored his 27th and 28th league goals of a remarkable first season for Preston that day at Brisbane Road to secure only the second promotion I had ever experienced. We had secured promotion in 1987 at exactly the same ground, but this time I would be there to see it.

As the final whistle blew, we were just about to pour onto the pitch with the other Preston fans, but just at that moment we saw our old friend from the pub again. He now looked more like a feral beast than he had done before the match. He was rattling the wire fencing, gnashing his fangs together, and snarling and salivating us. He was also screaming very nasty words at us, and we hadn't even done anything. If someone had a gun with a silver bullet in it, then it would have come in quite handy at that point.

We decided that it was probably best to just get as far away from him as possible, so instead of going onto the pitch, we legged it back across the marshes, making sure to stay on the paths. I was glad that it had been an afternoon match and not an evening one with the chance of a full moon.

We reached the relative safety of our flat and then it dawned on me what my team had just achieved. We had got promoted. We had not only baked the cake, but iced it too. All we had to do now was put the cherry on the top by becoming champions.

Preston had not won anything since 1971, two years before I was even born, and we were determined to change that. Two more 2-0 wins ensured that we finished the season as Champions, three points ahead of Gillingham. We had finally won something, even if it was the lowest division in the league, but who cared? We had won. We were the Champions. It was great.

I didn't know it then but that would be the last time Preston would be in the bottom division. Most of my footballing life had been spent watching Preston in the bottom division, and at the time of writing, we haven't slipped back down yet. We may well do again, but it won't be next season that's for sure.

Liverpool v Manchester United

FA Cup Final

May 11th, 1996   Wembley Stadium

Liverpool's suits had been duly chosen and fitted, and they frankly looked ridiculous. Alex Ferguson must have been laughing when he saw the opposition walking around Wembley in their white suits, looking like a third-rate boy band. Looking like a first-rate boyband (whatever one of those is) would have been bad enough, but Robbie Fowler, Steve McManaman, David James et al didn't even seem embarrassed by what they were wearing. Ferguson must have thought another Double was in the bag. But it proved to be much harder than everyone expected.

My flatmate and I were literally skint for the whole of May 1996. We had obviously been spending far too much on delicious and not at all greasy Dixy Fried Chicken. We could not even afford any beers to drink on Cup Final day, so we settled down for a feast of television viewing, which would not just involve the game, but also, as there was nothing else to do or watch, the Eurovision Song Contest later that evening.

Gina G would be performing her "classic" entry "Ooh, Aah, Just a Little Bit", and as we both had silly schoolboy crushes on her, we planned on watching her perform, along with many other awful songs by other awful "artists". We couldn't afford to go out anywhere so this seemed like a reasonable, if very sad plan.

The game started well for United, and they had quite a few chances early on, but just could not convert any of them. If they had, then they would have gone on to win much more easily. Instead, the game became very tight and very tense, and it was only in the 86th minute that Eric Cantona of course came up with the winner. A controlled finish from the edge of the penalty area through a crowd of players won the game for United.

Cantona's effort could so easily have been ballooned up over the bar, but the way he kept the ball down was very special. United had won another Double; their second in the space of three seasons. It had taken them only three years to achieve something that only one other club, Liverpool of course, had done in the entire history of English football.

After the FA Cup had been lifted and Des Lynam said goodbye to us all, I remember feeling a complete sense of deflation. It had been a remarkable season for United and Preston, both teams having won their respective divisions, and now it was all over. It had been the most tense of seasons, but now the tension was replaced by an almost profound sense of emptiness. What was I going to do now? Apart from watch Gina G of course.

After a sublime finish from Cantona, we moved onto the ridiculous part of our day. We watched every second of that Eurovision contest that night, completely and utterly sober, and had to wait ages for Gina G to do her thing. We even got mildly excited when we caught a glimpse of her knickers as she strutted about the stage. She came nowhere near winning, and our brief moment of titillation was over.

The only thing left to do was go to bed and ponder what the hell we were going to do until we both got paid at the end of the month. I think we both resolved that night to never be in the situation again where watching Gina G's knickers was the highlight of our day. With no more football until next season, how were we going to get through until August? Oh wait…Euro 96 would be starting soon. That might help us fill the void.

England v Scotland

European Championships

June 15ᵗʰ, 1996   Wembley Stadium

Up until this day my life in London consisted of work, planning lessons, marking books etc. as well as a couple of games of squash a week at the nearest sports centre in Finsbury Park. Friday evenings, after eventually getting home after an after-work drinks session, would usually consist of chilling out in front of the television, watching The Fast Show, Have I Got News For You, Shooting Stars, and the televisual highlight of my week, Fantasy Football League.

Baddiel and Skinner had released their "Three Lions" song by now and it would often be played in our flat in the run up to England's first game against Switzerland, to get me even more excited about England's first competitive match for over two and a half years. The song would take on a life of its own over the next few weeks, but the wave of national pride and expectation had not yet overtaken the country as we stepped out to open the tournament.

England were now managed by Terry Venables, and he had experimented with a Christmas tree formation in the last two years, which was essentially a 4-3-2-1 set up. It had worked to an extent, but by the start of the tournament England seemed to have reverted to what they knew best; a 4-4-2 formation with the SAS of Alan Shearer and Teddy Sheringham up front. It should really have been called the SHASH, but I'm guessing that Alan and Edward (as Brian Clough always used to call Teddy Sheringham) would rather have the cooler and slightly scarier acronym of SAS.

Shearer lived up to his name in that opening match and he gave us the lead midway through the first half, but we could not push on, instead conceding a penalty late on, which was converted for a very underwhelming 1-1 draw to kick the tournament off.

After the match my mate and I would do what we normally did on Saturday nights, which was to go into Camden, go to a club there and flail drunkenly around to Blur, Oasis, Pulp, and many other bands from the Britpop era. We would unsuccessfully try to chat girls up, and then usually fall asleep on the night bus home, waking up miles away from our flat, before walking back to our flat.

We were both ready for something different, something better than this rather sad routine. We'd both read Irvine Welsh's "Trainspotting" earlier in the year, just before the film version had come out, and we then went onto read everything else that Welsh had written, including "The Acid House" and his collection of three short stories entitled "Ecstasy".

After waking up with yet another hangover, with a whole week at work to get through until England's next game against the auld enemy, we both suggested to each other that maybe we should go to a proper club next weekend, a club where we would not be surrounded by drunken idiots like ourselves, where we could dance to repetitive beats, and not end up drooling all down ourselves as we fell asleep on the way home.

We made a few phone calls to various mates around the country and they were all well up for a weekend in London at our place, where we would all watch the England/Scotland match before hitting the club scene of London properly. The plan was sorted and we got through the week at work easily, knowing that whatever happened at Wembley the following Saturday, we would at least have a great night out afterwards. And what a weekend it proved to be.

Everyone arrived at various points on the Friday evening before the match, and we just stayed in drinking beers and catching up with each other. We were all just waiting for the next day to arrive, as this would be the day the tournament really caught fire. Everyone was expecting us to beat Scotland, but nobody expected a goal like the one Paul Gascoigne was about to score.

The first half proved to be fairly uneventful, but soon after the restart Shearer got on the end of a Gary Neville cross and scored his second goal in two games. We would surely go on to get a few more now, but then Scotland got a penalty after a clumsy challenge from Tony Adams. We were all unaware at the time, but have been shown the footage countless times since, of how the ball moved fractionally, seemingly of its own accord, just before Gary McCallister hit the spot-kick, which was then subsequently saved by David Seaman. Seaman had not been able to do the same thing the week before, but this week his save spurred England on to greatness.

It especially spurred Gascoigne on, as only a couple of minutes after Scotland's chance to equalise, he produced perhaps his most famous and glorious of goals. The way he lifted the ball over a completely bamboozled Colin Hendrie with his left foot, before firing the ball in on the volley with his right, has become almost legendary for England fans.

So too has the celebration which Gascoigne engineered, reenacting the infamous "Dentist's Chair" night out from their pre-tournament warm up trip to the Far East. The players and management had been prudishly vilified in the press for having a night out and getting very drunk, but nobody cared about that anymore. Gascoigne had produced a goal of footballing beauty, which sent the whole country into raptures and knocked all the stuffing out of Scotland.

The game would finish 2-0 and we all decided to go and celebrate with a few drinks down the pub near a local park. With loads of other people doing the same thing, an impromptu game of footy broke out. We all obviously joined in. It was a beautiful summer's day; the beers were flowing and we were all trying to recreate Gascoigne's goal. We were like kids again; it felt brilliant.

Later that night we would feel brilliant again, but this time by getting completely off our faces and dancing to electronic music for hours, surrounded by lots of other smiley people who were off their faces too. It was literally a life changing day for me and if I had the choice of a Groundhog Day, then that day would definitely be on my list.

England v Germany

European Championships Semi-Final

June 26th, 1996   Wembley Stadium

My first ever experience of the Tuesday Blues were alleviated somewhat with the knowledge that England would be playing their final group game that night. Our opponents would be Holland, and on paper this looked like the toughest match we would have to encounter. However, our performance that evening made the match look like our easiest game yet.

We played some of the best football I'd ever seen England play that night. We completely dismantled Holland, with the SAS getting two goals each, before we allowed Holland to get a consolation goal late on. I couldn't quite believe I was watching England that night.

271

The way we passed the ball and the clinical finishing was something other teams usually did to us, but here we were, putting a very good Holland team to the sword, just as St. George had done to the dragon. The Three Lions were starting to really roar by now, and the song was becoming ubiquitous. Everywhere you went it could be heard. It seemed to be constantly on the radio or blaring out from cars as everyone reveled in the sunshine. The atmosphere not just in London, but around the whole country, was fantastic.

After the previous weekend's shenanigans, I decided to pop back Up North for the weekend to see my parents and watch our quarter-final match against Spain with them. The expectation was flowing throughout the country, and it seemed just as feverous in Lancashire as it was in the capital.

Sitting on my parents' sofa, with them both in their armchairs, felt like it used to when I was a boy when we would all watch the Cup Final together. A game of few chances which finished 0-0 meant that we would have to go through the torture of a penalty shootout again, our first one since we had lost in the World Cup Semi-Final six years before. But this time everyone expected us to win it. Stuart Pearce certainly did.

After his penalty miss against West Germany six years previously, he was desperate to put things right. Most players would have shied away from the responsibility, but not a man whose nickname was Psycho, one which I'm sure he was proud of. We all understood why he'd been given that nickname after he'd slammed his penalty home when he let out the most guttural, almost feral roar I'd ever seen. The veins in his neck were bulging, his eyeballs almost exploding with sheer relief and passion.

After we'd seen that, we all knew that David Seaman would do what he had done against Scotland and save one of the Spanish penalties, which he duly did. We had won our first ever penalty shootout, but I think we all know that it would be quite a while before we would win another one, and it definitely wouldn't be against Germany a few

272

days later, in a repeat of that most intense of games at Italia 90. We didn't realise just how intense it would be this time either.

After returning to my home in London, work seemed quite irrelevant. Not just for me, but the whole country was just waiting for the Wednesday night to arrive. As soon as school finished, I got the first train home and settled down to watch the first semi-final, a match between France and the Czech Republic played at Old Trafford. Surely we would be able to beat either of these teams at Wembley, in front of 100,000 partisan fans all singing and actually believing that football was indeed coming home.

My flatmate would be due back around 6pm but at half time in the first match which had kicked off at four o'clock, he rang me to tell me that he wouldn't be home in time for the England match. One of his work colleagues had somehow got a couple of free tickets to the match in Manchester, and he had left work at lunchtime and driven up to watch it. He was actually at Old Trafford when he rang to tell me. I couldn't blame him really. I would probably have done the same if it meant I had the chance of watching a European Championship semi-final.

This meant that I would be watching the England game all by myself. I didn't fancy going to the pub. My PMT (Pre-Match Tension) was far too high. I'd rather suffer in my own company, and then go out to celebrate or commiserate at the pub later.

It would prove to be a case of commiseration, but before the game, the whole country believed we would do it, and put the ghost of 1990 to rest. I'd never seen Wembley so alive. David Baddiel and Frank Skinner were in the crowd to sing the most uproarious rendition of Three Lions yet, surrounded by fans singing it back at them. Football was definitely coming home.

Paul Young, popstar from my childhood, had been given the job of leading the players and the crowd in the National Anthem, but he was simply not needed. One of his most famous songs was "Love of the Common People", and that was definitely on display that night.

There was certainly a lot of love from the common people for their footballing heroes as the whole team, the whole stadium, the whole country came together during that rendition of "God Save the Queen." The country was going wild, and it became even wilder after only three minutes of the game, when the goal machine, Alan Shearer nodded in from a corner. If we didn't believe before, we certainly did then.

However, the aptly named Stefan Kuntz equalised thirteen minutes later to bring our tension levels up to an almost unbearable level. We had the better chances throughout the rest of the ninety minutes, Shearer unbelievably missing a glorious chance to win it for us, but the game went into extra time with the score at 1-1, just as it had done six years before.

Again, just like the previous match, we should have won it in extra time, Darren Anderton hitting the post and Gascoigne being millimetres away from winning it for us, but the ball rolled agonisingly past his outstretched left foot as he slid in with an open goal in front of him.

It was becoming almost a carbon copy of the game in 1990. Unfortunately so did the penalty shootout. Even though we had won our last match on penalties, this one was against the Germans; a team that simply did not miss penalties. They were just as ruthless, just as merciless, just as pitiless as they had been in Turin. But then again, so were we. Every penalty for both teams was scored convincingly, and now we would have to choose one of our less experienced penalty takers for the sudden death.

When Gareth Southgate stepped up I knew he wouldn't score. I don't understand why someone like Paul Ince didn't volunteer before Southgate, but he just did not look confident as he placed the ball on the spot. He struck the ball firmly enough, but it was too close to the keeper and was easily saved. I then understood why sudden death was so named. If I felt like I had suddenly died inside, I cannot imagine what Gareth Southgate was feeling. Sudden annihilation maybe.

Andreas Moller then converted his penalty and just stood there arrogantly looking at the despairing faces of the England players and fans. It had happened again, but this time with another fall guy in place of Stuart Pearce and Chris Waddle. Gareth Southgate was inconsolable after the game, and it took him many years to get over it. Unlike Stuart Pearce, he would not have the opportunity to atone for his sins. At least not on the pitch. He would have to wait until he had become England manager to do that. But at least he got a pizza advert out of it.

I couldn't be bothered to go to the pub. London was becoming slightly scary and there were reports of violence in the centre. I just sat there on my sofa, numb with disappointment, all by myself. If I had a copy of Eric Carmen's power ballad, I would have put it on as loudly as possible. I needed to wallow in my footballing pain. I don't think I had ever been so deflated after a football match before.

Yet again we had been so close. Yet again, another nearly moment. Yet again.

Season 1996/97

Tottenham Hotspur v Preston North End

Coca Cola Cup Second Round, Second Leg

September 25th, 1996   White Hart Lane

After the disappointment of Euro 96 I consoled myself with my new passion for clubbing. We went out again a couple more times before my first year as a teacher came to an end in mid-July and then I basically became almost nocturnal for the rest of the summer.

I would stay up through the night watching the Atlanta Olympics, and increasingly annoy my flatmate as he still had to get up and go to work in central London whilst I would enjoy my first ever summer of being paid without having to do any work.

Mates would stay over and we would have to make sure we were in bed before my flatmate would have to get up for work. It would have been flaunting my freedom a little too obviously if I was still watching the television as he left for work.

The new football season started as me and five friends were sitting around the pool of one of my mate's parents' villa in Spain. We had taken advantage of this opportunity to get some proper sunshine and had the best week ever, chilling by the pool and getting hammered either in the villa or in the bars of the local town.

As David Beckham was scoring from the halfway line against Wimbledon, I was recovering from a major night out. I knew that I would have to get my head around planning for the new school year when we got back to England, and this was the final blow out of what had been the best summer of my life.

The new year at school started and to my absolute delight, Preston were drawn against Spurs in the League Cup. The first leg was at Deepdale and live commentary was provided on the radio. After our glorious promotion only a few months before I was keen to see how we would fare against a Premier League team, and was thrilled when we held our own at Deepdale, drawing 1-1.

We had proved we could at least not get thrashed. The second leg at White Hart lane the following week would be different, but it would be played only a couple of short bus rides away from our flat. I finally got to watch my team play in a Premier League stadium, and really didn't mind that we got beat 3-0. Just seeing them at a great ground and not a dump like Barnet or Gillingham was such a treat.

***

I include this game for not just footballing reasons. If you remember, I had been to White Hart Lane once before, when I was nine years

276

old, and I mentioned that a twelve-year-old girl who lived just around the corner from the ground would become my wife. Well, this is where the next part of that wonderful story would start. She was now a twenty-five-year-old woman, married but recently separated, with the most adorable of two-year-old daughters. But I had no idea of that just yet.

She was now living in a flat near Bruce Grove station, two stops up from where I would catch the train at Stamford Hill. We would both get the train up to Enfield Town and I had no idea who she was or what her circumstances were.

I'd noticed and become quite intrigued by this very pretty girl on the train a few times in my first year, but because she was not on the same train every morning, I thought she may be a temp or something. As I got the train home after my first year of teaching ended, I wondered if I would ever see her again.

The answer was yes. As I started my commute again in the September of 96, she was still there, and she looked even prettier now. She was the sweetest, most gorgeous girl I'd ever seen and even better, I realised she worked in an office block just over the road from my school. I still had no idea who she was. She may well have been married with a kid for all I knew. I definitely didn't know that she actually was married with a kid.

My intrigue and curiosity built and built, and eventually I took the plunge and sat next to her on the train after work one afternoon. We got chatting and found out that she was called Emma, had a little girl, and a wanker of a husband who she had left the previous year.

I also discovered that whilst I had been sat at home when I was eight and nine years old watching Spurs win the FA Cup in consecutive years, she was actually out on the streets of Tottenham outside White Hart Lane watching her team bring back the Cup in an open top bus. She wasn't exactly a huge football fan, but remembered her childhood Saturdays being dominated by the noise from the stadium, the fans walking past her house on their way to and from one of the

Spurs pubs, The Antwerp Arms, which was at the end of her street, and how the whole atmosphere of where she lived being changed when there was a game on.

I told her how I'd just been to White Hart Lane to watch my little team from Up North play against her Premier League giants, and thankfully she didn't seem bored at all. It must have been my innocent Northern charm, but I was amazed when she actually seemed to enjoy talking to me.

From then on, my commutes to work changed forever. Instead of dragging myself out of bed to catch the train, I would leap out and get ready as quickly as possible to ensure that I would be on the same train as her. The thought of just being able to chat with her on the train was the only incentive I needed to get to work, and I would have a spring in my step in all my lessons after our morning train ride together.

We eventually exchanged numbers and we arranged for me to come around to her flat. She offered to cook me something nice to eat. After eating mostly Dixy Fried Chicken for the past year, this sounded like the most wonderful evening ever, but there was a slight problem. I was due to play squash that night and I knew that my flatmate would not be too pleased if I cancelled, so I told her that we would have to do it another evening.

By the time I got home, I realised what a dick I was. Here I was, putting off an evening of gorgeous food, gorgeous company, and maybe even gorgeous something else, all for a game of squash with my mate. I wasn't going to let an opportunity like this slip by. I rang my flatmate and told him that I was mugging him off for a girl, and, as predicted, he wasn't pleased. We'd both been looking forward to resuming our battle on the squash court, but that could wait. I had a date.

I rang Emma and told her that unfortunately my mate's squash racquet had broken and so we couldn't play anymore. As such, I was now available to come round for dinner after all if she so desired.

The rest is history as they say. I was falling in love. Truly, madly, deeply.

***

I'm not writing about any more games for this season as frankly football was substituted for a new, and even more wonderful passion. I still played for the staff football team. I still watched Match of the Day when I wasn't staying at Emma's, and even when I was there, she was quite happy for me to watch it. I already thought she was perfect, but now she was even more perfect.

Football seemed inconsequential somehow now. Man United won the Premier League again, much more easily this time, and Preston found it quite tough in their new higher division, but eventually finished a respectable 15th. Gary Peters had taken us about as far as we could get. I don't remember going to any more games that season at all.

The only other game I vaguely remember is the Cup Final which I always watched. I'd been out clubbing the night before and hadn't had much sleep really. I saw Roberto Di Matteo's goal after only 42 seconds, but then must have nodded off. At least I did see it though, unlike many people there who hadn't taken their seats for the match yet. Chelsea went onto get another in the second half to beat Middlesbrough 2-0, in what must have been a dull game. It certainly didn't keep me awake.

My life now consisted of work, clubbing with mates, and falling in love with my new girlfriend. I would also fall in love with Emma's daughter, Lottie. I was fully aware that my relationship with Emma would depend on how her daughter responded to me being in her life. She still went to stay over with her father every other weekend, which meant that Emma could come out clubbing with me too, but the more time I spent at Emma's, the more I fell in love with Lottie too, and the closer we would get.

I had basically got myself a ready-made family, with a dog included too. My year at work flew by, and as I was spending more and more time at Emma's, it became inevitable that I would move out of my flat, and in with her. It felt like the easiest and most natural decision I ever made.

Thankfully, my goalkeeper mate from all those years ago had finished his degree at Aberdeen University and had come down to live with us, making his bedroom behind the sofa in our front room. If I moved out, he would be able to have my room and I wouldn't be leaving Rob, my original flatmate, all by himself. It was a no-brainer.

So, at the end of my second year, I moved my very few possessions into Emma's flat and started the next phase of my life, a phase that is still going strong to this day.

Season 1997/98

Arsenal v Newcastle United

FA Cup Final

May 16th, 1998   Wembley Stadium

After moving in with Emma and even doing a bit of decorating to make the flat feel like ours, I had the whole summer holidays to spend with Lottie. Emma would still be working and rather than find childcare, we both realised that we already had some: me. Lottie and I would spend our days either at the local park and playground, or we would go into London and be tourists. I'd pack a little bag and put her in her buggy and off we would go. Both Emma and Lottie obviously trusted me and we had a wonderful summer.

The new school year loomed and we would have to find a nursery for Lottie as she was now nearly four years old. After we had shown her our preferred choice, which she loved too, she asked me if that meant she could call me daddy now. I didn't object. I basically was her dad now. I did everything a dad should do and loved her. I was in what some people may think of as a strange situation of being a dad before I had become a father, but to me it felt perfectly natural. I was the happiest I think I had ever been. I knew this was the life that I wanted and wanted to make sure it continued.

One evening after work, me and Lottie were sat on the sofa watching Scooby Doo, with Emma doing a bit of ironing, when it suddenly struck me that the way to ensure this happiness was to make it as difficult as possible for them to not be with me. I could do this by marrying Emma, then there would be a huge legal process for her to go through if she ever did want to get rid of me. With them in my life, my life felt complete. Without any thinking, without any planning, it suddenly popped into my head and out of my mouth, "Will you marry me next summer?" I had no ring, I was not on one knee, I didn't even have a cage full of doves to release when she immediately said yes.

To this day my "proposal" is a way for Emma to affectionately mock me. I know it wasn't romantic or minutely planned; it was purely instinctive and a little bit self-protective too. This ordinary scene on an ordinary school night was bliss to me, and if I could feel blissfully happy in this situation, then I simply wanted to carry on doing it for the rest of my life. The only problem was that she was still married to the wanker. Before we would be able to get married, she would have to get divorced.

With a goal to now fix on, the school year again flew by. Emma and Lottie by now had met my parents and they had fallen in love with both of them too. We spent a lovely Christmas with them and by Easter, Emma's divorce had come through. The wedding plans were also well on their way now. We also had to start thinking about which primary school Lottie would attend in September. The ones she was likely to be offered places in were all in Tottenham and they all had barbed wire on the tops of their fences.

Emma had heard about my childhood Up North and we suddenly realised that we could move up to Lancaster. The schools were not lined with barricades, and my parents would be there to help us. House prices were much cheaper and we would be able to give our daughter, as she now was, a much better childhood if we got out of London.

Even though it would mean moving 250 miles away from her mum, all her friends and her other family, Emma did not hesitate. It was the bravest decision she had ever made, but again, it felt like the most natural thing to do for our daughter. I'd just have to get a job now, in a school completely different to the one I had been teaching in for the last three years.

There were vacancies at schools I knew when I was growing up, schools that I had played football or rugby against, and after one unsuccessful interview in early May, I knew I had another opportunity the week after. The interview would be on the Friday before the Cup Final. I could bring Emma and Lottie and make a weekend of it. I would also be able to watch the Cup Final with mum and dad, just as I had when I was a few years older than Lottie now was.

We travelled up the night before and whilst I was out at my potential new school, being shown around very politely and then grilled by a panel of four senior teachers and governors, Emma, Lottie and my parents waited on tenterhooks. If I could get this job it would mean our dream of starting a new life as a family Up North would be able to happen.

I returned to my parents' house around mid-afternoon but still had not been told of the school's decision. We were waiting with bated breath now, but eventually the call came through and to everyone's huge relief and delight I had been successful. My dad even pulled me to one side, hugged me and had to wipe the tears away from his eyes. His prodigal son was returning, but this time with a little girl for him to dote on. He'd never experienced a daughter or granddaughter before, and he knew this was his chance to be a grandad to a granddaughter. He couldn't wait. He was more excited than me.

The following day I sat in my parents' front room, next to my future wife and daughter, watching Arsenal comfortably beat Newcastle 2-0 with goals from Marc Overmars and Nicholas Anelka. I'm not sure how much of the game was actually watched by my parents; they were transfixed on Lottie and had already bought her lots of presents to play with.

Instead of watching the game, my dad was having his hair put into pigtails, which looked like horns protruding from his balding head, whilst pretending to eat food made out of play dough. I say pretending, but I'm sure he did actually eat a fried egg that was offered to him by Lottie.

Arsenal won the Double that day, after having beaten Man United to the Premier League title. They had now joined the club of being double Double winners. This was the first time that United had lost the title because they had not been the best team. Back in 1995, Blackburn won it, but that was because Eric Cantona did not play for the second crucial part of the season. With Cantona, United were a better team than Blackburn.

He had rather bewilderingly retired from football the previous summer at the age of 30. He was always going to go out on his terms and no one else's, and so without Cantona, Arsenal proved that they were a better team than United.

As for Preston, Gary Peters, our manager who had got us promoted as Champions, left in January and was replaced by David Moyes, who started the job in a player/manager role. We would end up 15th again, exactly the same position as the previous year. Moyes would continue a strong tradition of Scottish managers and players at our club, going all the way back to Bill Shankly. He used the second half of the season to get to know his new role before we would make a concerted push for promotion the following season.

After spending a lovely weekend with my parents, we travelled back down to London knowing that our future was now set. All we had to do was find somewhere to live, get married, move 250 miles North, enrol Lottie into a primary school, and start new jobs. Easy peasy. And we'd have to fit all these minor details around the most important event of the summer: England had once again qualified for the World Cup, and we now had a potential new weapon, a certain 18-year-old called Michael Owen.

World Cup Finals France 1998

England v Argentina

June 30th, 1998   Stade Geoffroy-Guichard, St. Etienne

I wasn't able to watch the first game of our campaign against Tunisia as it was on a school afternoon. As it was exam season, I had been placed on invigilation duty that afternoon whilst the rest of the school all piled into the school hall where it was being shown on a big screen. I couldn't help knowing the score though as amidst the silence of the exam room, when Alan Shearer put us ahead, a huge roar went up from the hall, emanating around the whole school. The lads in front of me, all at their individual exam desks, doing a physics exam I think, all looked up from their papers and at each other. They too would rather have been in the hall watching the match with the other students and teachers rather than answering questions about forces and pressure.

As soon as the clock told us that time was up, the papers were collected in, much more quickly than usual, so we could all rush down to the hall and join in the fun. We at least got to see Paul Scholes score a fabulous second for England to get us off to a great start; the first time we had won our opening game of any tournament since Bryan Robson's 27 second goal against France all those years ago.

Our second game against Romania was much more conveniently played in the evening, but this time the game did not go to plan. We were 1-0 down with only about a quarter of an hour to go. There had been calls for Glenn Hoddle, our manager by now, to unleash Michael Owen much earlier, and he finally relented. The wonderkid came on and immediately grabbed an equaliser, latching onto a loose ball in the Romanian penalty area and firing it in.

We should have at least held on for the draw, if not gone on and won the game, but in the last minute of the game, Graeme Le Saux was not strong enough against the Romanian forward. He just stopped, clutching his face after an inadvertent arm had brushed against his hair, and the ball was poked home for a winner.

We would now have to beat Colombia in the final game to ensure second place in our group. But this would also mean that we would have to play against one of the group winners in the second-round knockout match, potentially Argentina, the first time we would have met since the cheating bastard Maradona knocked us out twelve years earlier.

My mate, whose parents' villa I had stayed at two summers ago was now living in London, and he suggested we all go into London to watch the game in a packed bar. I was still not a fan of being surrounded by drunken people who rarely even watched football, particularly when it was such a crucial game, but it turned out to be a good decision.

We had a great night, watching David Beckham score what would become one of his trademark free kicks to put us 2-0 up. My mate decided to flash his cash and bought champagne for everyone in the bar at half time. We all had a great second half, even though not much else happened on the field. England won comfortably in the end and set up the match that we all wanted and yet dreaded; England v Argentina.

It would prove to be another case of serious PMT for the whole country. Not only was it Pre-Match Tension, but it was also a case of

285

Post-Maradona Trauma. But with Alan Shearer still being a goal machine, and young players like David Beckham and Michael Owen firing on all cylinders, I was quietly confident we could get revenge.

On the night of the match I played squash against my flash Champagne Charlie mate to try and ease the PMT, and we then went back to our flat. Emma and I got Lottie into bed early that night and settled down with my mate in front of the television with a definite sense of trepidation. This game could go either way.

It seemed to be going the wrong way after only six minutes when Argentina got a penalty and The Angel Gabriel, Gabriel Batistuta, converted; only just though as David Seaman almost saved it. Only four minutes later Michael Owen showed how adept he was at using similar tactics to Argentina when he felt the slightest brush in the penalty area and instantly went down. The referee believed he had been fouled and pointed to the spot. Shearer slammed the ball home with much more aplomb than Batistuta had done. Game back on. And then something extraordinary happened; the pizzas we had ordered turned up.

Just as I was getting out of my seat to answer the door and take delivery of the pizzas, Beckham played a through ball towards Michael Owen who was only just inside the Argentinian half. As Owen got closer to the goal, I got closer to the television, and the pizza delivery guy got closer to our window from which he could see the television. As Owen finished off a truly wondrous goal, three of us inside the room and one guy standing outside were all leaping around in unison, partly in disbelief as to what we had all just seen. Michael Owen was a boy, and he had just skipped past men as if he was still a kid in the playground.

However, by our third slice of pizza, Argentina were level again. Just before half time, a beautifully deceptive free kick allowed Javier Zanetti to make it 2-2. The game was still anyone's and was there for the taking. We had played some brilliant football, and if we continued in the same vein, then we would win this time. That is as long as one of our best players didn't get himself sent off for the most petulant and stupid of offences.

We all know what happened as David Beckham was lying on the ground following a heavy challenge from Diego Simeone. And we all know that we would have won the game if he had remained on the pitch. Some people moaned that he should not have been sent off for such an innocuous kick, but none other than Zinedine Zidane had been sent off earlier in the tournament for a similarly stupid thing, and so Beckham's red card was warranted.

The game changed completely at that moment. It had been the most pulsating game before his sending off, but now it became a case of backs to the wall defending, and hopefully we would get a chance from a set piece.

The game entered extra time and our plan was working. Sol Campbell even managed to score from a set piece to send us, and all the players into disbelieving raptures. None of us, players included, realised in our celebrations that the goal had been disallowed for some reason and play had already restarted. As we were still all celebrating and then confusedly wondering why the ball wasn't on the centre spot, Argentina went straight up the other end and almost scored themselves.

It became as tense a period of extra time as the semi-final matches against the Germans of 1990 and 1996. And like those two matches, the game would go to penalties. And like those two games, there would be a fall guy for England. After Hernan Crespo's effort had been brilliantly saved by Seaman, Paul Ince showed maybe why he hadn't volunteered instead of Gareth Southgate in Euro 96 as his penalty was also saved.

No more penalties were missed by either team, meaning that this tournament's fall guy was to be David Batty. The keeper guessed right and saved it to knock us out yet again on a penalty shootout. Batty, Yorkshire through and through, was not going to show any emotion, but I'm sure he was feeling just as gutted as everyone else.

But maybe not as gutted as David Beckham was feeling. He felt, quite rightly, that he had let not just himself down, but his team mates and the whole country down. He had been a very naughty boy, but the vilification he suffered in the press, some of it obscene to be honest, was not justified.

That game, even in defeat, would be the last time I felt any real thrill watching England at a major tournament. It was one of those games that even when we lost, as we had done in 1986, 1990 and 1996, you knew that you had just witnessed a game that would stay with you forever. England showed not just grit and determination, but also real flair and skill. We went down fighting, playing as if it mattered just as much to the team as it did to the fans. Yes we've had memorable moments since, but never really at the World Cup or European Championships. Not for me anyway. But that night in St. Etienne was truly memorable.

At least Argentina would go out in the next round to one of the most beautiful pieces of skill ever, Dennis Bergkamp controlling, turning and finishing off a 40-yard pass in the final minute of their quarter-final. Even if we had won that game against Argentina, we would never have won the tournament. It was destined to be France's, and particularly Zidane's tournament, just as it had been Maradona's in 1986.

Despite another failure in footballing terms, I could now concentrate on the second most important event of the summer, and console myself with the fact that I was about to marry the most beautiful woman in the world.

Season 1998/99

Luton Town v Preston North End

August 15th, 1998   Kenilworth Road

As no one could find any just cause as to why we should not be lawfully joined together in matrimony (Emma's divorce had gone through without a hitch), the wedding went very smoothly. My parents had kindly offered to take Lottie back to theirs whilst we went on a honeymoon, and even though it was doing us a huge favour, allowing us to enjoy a couple of Greek Islands in matrimonial bliss, they secretly wanted her all to themselves. They had a great time whilst we were sipping our drinks overlooking the beautiful bay, almost a lagoon, of the island of Sifnos, before heading to the busier and more vibrant island of Paros.

The new season had kicked off whilst we were away, David Moyes' first full season as Preston manager getting off to a great start with a 3-0 win at home to York. Our first away match would be a couple of days after we arrived back in England. Seeing as we still had a few days before we would be reunited with Lottie, I felt like spoiling my new bride and thought it would be a lovely romantic gesture to take her for a day out in Luton. Ever the romantic. How could she refuse such an offer?

So off we went in our new, third-hand little car to watch Preston play at another dump of a ground. Another one to be ticked off the list for me, but this would be the first time Emma had ever gone to a game not at White Hart Lane. She had been to a few games when she was younger, but she had never been to such a ground as Kenilworth Road. She also had never been abused by Southerners before, but seeing as we would be sitting in the away end, she was now fair game for abuse from the Bedfordshire fans.

The game ended 1-1 but the main incident was when Michael Appleton got sent off for a high challenge. The Luton fans spontaneously burst out into the chant of "You Dirty Northern

Bastards" at us Preston fans, before we responded with the usual riposte of "You Soft Southern Wankers".

It must have felt very bizarre for my wife to be called such names. She was less northern than any of the people she was sitting amongst, and more southern than the people we were admonishing for their geographical positioning in the country, as well as their self-pleasuring tendencies. She had never been further north, before she met me of course, than Luton's rivals Watford, and here she was being called northern by a few thousand people who lived further north than where she had lived all her life. It was a great introduction into the weird world of lower league football fans, but funnily enough she has never been to a football match with me since.

As soon as the game finished we got the hell out of Dodge City and headed back Down South as all the other Preston fans headed Up North. We had planned a last clubbing night in London with friends before we would have to start packing and preparing to move up to the enlightened land of The North. The thought of leaving the urban sophistication of Luton (and London of course) behind and moving up to a place where no one knew what a saveloy was, or where Pie and Mash was not considered a delicacy may well have entered her head at that point.

But to my everlasting gratitude, she rose above these concerns and at the end of August, within the space of five days, we drove 250 miles, with our dog and daughter almost imprisoned by items that hadn't fitted in the van that dad had offered to drive for us, moved into our new house, started a new job in a new school, whilst Lottie started primary school. It was bit hectic to say the least, but I could now say that my wife and daughter were officially Dirty Northern Bastards just like me. All I had to do now was change those accents of theirs. Bloody cockneys.

Preston North End v Arsenal

FA Cup Third Round

January 4ᵗʰ, 1999   Deepdale

One of the best things about being back home was that I could resume going to Deepdale with my dad on a regular basis. In amongst settling into our new lives and what seemed like endless decorating, we went to most games and watched our team look as though they had a chance of promotion again.

David Moyes had turned us into a resilient team with a touch of lower league flair. Our biggest test came when we managed to get through to the third round of the Cup, and to my absolute delight were drawn at home to the cup holders themselves, the mighty Arsenal.

Their team had just won the Double, and had two World Cup winners in their side, along with one of the most elegant players I had ever seen play, in Dennis Bergkamp. Throw in the England keeper and most of the England defence, along with a Dutch winger who had electrifying pace, and you've got a half decent opposition. And Ray Parlour was in the Arsenal team too. Why should we have been worried?

It would be a brilliant test of just how far we had come since we got promoted. I knew we would get beaten, but I wanted to at least give a good account of ourselves, especially as it would be live on the television (well, live on Sky) and so a few hundred thousand more people would be able to see what we were like too.

Deepdale was now on its way to becoming the wonderful stadium it is today. In fact it was exactly halfway there. In 1995, the magnificent Sir Tom Finney Stand had replaced the old West Stand and Pavilion, where me and dad mostly used to watch, and we had just opened up the old Spion Kop's replacement, The Bill Shankly

Kop. Both of these legends' faces had been depicted with different coloured seats, and the ground, from one angle, looked beautiful.

From the other angle it still looked tired and dated. Opposition fans used to sing "You've only got two stands", and frankly we couldn't argue. Saying that, most fans of League One clubs back then were as impressed as we were with what was happening at Deepdale. Our ground was becoming one of those grounds players love to play at, but only when they were facing a certain way. Even though the facilities and the view were much better in these wonderful new stands, it was nice to be in one of the old parts of the ground just so we could admire the new ones properly.

The night Arsenal came to town, me and dad had tickets in the new Bill Shankly Kop, near to the top of the great man's right ear if I remember rightly. We had never seen these new stands as full as they were that night. Everyone wanted to see the great Arsenal players, as well as our own slightly less great players. And like me, I'm sure that everyone else was just as disappointed when the teams were announced and there would be no sight of David Seaman, Nicolas Anelka, and worst of all, no Dennis Bergkamp. But at least Ray Parlour would be playing. Without these players we would obviously be able to beat them 4-0 instead of just 3-0.

To everyone's amazement, we were halfway to four after only 21 minutes. It could possibly have been even more after Lee Dixon had to clear off the goal line. The two we did get though were scored by Kurt Nogan and his face, just like ours, was disbelief personified. We were 2-0 up against the Premier League Champions and FA Cup holders. But we'd just made the Gunners slightly annoyed and they went up a gear or two to show their real ballistic powers.

They crucially pulled one back on the stroke of half time, and at that point we all probably knew that the second half would be much different. We didn't help ourselves though after David Ayres got sent off for bringing down Marc Overmars. Ayres had no chance against the flying Dutchman. He was like Dash from The Incredibles and the only way to stop him was by tripping him up. Down to ten men, the inevitable happened and we conceded three more to lose 4-2 in the end.

Despite the defeat, we had done what I hoped we could do; to impress a few people and show off half a great stadium, as well as giving the best team in the country a right good scare. They still beat us convincingly and I dread to think what the score might have been had they played a full-strength side, Bergkamp included. But it would have been nice to find out.

We grew in confidence for the rest of the season, and eventually qualified fairly comfortably for the play-offs, finishing in 5th place, meaning that we would be facing our would-be nemesis, Gillingham. They proved to be our bogey team yet again, as we could only draw with them at home, and as we all watched on a big screen at Deepdale, lose 1-0 at The Priestfield Stadium.

Soft Southern Wankers.

We had now lost four times in the play-offs. If we'd have beaten Gillingham we would have had the chance of stopping Manchester City from making their way back to the Premier League. Whatever did happen to the other team from Manchester?

Preston North End v Bristol Rovers

February 6th, 1999   Deepdale

If Preston were having another nearly season, then Manchester United would have not only the best season in their history, but also the best season any English team would ever have. I pick this rather inconsequential game not because Preston fought hard for a 2-2 home draw, but because as me and dad were driving home from Deepdale listening to Sports Report, James Alexander Gordon read out one of the most remarkable and eye-catching (well, the aural version of eye-catching anyway) results I had ever heard: Nottingham Forest 1, Manchester United 8.

On the old vide-printer on Grandstand, if there was a score which seemed unlikely, then after the score the number of goals would be written in words in brackets, just so we didn't think there had been some sort of misprint. That old vide-printer would definitely have written (eight) after that score.

It was just one of those results you never hear. Yes, on a few occasions, you hear huge home wins read out by the now dearly departed James Alexander Gordon, such as Man United's 9-0 thrashing of Ipswich in 1995, but the inflection of his voice this time let us all know that it would be an expected away win for United. No one expected the word (eight) to follow.

I could have picked any one of many remarkable results for United in this now fabled season. I could even have used their opening weekend fixture where another of David Beckham's free kicks rescued a point at home to Leicester in the final minute. This was the first game he had played since his antics in the World Cup and he at least redeemed himself that day with the United fans, but certainly not with every other England fan around the country.

I could have picked any of the three defeats they had by Christmas, particularly the 3-0 defeat away to Arsenal where they looked outclassed on the day. Or I could have picked either of the 3-3 draws against Barcelona in the group stage of the Champions League, both games being almost mesmeric to any football fans, not just of the United persuasion.

I could have picked their FA Cup fourth round win over Liverpool, where they were 1-0 down with only two minutes to go but still won 2-1, with Ole Gunnar Solskjaer getting the winner in injury time. This game at least gets an honourable mention as it would almost be a practice for what would happen in their final game of the season.

Maybe I should have picked their FA Cup Semi-Final Replay (the last ever one) where Roy Keane got sent off, Peter Schmeichel saved a penalty and Ryan Giggs showed off his hairy chest after scoring one of the greatest goals of any season, by any player, in any era.

The two Champions League ties, now known as "The Italian Job", should also get a mention. After knocking out Inter Milan in the quarter- finals, they then went 2-0 down in Turin in the semi-final second leg, a game they had to win, or at least draw 2-2. They not only drew the game, but went on to win it, dumping out the mighty Juventus.

The fact is that from Christmas they did not lose another game all season, in any competition. They'd been knocked out of the League Cup by Spurs in early December, but they had bigger games and bigger competitions to concentrate on. By Christmas they were ready to make their assault on all three competitions they cared about, and this game against Forest in early February showed just how rampant they were becoming.

The match itself looked like it was going to be a close game, United leading 2-1 at half time, after a spate of early goals by both teams. I'm not sure what happened in the dressing room at half time, but United just blew their opponents away in the second half. Dwight Yorke and Andy Cole, who were becoming the SAS of United, scored one more each, and everyone wondered which one would get their hat-trick first. The answer was neither.

The Baby-Faced Assassin, Ole Gunnar Solskjaer was put on in place of Dwight Yorke after 72 minutes, if only to give him some game time, and was told to just play the ball around conservatively and see the game out. He took no notice of this advice.

He'd been on the pitch for eight (eight) minutes, before he obviously thought, sod this I fancy some goals. Within the space of the next ten or twelve minutes he scored not just a hat-trick, but four goals. It was as if he was scoring goals to ease the boredom, after having spent most of the match on the bench.

In that match there were only ten shots on target in the whole match, and nine of them went in. Solskjaer scored 44% of the goals that day in just 11% of the whole match time, there or thereabouts. No wonder my ears pricked up when I heard the result on the radio. United had laid down a marker for the rest of the season, and by now Ole Gunnar Solskjaer was getting a taste for late goals. It was a taste he would have to wait some time to enjoy again, not until the final seconds of the final game one evening in May, at a certain stadium in Barcelona.

Bayern Munich v Manchester United

Champions League Final

May 26th, 1999

Camp Nou, Barcelona

The eleven days between May 16th and May 26th, 1999 would be when Manchester United's team become a legendary one. They would do something that no other English team has done before, or since. In fact only three other clubs had done the same thing previously: The Lisbon Lions of Celtic were the first team to do it in 1967; the great Ajax team of the early 70s were the next, and their Dutch rivals PSV Eindhoven did it in 1988.

Only three teams have done it since: Jose Mourinho's Inter Milan team did it in 2010; Bayern Munich in 2013, and of course Barcelona have done it twice, under Luis Enrique in 2015, and also under Pep Guardiola in 2009, beating Man United in the Champions League Final to complete it. At the time United did it, I would firmly have said that it will never be repeated in England, but with Pep Guardiola around, then if anyone will do it again, then it'll be one of his teams, most probably the current Man City side.

As you can see, it's not easy to win a Continental Treble, but that is what Man United did in those eleven wonderful days for not just

United fans, but football fans everywhere (although I doubt Liverpool fans would agree). The memories that those eleven days created for anyone who watched the three games included will never fade. Not for me anyway.

It all started with United's final game of the Premier League season, at home to Spurs. The mathematics were simple; if they won, they would win the league; if they did not win and Arsenal won, then Arsenal would deny them the chance of this piece of history at the first hurdle. It was in United's hands.

But Spurs were not about to roll over, even if it meant they could hand their North London rivals the title. Spurs went 1-0 up and everyone started to get the jitters. But not David Beckham, who had endured abuse at every away ground he played at throughout the season. But in front of his adoring home fans, he curled in a lovely right foot shot just before half time and everyone could calm down a bit.

United, with steely determination running through their veins, forged on the banks of the River Clyde in Govan where Alex Ferguson had grown up, were not going to let this opportunity slip away from them. Andy Cole's delicate lob won them the game and the Premiership and everyone could get ready for the Cup Final six days later.

This match, on paper, looked to be the easiest of the lot, and proved to be exactly that. Teddy Sheringham and Paul Scholes got a goal in each half at Wembley to win yet another Double for United, and deny Alan Shearer his last ever chance of winning the FA Cup. Gary Lineker never fails to remind him of this missing piece of silverware, much to Shearer's annoyance. But then again neither has Gary won a Premier League title, nor any league title for that matter for any of the clubs he played for, including Barcelona.

Two down, one to go. The previous two games had been expected to be won. United had had a full-strength side available for both games, although Roy Keane did get injured early on at Wembley. But that just proved to be the catalyst for victory as Sheringham was the one who replaced him and scored almost immediately after coming on.

The Champions League Final against Bayern Munich was anybody's guess though. They had already drawn twice with each other in the group stages, but this time United would be without the already suspended and now injured Keane, and also would miss the suspended Paul Scholes. Half of their midfield had been taken away from them. This probably pushed Bayern into the favourite's slot. Just about.

Nicky Butt came in for Roy Keane, and Jesper Blomqvist played wide left, which meant that Ryan Giggs was on the right, in an unnatural position for him. David Beckham had also been pushed more centrally which was not his favoured role. For the whole of that season, United had been as close to a finely tuned machine as you could get, each player knowing their role perfectly and how their cog would make the whole machine work.

That night in Barcelona, there was a sense of United trying to fit square pegs into round holes, and they looked completely disjointed. This lack of cohesion led to Bayern taking the lead early on with a free kick from the edge of the area which left Schmeichel statuesque on his line.

Bayern had so many chances to put the game out of United's reach, hitting what seemed like every bit of woodwork available to them, and peppering the United goal constantly. United on the other hand created no real chances at all, and those that they did create were not even half chances.

In almost desperation, Sheringham and Solskjaer were sent on and the Norwegian almost scored with his very first touch. Well, he got a header on target at least which forced the Bayern keeper into making a meaningful save at last. Half chances, and even some that were nearer to three-quarter chances, started to be created, as Bayern simply could not kill the game off. Even Big Ron Atkinson, who was co-commentating that night with Clive Tyldesley, was becoming an oracle. "If they can equalise, and I'm not betting against them, I think they'll win this," were what turned out to be very accurate and almost prophetic words. Ferguson and his team were also thinking the same thing.

United were still only one goal down. If they could stay within touching distance, Alex Ferguson had instilled the belief into his team that they would always get one chance. It turned out to be two. Three minutes of added time were signalled and it was now time for even more desperate measures. Peter Schmeichel went up for a corner to at least cause confusion in the box, which he certainly did. A sliced clearance, a hopeful shot from Giggs and there was Edward Sheringham to put the ball in. Even his shot was not cleanly struck, but it still crept in. "Name on the trophy!"

The never-say-die mindset which Ferguson had hammered into his players, right from the beginning of the season when David Beckham had rescued a point against Leicester, would now put them in the driving seat. They had been in ominous positions throughout the whole season, but had come back from the dead so many times that they made Lazarus look like he needed more practice.

Once they scored, we all knew that they would go onto win it, we just didn't expect it would be so soon. We were all just trying to mentally prepare for extra time, but United wanted it over and done with. Bayern were now mentally, emotionally and physically spent. Another Beckham corner, another Sheringham flick, and there was little Ole to put the ball in.

Clive Tyldesley said in commentary that "nobody will ever win a European Cup Final more dramatically than this," and I completely agree with him. United should have been beaten that night. They should have been not only dead, but buried. Not just six feet under, but sixty feet under. But they still won.

The irony is that after the season they had had, in which they had played some of the best football ever played, their performance in the final match of the season was one of their worst. But they still won.

I certainly had never seen a game like it. I doubt many other people had either. Alex Ferguson summed the chaos, the confusion, the bitten nails, the anguish, the faltering hope, the relief, and ultimately the glory up in one fantastically simple phrase: "Football, bloody hell!" We all knew exactly what he meant.

***

The day after, I returned home from school and was watching the United team parade their three trophies through Manchester. What that team achieved changed their lives and the lives of so many fans. I called my wife to see what time she would need picking up from the station, and at that moment she changed my life too. Again. I was already a dad, but now I was going to be a father.

Part Three

Grandad and Me

2000-2019

During the previous twenty seasons or so, before I became a father, I could remember many things about most games, and could easily recount each season chronologically, which of course is what I have just done. If I had to pick a specialist subject on "Mastermind", then it would probably be either FA Cup Finals of the 80s and 90s, or World Cups of the same period.

If such a topic came up on "Pointless", I would be confident of getting quite a few pointless answers. As a boy and a young man, my mind had always seemed to be able to recall pointless information. My wife certainly seems to think that it's pointless anyway.

However, as I have got older, my memories are not quite as vivid. On certain games anyway. Maybe the fact that I became a father made my memory go a bit hazy. Lack of sleep tends to do that.

Maybe it is the fact that back then my life was constantly changing. Each year was different. My brain could take in much more detail then and now perhaps it has become saturated with pointless details. There's only so much it will retain now as it's got quite full.

Maybe it is the fact that I have lived in the same house for over twenty years now, and have watched games in the same front room. When I was a kid, we were forever moving house. By the time I left for university, I had lived in seven different houses, and my memories are sparked off because I remember which front room I was in and which television I watched the games on.

Or maybe it's because each year now does not feel that different from all the others. I remember things through my kids rather than just me. Their lives are changing constantly whereas mine has remained fairly constant. I've just got on with being a dad, a husband and a teacher, probably in that order. I've watched my kids grow up into lovely young people who I am immensely proud of, and my wife might even say that we've got on quite well for over twenty years now too. I don't use football matches as reference points as much anymore. My kids provide these for me.

I've still religiously watched every Cup Final and World Cup, but the pinpoint accuracy is no longer there. As a result, I won't be chronicling each and every season, just recalling key moments and key games, starting with Preston's amazing rise to the highest position I had ever seen them in. I had already seen them at their lowest, and now it was about time things were different.

I'd like to think my son played his part; after all, he'd been named after Tom Finney.

Preston North End v Millwall

April 29th, 2000   Deepdale

When I say that my son was named after the great Tom Finney, it wasn't completely true. Mostly true, but not completely. Once we had found out that we were going to be having a boy, another boy in a long line of boys on my side of the family, thoughts turned to what we should call him.

Our daughter Lottie was, at the time, a big fan of Rugrats, the cartoon from Nickelodeon, and I would spend many hours curled up on the sofa with her as she watched this sweet little cartoon series. Her favourite character was the baby named Tommy Pickles, so when we asked Lottie her opinions as to what her little baby brother should be called, she naturally said Tommy.

I was instantly in agreement with her as I could claim that we were naming our son after Preston's greatest ever player, and not some freaky looking baby who despite still being in nappies, could converse very well indeed. His name even gave me an excuse to chat football with one of the guys in the operating theatre who helped to deliver my son.

He had proved to be a real pain in coming out (well, not for me anyway), and had to be delivered by Caesarean section. Whilst I was holding Emma's hand and definitely not looking over the other side of the sheet that was thankfully put up just above her belly, the very friendly nurse had enquired as to what his name might be and I mentioned how I was a Preston fan so Tom seemed appropriate. The nurse, who turned out to be a Man City fan, chatted away with me for the next few minutes about both clubs' fortunes, whilst my wife was being cut open and our Tom was being brought into the world.

Tom was born two weeks after the dawn of not just a new century, but a new millennium. It most definitely felt like a new dawn for me. As soon as I was ushered into a room, with Tom in my arms, whilst my wife was being stitched up, that new dawn completely overwhelmed me. I held him and looked at him with tears streaming down my face.

I had already become a dad, but now I was a father. I had never experienced Lottie as a baby, and definitely not as a newborn, but with Tom in my arms I could not control any of my emotions. The relief and love I felt was the strongest emotion I had ever felt, and probably will ever feel. I was in a bubble and nothing could pop it. Nothing seemed to matter anymore. Whatever happened in life, I would always have him and the memory of that first feeling as I held him.

I didn't care about anything else apart from him and my family. I certainly didn't care that Preston were live on Sky that night, away against Stoke. I didn't care that we lost 2-1. I didn't care that this would be only our third league defeat of the season. I didn't care that we had just missed the chance of going top of the table. It all just seemed superfluous.

The bubble eventually broke once I returned to work and the real hard work of being a parent kicked in. I also returned to my senses and realised just how close my team were to getting promoted. Again.

After reaching the play-offs the previous season, and losing for the fourth time, we realised that our best chance of promotion was to go up automatically, preferably as Champions. And that is exactly what happened. I was convinced that the birth of my son, who after all had most definitely been named after Tom Finney the legendary footballer, and not a cartoon character, was my lucky charm. After his birth and the defeat to Stoke, we would only lose three more games all season, and won thirteen.

By the time my 27th birthday arrived at the end of April, my first one with Tommy, Preston had already won the league. The team included, among others, Sean Gregan as captain, Graham Alexander, Mark Rankine, Jon Macken and Michael Jackson (no not that one). We were already seven points clear with only two games left to play. As for the details of the match, I don't remember anything. I hadn't been going to as many matches since January, preferring to spend as much time with my boy as possible. But I still wanted, or more likely needed a break occasionally, and as this match was the closest to my birthday I deserved a break, especially as Preston were going to be presented with the League One trophy.

But, as I said earlier, fatherhood has a knack of fuzzing your memories up, and I do not remember anything about the game at all; the result, the score, who scored, if anybody scored at all. Apparently we won 3-2 so it must have been a cracking game. The most important thing was that my lucky charm, my boy Tom, had made it all possible. His luck would continue all the way up to the final match of the following season too. That's my boy.

England v Germany

World Cup Qualifier

October 7th, 2000   Wembley Stadium

This would be the last ever game at Wembley Stadium, before it would be completely demolished and replaced with a shiny new one. However, before I get all dewy eyed, there was one final Cup Final to be played there.

A week or so after Preston had lifted the League One trophy as Champions, Aston Villa played Chelsea, and for the life of me I cannot remember a single thing about the game. As I said earlier, this may have had something to do with my lack of sleep, but I doubt whether anyone who does not support either of the two teams remembers anything about it either. In fact, I wouldn't be surprised if many people who were actually at the game couldn't recall anything either.

I just remember that Chelsea won it 1-0 and it was dull. The weather may well have been dull too; it would have been appropriate for such a dreary game. It was as though Wembley was in mourning for itself; as if it wanted to be remembered for all its past glories already.

I've mentioned every Cup Final since 1980 now, and I promise that this will be the last one I do mention after this chapter, well apart from the latest one between Man City and Watford. As alluded to earlier, if someone had given me a year between 1980 and 1999, I would easily be able to tell you the two teams, the score, the scorers, what times the goals were scored, and a range of varied and interesting facts about each game. But since then I will struggle to do the same.

Since the new millennium, the FA Cup has been won by just seven clubs. Apart from the odd rogue years when Wigan and Portsmouth won, only Arsenal, Liverpool, Chelsea and both Manchester clubs have won it. I only remember the Portsmouth win because I had just walked up and down Helvellyn on my mate's stag do. We had been trying to recreate a day when we were all 17 or 18 when we walked up the mountain for the first time together and had an awesome day out. In 2008, our day out was not so great. The weather was misty and gloomy and we got back down and into the pub to watch the match just as the weather became even more wet and horrible.

I vaguely remember Wigan's goal to beat Man City, and I don't think any football fan will ever forget Steven Gerrard's wonder strike in the 2006 Final. I also remember that smaller teams like Cardiff, Hull and Millwall have also featured somewhere in the last twenty seasons. And Stoke. Can't forget Stoke of course. But the FA Cup has lost its unpredictability, at least as far as the final goes. The odd odd result occurs every now and then, but basically one of five teams always wins it.

I know the new Wembley is a wonderful stadium, with world class facilities. I know the gleaming arch looks more sleek and modern than the two, rather militaristic towers, but maybe I just miss the old stadium, as far as Cup Finals go anyway. Maybe it's because the time of kick off has changed and that the stadium is always used for the semi-finals too. I don't know what it is, maybe a combination of lots of different things, but the FA Cup Final does not excite me as much as it used to do.

The old stadium provided so many boyhood memories for millions of us, and it was a shame that its last ever final was such a damp squib. But not as damp as the last ever match there.

England would start their qualifying campaign for the 2002 World Cup Finals with one last game at Wembley. It would be against our fiercest rivals Germany, who would come over here and perform a classic case of smash and grab.

The weather was miserable, with Wembley now almost willing to be put out of its misery. Kevin Keegan was ready to be put out of his misery too. He had taken over as England manager after Glenn Hoddle's sacking for rather dubious comments about reincarnation, and only just steered us to Euro 2000. We scraped into a play-off position and then needed to beat Scotland over two legs. We nearly messed this up too, managing a solid 2-0 win at Hampden, but then only scraping through after the Scots beat us 1-0 at Wembley.

Once at the tournament, we got off to a flier, going 2-0 up against Portugal before inexplicably losing it 3-2. We did manage to beat Germany, who were going through the worst spell I can ever remember for their national team. Then we lost to Romania and we were out, along with Germany. But Germany did something about their predicament. We just carried on believing that Kevin Keegan's brand of attacking play and heart on the sleeve patriotism would be enough to get us out of our rather dire situation.

I've got every respect for Keegan as a man and a player, he was one of the greatest our country has ever produced, but as a manager, he was simply not good enough. Newcastle should have won the Premiership in 1996. End of. No other manager would let such a huge lead slip from their grasp. With England he was just as bad, and he knew that he wasn't the man for the job after this game. I think we all already knew that though.

On paper, England still had a really good team, despite Alan Shearer's retirement from England duty after Euro 2000. Beckham, Scholes, Seaman, Adams, Neville and Owen all played in this game. And Martin Keown. We should have been able to beat a poor German team which was "in transition" shall we say. But after Dietmar Hamann scored with a long-range free kick after just 14 minutes, we never looked like scoring. The game was another heart stopper, but not because of the sheer excitement being too much for us, but because it was so crushingly boring that our hearts just couldn't be bothered to carry on any more.

We lost 1-0 and as Keegan trudged after his team of superstar failures down the tunnel, fans shouted abuse at him. I hope it wasn't anything personal because he did not deserve that, but I'm sure these fans were questioning in not too polite a manner whether or not Keegan had any clue whatsoever what he was doing in this job. He obviously agreed with them and resigned soon after. It summed the whole match up; dismal failure. Another completely unfitting way to say goodbye to Wembley.

Once Wembley was finally put out of its misery and knocked down, England would enter a new era. An era of travelling around the country and playing at different grounds, like a boyband on tour. And for this new era, we would need someone new; someone with bold, creative ideas, someone with any ideas actually. Someone who did not even need to be English any more. Someone who came from the land of Sweden; someone called Sven.

Preston North End v Birmingham City

Championship Play-Off Semi-Final, Second Leg

May 17ᵗʰ, 2001   Deepdale

As I said earlier, the good luck which my son had brought to Preston's fortunes continued. We were now in the highest division I'd ever seen us in since my very first season watching Preston, and had brought in another very useful striker in David Healy. We would end up at the dizzying heights of fourth. Fourth! Our first season in the division below the Premiership was maybe a bit of a fluke; we still couldn't beat our bogey team Gillingham, losing 4-0 in Kent and only drawing 0-0 at Deepdale, but we did beat Wolves, Palace, Burnley, Norwich and Sheffield United that season, all of whom are now Premier League teams.

Our fourth-place finish meant that we would need to beat Birmingham in order to reach not Wembley, but the Millennium Stadium in Cardiff, which was the new temporary home of the play-offs and Cup Finals.

With our new Alan Kelly Town End stand in the process of being built ("We've nearly got three stands!") our luck continued even then, winning 2-1 at home after losing 1-0 at St. Andrew's. David Healy had put us one up to make the tie level before we conceded on the hour mark to make it all square again on aggregate.

We even missed a penalty, Graham Alexander hitting the bar from the spot in what was for him his first ever failure as a penalty taker. He was always Mr. Dependable but he chose the wrong night to miss his first ever penalty for us. The luck seemed to have run out but then Birmingham had a shot which trickled along the goal line but crucially did not go in. Our luck was back and from our own penalty area, we pushed forward and got the goal which would take the game into extra time, Mark Rankine latching onto a save which hadn't been held by their keeper.

We had chances to win the game outright but just couldn't finish it off. Thankfully the away goals rule did not count in domestic competitions and so our ticket to Cardiff would have to be decided with a penalty shootout, the first one I had ever seen live, and certainly the first one I had ever seen at Deepdale. But before the penalties would begin there was something I'd never seen before either.

Trevor Francis, the Birmingham manager at the time, threw his dummy out of his pram when he didn't get his own way about which end the penalties would be taken at. He wanted them to be at the end where there were no fans at all due to the demolished stand, and he even led his players off the pitch in a right old hissy-fit.

Francis was famously managed by Brian Clough at Nottingham Forest and one of Clough's most famous quotes is about how disagreements would be resolved. He told of how he would sit down with a player, "talk about it for twenty minutes, and then we decide I was right."

Francis realised that he was in the same situation again and decided all along that the referee was right; the penalties would be taken in front of the Preston fans in the Bill Shankly Kop after all. Graham Alexander made amends for his miss in normal time by scoring the most emphatic of opening penalties. Birmingham missed two, we missed one and it was then up to Paul McKenna to use his hypnotic powers to score our last penalty and take us through to Cardiff. We were all mesmerised anyway.

And so in our first season back in the second division out of four, we were now just 90 minutes away from the promised land of the Premier League. One game away from glory. One game away from being back in the top flight, somewhere we had not been since 1961 when my dad was just fourteen. All we had to do was beat Bolton, now managed by our former player and one-time manager, Big Sam Allardyce.

Mum and Dad both came round to my house with Tommy in his tiny little PNE kit which dad had bought for him. However, we must have used up all our allotted luck as we were soundly beaten 3-0 on the day. I don't think I ever really expected to win. We were completely new to this kind of situation, and Bolton back then had a very strong, powerful side who played in the same manner their manager always did.

They steam rollered us and deserved to win. They would actually start the following season in the Premiership with three straight wins, and be top of the whole league for a short while, before ending up 16th. Their brief spell at the top included a 5-0 win against Leicester on the opening day, and a 2-1 win against Liverpool, who had just won the FA Cup, League Cup and UEFA Cup to give them their own less prestigious version of the Treble.

Even though we had lost (now for the fifth time in play-offs) and were all disappointed, we had to keep pinching ourselves. At the start of the season we would have been happy to just survive. To get not only into the play-offs, but actually into the final was a huge achievement. It was a nearly season which we could all accept.

Only fifteen seasons ago we had been almost kicked out of the league and here we were, one game away from being a part of the richest league in the world. We'd had a taste and we wanted more. But so would our manager David Moyes.

Everton came calling for him the following season and off he went. No one blamed him. He had been a fantastic player and manager for us and would go onto do greater things, until he was chosen by Alex Ferguson to be his successor at Old Trafford. Then it all went a bit tits up really.

Germany v England

World Cup Qualifier

September 1st, 2001 Olympiastadion, Munich

And so Sven from Sveden became the first ever non-English manager of the England national football team. After Howard Wilkinson had overseen the team draw 0-0 in Finland, Sven Goran Eriksson took up his post in January 2001, and instantly had an impact. He won the return tie against Finland along with victories over Albania and Greece. But these were games we were expected to win whoever was the manager.

It would not be until our game away to Germany that Sven would become universally loved and lauded. Before the game we were still six points behind Germany with the Germans having played one more game. Only the winners of the group would qualify without the need of a play-off and so if we could win this game then qualification would be a distinct possibility again. And boy did we win it.

England's team would be in the early stages of what should have been their golden years, filled with top quality, maybe even world-class players. Seaman, Cole, Neville, Ferdinand and Campbell at the back, with a midfield of Scholes, Beckham, Gerrard and Nicky Barmby. Up front would be Michael Owen, who had just won the Ballon d'Or after being voted the world's best player. Partnering him was someone who never quite managed the same feat: Emile Heskey, but even he looked world-class that night in Munich. Well, almost.

Things got off to a bad start after we went behind after only six minutes, but then we played the most brilliant 80 minutes of football I'd ever seen an England team play, even better than our thrashing of Holland at Euro 96. And this time it was in the Germans' own backyard.

Owen equalised after 12 minutes and the game remained quite tight until Steven Gerrard unleashed what would become one of his trademark right foot piledrivers just before half time to make it 2-1 to us. It was possibly his best ever goal for England, especially as it was his first ever England goal too.

We came out all guns blazing after half time. Maybe Sven had given them all a personal massage, but whatever he did or said, it worked. Owen got another soon after the restart, and then on 66 minutes he completed his hat-trick. He was showing the whole world why he had been given the Ballon d'Or, and he was still only 21 years old. Even Emile Heskey joined in the fun, slotting home a fifth goal to make the final score Germany 1 England 5.

Liverpool had provided the scorers of all five goals but the whole country went Sven crazy, with headlines like "Svennies From Heaven" capturing the mood perfectly. Even Ant n Dec released a song with the scoreline as its chorus. Let's just say that the song was not quite as good as the football though.

It really was a remarkable result, considering that just less than a year before, we had been humiliated at home by Germany. But Sven had changed us. We were now playing with more intelligence, more freedom, more creativity, and definitely more confidence. Another win against Albania four days later meant that we would only need a draw in our final game against Greece to qualify.

If the game in Munich had been a great team performance, then the game against Greece would see the greatest individual performance by one player that I have ever witnessed. But before that, David Beckham would be involved in another ridiculous game of football, this time at White Hart Lane.

Tottenham Hotspur v Manchester United

September 29th, 2001

White Hart Lane

Dad made the mistake on his own wedding day. My brother did it for my first nephew's christening. My headteacher did it for a school Open Evening. And my brother-in-law did it for his wedding day: none of them checked the fixture list first.

My dad was berated by the rest of his family for allowing my mum to book their wedding on the first day of the season in 1968, causing them all to miss Preston's opening game.

I had to sneak out early from my nephew's christening just so I did not miss the first part of United's Treble extravaganza, when they beat Spurs to win the Premier League in May 1999.

My Headteacher had to change the date of the school Open Evening, where all the little primary school kids have a look around and see whether they want to grace us with their presence the following year. I'd warned him that if results went as expected, then one of England's key games at Euro 2012 would fall on the same night. Wisely I feel, he took my advice, otherwise we would have had a lot of grumpy kids and in particular, grumpy dads trailing around the school, asking their wives if they could go home yet.

I didn't make the same mistake. I made sure our wedding was slap bang at the end of July when any summer tournament would be finished, and the domestic season would not yet have started.

My brother-in-law, however, had his wedding six weeks into the season, in the middle of Tottenham, when Man United were in town. He annoyed not just his own side of the family, but also the Spurs supporting family of his future wife. Not only that, but the ceremony would take place whilst the game was on so nobody could even listen to it on the radio. This meant that the limousine journey to the reception would take the newly weds down Tottenham High Road

314

just after the game had finished, where lots of either angry or exuberant fans would be. Let's just say that it did not go well.

This wasn't just any old game between Spurs and United. At the end of September 2001 they played a game which has gone down in the annals of Premier League history. It has definitely gone down in the annals of our family history due not only to the bizarre freakish scoreline, but also the bizarre freakish weather that day in North London.

The wedding ceremony was to be held at a church in Tottenham, not far from where I moved in with Emma. The reception was to be held afterwards at a nearby restaurant with drinks and dancing next door in a function hall. Not much different from countless weddings that would be happening up and down the country that day. But this wedding would be held less than a mile from White Hart Lane, and Man United would have just claimed a very famous victory.

The events of that day started off pleasantly enough. The sun was shining and it was a beautiful day. As the guests were waiting for the ceremony to start and the blushing bride to arrive, the whole church was buzzing with the news that at half time, Spurs were 3-0 up against United, who had just claimed their third consecutive Premier League title. That feat had only been done three time before in the history of English football: Huddersfield in the 1920s, the great Arsenal side of Herbert Chapman in the 1930s, and the even greater Liverpool team of the early 1980s.

This was a huge deal for a church load of Spurs fans. I was not only the only northerner there, but I also had strong affections still for United. Thankfully, none of my fellow guests knew this and so I had to join in with the cockney banter about how the Champions from Up North were being taught a lesson in football by the more sophisticated Londoners.

The weather had suddenly turned and the clouds looked very heavy. Just as the bride's car arrived, the heavens opened, in an almost biblical way, but thankfully the bride had got inside the church before it really got going. She arrived on time. The groom looked deeply into her eyes. The vows were read.

I promise I am not embellishing this in any way, but literally at the point where the couple were saying "I will" to each other, there was the most almighty crack of thunder and the rain seemed to go up another notch. It was difficult to hear the ceremony as the rain battered the stained-glass windows. I thought they were going to be smashed at one point. The whole congregation looked around at each other then chuckled sheepishly.

Just as the happy couple were pronounced husband and wife, the rain stopped. We all followed them out into the churchyard and chatted about how lucky we were to have been inside the church when the torrential rain was falling. The conversations then suddenly turned as gloomy as the clouds that had just passed over, as the scoreline from White Hart Lane became known.

Man United, whilst the ceremony was taking place in the rain, had not only seen the three goals of Spurs, but raised them. The game had finished Spurs 3 United 5. I couldn't help but blurt out with laughter in front of many irate Spurs supporters as the wedding photos were being taken.

With lots of grumbling, and not much love all around me, the now not-as-happy couple stepped into their limousine to be driven to the reception. The rest of us would either follow in cars, or walk, as it was less than a mile away. My wife had gone in a car with her mum and her rather frail and elderly nan, so I pushed Tom in his buggy. It turned out to be just as quick to walk due to all the football traffic.

As I was waiting to cross the High Road, with the limousine and following cars all stuck in the traffic a few yards away from me, I heard a noise. It sounded like the thunder we had heard earlier, but by now the sky was clear blue again. Then I looked up the High Road and saw a large horde of United fans who were in very high spirits to say the least. Their team had just come back from the dead once again and instead of being taught a lesson, had provided the footballing lesson themselves.

The marauding horde of fans were going along the line of cars in the traffic jam banging on the windows and generally being loud and exuberant. There was no real sense of threat or danger, but it would have been annoying had I been sitting in one of the cars as a load of excitable and rowdy Mancs banged on my windows and called me a soft, southern wanker (now I knew how my wife felt at Luton).

They were getting closer to the limousine and had reached the car my wife, mother-in-law and grandmother-in-law were all in who all had the shock of their lives when a leering northerner (not me I might add) banged on their window and shouted that afternoon's scoreline at them. But then the horde saw the limousine in which were sitting the bride and groom and they all descended on it like piranha fish in a feeding frenzy.

The now petrified couple had about twenty Mancunians bashing on their windows and bonnet, with not so very congratulatory comments being shouted at them. I seem to remember that the United fans did not think that today was the best day for a wedding to take place. I couldn't have agreed more with them.

They continued down the queue of cars and we all heaved a sigh of relief. But as I was just about to cross, two mounted police officers charged down the road, narrowly missing pedestrians and wing mirrors as they chased the now fleeing group of United fans. I finally got to cross the road and make it to the safety of the restaurant to await the people stuck in their cars.

My wife arrived looking shaken but not stirred; my mother-in-law looked stirred but not shaken; my grandmother-in-law was just shaking. The rest of the evening went according to plan, if the plan meant that the newlyweds got absolutely hammered along with many others who, as Spurs fans, were all drowning their sorrows. I just wanted to get back to the in-laws where we were staying so I could

317

see what had actually happened at that afternoon's game on Match of the Day.

If that game was the football match of the day, then it may come as no surprise that the other match, the matrimonial match of the day did not last the course. After what had felt like an omen from God Almighty himself with the thundercrack and torrential downpour during the ceremony, and the post-nuptial romance of being abused by lots and lots of Man United fans on the run from police horses, it was fairly inevitable that the marriage would not last. They lasted eight years though. As many years as there were goals that strange afternoon in Tottenham on a stormy September Saturday afternoon.

England v Greece

World Cup Qualifier

October 6th, 2001　　　　**Old Trafford**

A week later and David Beckham would be back at his club ground, but this time he would be captaining England. A draw would be enough for England to qualify for the World Cup the following year in Japan and South Korea, the first time it had been held outside the Americas or Europe. After being such a naughty boy at the last World Cup, he had been granted redemption by his own Manchester United fans during their Treble winning season, but the rest of the country still had him sitting on the naughty step. He would finally be allowed off it after this game.

We had beaten Greece convincingly earlier in the qualification games but since then Greece had changed their manager. They now had the German Otto Rehhagel in charge who had made his new team much tougher and harder to beat. Nevertheless, this game should have been a formality. But as very often happens with England, nothing is ever a formality. We always seem to make it harder for ourselves. Harder, but ultimately more special in a way. If we'd just simply won 2-0 then we would have missed out on one of the great England moments of our lives.

The game was as tight as they come, with Greece fighting to impress their new manager (they would go onto win Euro 2004 under Rehhagel, one of the most remarkable achievements ever in International football). The England players seemed strangely out of sorts and nothing was working for them. After the freedom they had been playing with, they now looked constricted, as if the pressure to qualify was choking them.

After 36 minutes the Greeks took the lead (Malaka!), but we still had half time to reorganise and the whole of the second half to put right what had gone wrong so far. It didn't work; the game continued in the same vein, with England huffing and puffing, and Greece trying to hold onto what they had (they seemed to win every game of their Euro 2004 success 1-0). Our players looked bewildered, as though they did not know how to break through this German built Greek wall.

David Beckham was the only player to do anything about it. He seemed to cover every blade of grass on the Old Trafford pitch that afternoon. He was tireless. He knew that if we did not qualify he would forever be damned by the fans he was playing for. It would also nullify the astonishing performance and result in Munich the previous month. He had to do something.

In the 68th minute, Beckham won a free kick out wide on the left after being unceremoniously dumped to the ground at the third attempt. As he was waiting to take the free kick, Teddy Sheringham was brought on and he made an immediate impact. Beckham flighted one of his inswingers into the area and Sheringham, with his first touch, looped a header over the Greek keeper to pull us level. All we had to do now was hold on for the draw for the next twenty minutes or so. Easy. Apparently not.

We couldn't even hold on for more than a minute. Soon after the equaliser, our defence looked like rabbits stuck in headlights, and we just could not deal with a hopeful ball knocked into our area. The loose ball was gleefully put away to leave us in exactly the same situation as two minutes before. We needed a goal from somewhere, and it did not look like it would come from any of the England players, except David Beckham.

A free kick from the edge of the area was just wide from Beckham, but he was obviously just using this as target practice. His sights were not quite perfect yet.

The game ticked away into added time. Beckham had been in a similar situation before, needing a goal in added time in the Champions League Final two years before. He was used to that sort of critical high-pressure scenario, and as had been drilled into him by his manager at United, a chance will always come.

With the game entering the 93rd minute, the chance arrived; another free kick, but this time more central than the last one. You could almost hear Elvis singing "It's Now or Never" as Beckham lined his sights up.

What happened next has become possibly the most iconic moment of David Beckham's career, certainly as an England player. His free kick was perfectly weighted and flighted. All those hours of practice paid off in that one moment as the ball flew into the top corner. As John Motson said in commentary, it was "a fantastic ending to a very very poor performance". It may well have been poor for every other England player, but for Beckham it was his crowning glory so far. From being the ultimate villain with effigies of him being burned in the streets, he was now the saviour of the nation.

We had qualified for the World Cup, and guess who we would be playing in our group once the draw for the Finals had been made: Argentina. If Beckham's redemption was not complete yet, he would have the chance of full redemption and a certain amount of revenge the following summer in Japan. He just had to stay fit and unquestionably, undeniably, most definitely not fracture a small bone in his left foot. That would be very naughty of him.

England v Brazil

World Cup Quarter Final

June 21st, 2002   Shizuoka Stadium, Shizuoka

Between Beckham's miracle free kick and the start of the World Cup, I became a dad again, this time to a baby girl. We didn't have any appropriate PNE legends to name her after, so instead we went for Becky. She was the first girl for many generations on my side of the family, and was considered our little miracle. The only miracle with her is how I've stayed sane since then. I'd always wanted two kids of my own, and now I had them, plus a bonus child of course. I assumed in my rather old-fashioned way that my son Tom would be my little Preston supporting buddy. It turned out to be Becky who would suffer with me once she was old enough.

However, she was only three months old when the World Cup kicked off and had no idea yet what being a Preston supporter would entail. Early mornings were now firmly established in my life as Becky tended to wake up at the crack of dawn, but early starts would have to become quite frequent for football fans throughout June 2002, at least for those of us in Europe.

This World Cup would be the first time anyone here had experienced the Eastern time differences. We had all watched games late at night from the tournaments in Mexico and America, but now we had to get used to games kicking off at 7.30 in the morning. It would prove to be a headache for not just us fans, but also the England team.

Another thing we would have to get used to would be the daily updates on David Beckham's foot. In early April, he had been naughty after all and had done the very thing he was not supposed to do: get injured. We all became experts in the skeletal structure of his left foot, the consequent healing process, and the expected date of when he would be fit. He had fractured the second metatarsal bone in his left foot and would be out for six to eight weeks. It was touch and go as to whether he would be fit for our opening game against Sweden on Sunday June 2nd.

Without a fit David Beckham we had no chance of performing to our potential, and even though he was pronounced good to go, he was not fully fit. He lacked match practice and sharpness, but an almost fully fit Beckham as captain was better than no Beckham at all.

The Sweden game kicked off at 10.30 that Sunday morning. It felt like the whole country was worshipping in front of their TVs instead of at church. As usual, we got off to a rather hesitant start and only managed a 1-1 draw against Sven's home nation.

The real test for us, and Beckham, would come the following Friday against Argentina. But the real test was how we were all going to watch it as it would kick off at 12.30 in England. Many people either did not turn up for work that day or they left for lunch and simply did not return. I can't remember what happened at school for me that day as I definitely watched the game at home. Either we had been all allowed to go home early, or it may have been during half term. I may even have developed a 24-hour sickness bug which had prevented me from going to work that day, but if I had pulled a sickie that day then it would have been too obvious.

Whatever the circumstances of me watching the match at home, it turned out to be a very tight game but the only moment anyone remembers came just before half time. It would be the moment David Beckham would finally gain complete absolution for his sins at the last World Cup.

Michael Owen, who was now becoming very adept at falling over even when he had not been touched, this time fell over Mauricio Pochettino, the former Spurs manager's outstretched foot and a penalty was awarded. This was Beckham's chance and he took it emphatically. He just smashed the ball as hard as he could, and the ball flew past the keeper before he had even seen it.

The outpouring of relief was obvious on Beckham's face, though nowhere near the warped and twisted face Stuart Pearce had pulled after scoring his redemptive penalty against Spain at Euro 96. We held on throughout the whole of the second half for the 1-0 win. Now all we would need was a draw against Nigeria the following Wednesday. This would not only mean our progression to the knockout phase, but it would also send Argentina home, something that was always desirable.

The Nigeria game would be the first game in which we would kick off at 3.30pm in Japan, which meant a 7.30am start in England. This time I remember distinctly how I managed to watch the game as my Headteacher at the time decided he wanted to watch the game too and announced that school that day would not start until 9.45 rather than 8.45. We would all have the chance to watch the game first before teaching, and of course learning, commenced. The Headteacher who had suddenly gone up in my estimation was due to retire the following month so he didn't care less whether it was legal or not.

I think I'd rather have been teaching actually as it was one of the worst games I have ever watched. There is literally nothing about the game I can recall, apart from the 0-0 scoreline. But who cared? We had got into the second round and Argentina hadn't. We were now growing in confidence and the following Saturday (thankfully) we dispatched Denmark easily, winning the game 3-0, with all the goals coming in the first half. This set up a quarter final against the mighty Brazil, the first time we had met each other in the World Cup since Bobby Moore and Pele had battled it out in Mexico in 1970. We had lost 1-0 back then, and unfortunately for us, the result, if not the score would be the same this time.

The game was due to be played on a Friday again, with a 7.30 am kick off, as with the Nigeria match. However, I think my Headteacher had had his knuckles rapped by the educational powers that be. This time school would have to open as normal, but he had a plan. A big screen would be provided in the main school hall for anyone to watch the game if they wanted. This meant that only the first half of Period 1 would be disrupted. I decided to go for a slightly different approach.

The plan was to get up and get ready for school, suit and tie on, and watch the first half at home. During half time I would be able to rush to school ready for the second half. This was the biggest World Cup game we had played in for twelve years, ever since we had lost on penalties to West Germany in the semi-final of 1990, and I wasn't prepared to miss any of it. So, I was up earlier than usual on the longest day of the year. It would certainly feel like the longest day ever by the end of it.

In North Lancashire, the weather, instead of being bright and sunny, was dismally overcast. As soon as the sun had risen at about 4am, it never managed to break through the ashen grey cloud cover. It would remain like this for the entire day, and instead of giving us the longest day of sunshine, all we got was the longest day of greyness. It seemed fitting of the mood after the match.

The match itself started brilliantly for us, with Michael Owen continuing his record of scoring in every major tournament he had played in so far. Halfway through the first period he scored with a lovely finish to give us a rather improbable lead. The sun almost came out, but by half time it had thought it wasn't worth the hassle and gave up for the day. A bit like England.

Just before half time, David Beckham showed that he wasn't actually completely fit. Instead of going in wholeheartedly for a challenge, he chickened out and the ball was passed to Brazil's version of Pele this tournament, Ronaldinho. He streaked through our defence and laid a perfectly weighted ball through to Rivaldo, who calmly side footed the ball past David Seaman. My mood became as black as the clouds overhead, and rushed to my car to get to work, cursing the whole way.

I arrived just in time, and as promised, the big screen was set up, with many students all sitting there watching. I took a seat on the front row and tried to block the hordes of chattering kids out. To them this was just a bit of a jolly, a much better way of spending their time than sitting in a maths lesson, or even one of my lessons.

To me this was more important than anything. With many big teams already knocked out of the tournament, it was being said that the eventual winner would come from this game. It was certainly more important than finishing off a piece of coursework on "Of Mice and Men" with my Year 10 class.

But as I had taught my students, and as Robbie Burns had written, "the best laid plans o' mice an' men gang aft a-gley," which basically means that dreams often do not come true. They certainly didn't in that second half anyway. Only five minutes into the second half, Brazil got a free kick about 35 yards out, surely too far to have a direct shot on goal. At least that's what David Seaman thought as he stood waiting for Ronaldinho to take the kick. He was only a couple of yards off his line, but too far to reach the Brazilian's sublime looping effort.

Many people say what Ronaldinho did was a fluke, that it was a misplaced cross which freakishly and luckily for Brazil, went in. I do not agree. Ronaldinho knew exactly what he was doing, and he did it with such precision that it knocked the wind completely out of our sails. At that moment, I let out a very audible and very inappropriate expletive which every student and every other teacher must have heard, and I stormed out of the hall. I needed to find somewhere else to suffer.

I knew there was a TV in a Media Studies room that had an aerial and so could pick up the game. I went up to find a few other teachers all sitting there, all in the same predicament as me. Watching England lose to Brazil would be something I'd prefer to do away from the students. I could now swear to my heart's content.

I swore a lot that game as we simply had no answer. We never really threatened the Brazilian goal at all for the rest of the game. It just petered out into nothing and then suddenly we were out, beaten again by a team from South America, just as we had been in 1970, 1986 and 1998.

I now had to try to be an enthusiastic teacher for five lessons, with a lunch duty to do as well. It's safe to say that my enthusiasm for not just teaching, but everything that day seemed to have gone. I just wanted the day to be over with, but we still had about fifteen hours of supposed daylight to endure.

The dream of winning the World Cup had yet again gang a-gley. We weren't gonna live off the fatta the land after all. But at least the pundits had been right about the winner of that game being the eventual winner of the whole tournament, as Brazil went on to claim their fifth World Cup, with a certain player called Ronaldo making up for the disappointment of the previous tournament, scoring twice in a comprehensive 2-0 win against Germany in the final, the same German side that we had hammered 5-1 away in a game that now seemed like years ago.

Everton v Arsenal

October 19th, 2002   Goodison Park

I wasn't at this game. I don't support Arsenal or Everton. But it was a game which introduced me and everybody else in the country to a certain 16-year-old lad who had supported Everton as a boy, and now, even though he was still just 16, became a man by scoring a last-minute winner for his team against the then Premier League Champions, Arsenal.

Wayne Rooney's goal that day summed up everything about him as he burst into our collective conscience. It was instinctive, powerful, audacious, unstoppable and showed no sign of respect for its illustrious opponents.

Those first few years of Wayne Rooney's career were a thing of shock and awe. I remember one pundit describing him as a streetfighter of a player, and he did remind me of a young Mike Tyson at his most scary and most brutal. Rooney was like that in footballing terms. He did not fear anything or anyone. Why should I be scared of Arsenal? So what if they were the so-called Champions? So what if they haven't lost for the last thirty games. How dare they think I won't be able to score from here. I'll show them what a real punch is…have that! And he smacked the ball in off the crossbar from 25 yards out, leaving the England keeper reeling.

That goal made him the then youngest ever Premier League goal scorer, and instantly the whole of England knew that this boy, this 16-year-old man, was a player.

Over the next few months he would score a few more goals, including the winner against Blackburn less than a week after he had won the BBC Young Sports Personality of the Year. He would also show another side of his explosive style of play when he got his first red card a few days later. It would not be his last.

Soon enough he was picked for England and made his debut in February 2003, before becoming the youngest England goal scorer the following September. He instantly became a regular in the national team scoring some phenomenal goals. Those first few early England goals were quite frighteningly good. His right foot was like a piledriver, hammering the ball into whichever part of the goal he fancied. It did not seem to matter how far out he was, or what the angle was. He just leathered the ball and in it went. His last goal before Euro 2004 against Iceland is just ridiculous. He even looks a bit sheepish afterwards, as though even he didn't realise how good he was.

His name was probably first on the sheet when Sven announced his squad for Euro 2004, and nobody could have argued. He had rapidly overtaken David Beckham, Steven Gerrard, Frank Lampard, Michael Owen to name but a few as England's most important player. He proved this in our group game against Switzerland, becoming the youngest ever scorer in the history of the tournament, at least for a short while as one of his even younger opponents that day would score only four days later.

He scored a second that game against Switzerland that day. Or so the records show, but his shot came back off the post and went in off the keeper. Many similar goals before and since have been credited as own goals, but not this one for some reason. I'm just glad he broke Bobby Charlton's England goals record by more than one, otherwise there would have been a bit of a dispute over who the record holder actually was.

He bagged two more goals in the next match against Croatia, including another thunderous piledriver which just went through the keeper's hands it was that powerful. With him in our side we could beat anyone. That's how the whole country felt. Take him out, and we would probably be beaten.

Which is exactly what happened in the quarter-final against Portugal. Michael Owen scored his now customary tournament goal, and we were in control. But Rooney suffered almost exactly the same injury as David Beckham before the last World Cup, fracturing his fifth metatarsal and that was it. He was out of the tournament.

An hour or so later so were England, losing yet another penalty shootout, with this year's fall guy being Darius Vassell (although Saint David of Beckham had already missed our first). It was simple, keep Wayne Rooney fit and hungry and England would win.

During his recovery, he signed for Man United and scored a hat trick on his debut for the club, which also happened to be his first ever Champions League game. He had stepped up a notch or two, and had simply got a notch or two better. Nothing phased him at all.

He would become not just England's leading goal scorer with 53 goals, but also Manchester United's, his 253 goals in 559 appearances surpassing another of Bobby Charlton's long-held records. He won the Player of the Year four times. He won every trophy possible at club level, either in domestic or European competitions. He is the most capped outfield England player ever.

So why the hell did he fail to win anything with England?

The answer to this question would take a whole other book to answer, one which no doubt has already been written. All I know is that for the rest of his International career until he announced his retirement in 2017, England woefully under-performed.

Had he not been injured in that game against Portugal in 2004, I have no doubt he would have won the Golden Boot and helped England win the tournament. His right foot would surely have been able to beat even the impenetrable Greek defence, smashing through like a thunderbolt from Zeus. But even super heroes like Rooney can get injured and we would never see quite the same player again for England.

Two years later we would all have a case of deja-vu as it would be Rooney and not Beckham who would be in a race to get fit for the World Cup in Germany. Another pesky metatarsal would be the problem again and even though he returned for the second group game, he was palpably not fit and did not score at all in the tournament, instead getting himself sent off after an altercation with his United teammate, Cristiano Ronaldo, as England crashed out again on penalties, with Jamie Carragher taking his turn this year to be the fall guy.

We did not even qualify for Euro 2008 under Steve McLaren, who had taken over from Sven, crashing out on a wet night at Wembley by failing to beat Croatia, with McLaren hiding away under his umbrella, causing the possibly justified headlines of "The wally with the brolly".

In 2010, under the sergeant major style control of Fabio Cappello, England scraped through the group stage, enduring booing by their own fans as they were that boring, before being humiliated by Germany in the second round. Even if Frank Lampard's "goal" had been given (it was only about two feet over the line), we still would have got beaten. Rooney would still not score a World Cup goal.

At Euro 2012, Woy Hodgson saved the day by taking over from Cappello after the FA got bored with his over officious and ultimately stultifying approach, but still could not do anything with the team, losing again on penalties to Italy in the quarter-final, with Ashley Cole drawing the short straw this time.

Rooney finally scored his one and only World Cup goal in 2014 in Brazil, but could not prevent us from losing to Italy and Uruguay and going out of the tournament with one group game still to play. We all thought this was our lowest point, but at Euro 2016, even though we got through to the knockout stage, we probably wished we hadn't bothered as we were humiliated by Iceland in the second round, losing 2-1.

And that was it. We would never again see Wayne Rooney play for England at a major tournament. Ironically it would need the retirement of possibly our greatest ever player to make us a better team. Without him we would get to the World Cup semi-final again, but more on that later.

Rooney has to go down as the one player with the most unfulfilled potential ever, at least on an international level. I have never seen him play live, and this is one of my biggest footballing regrets, I might still have a chance early next year. He's due to become Derby's player/manager in January, and when Derby come to Deepdale next March, I so hope he decides to be a player and not just a manager that day.

I just wish I'd seen him when he was in his prime. I dread to think how many he would have put past Preston back then. But it would have been a privilege to have seen him do it.

Preston North End v West Ham United

Championship Play-Off Final

May 30th, 2005   Millennium Stadium, Cardiff

David Moyes' departure came just before the arrival of my daughter Becky, but unfortunately she did not bring the same luck as her brother had done. That was how I knew she was going to be a true North End fan. Preston carried on the tartan theme and appointed the former Scotland manager, Craig Brown. We had two respectable if uneventful seasons under him, finishing 12th both times.

His replacement would be another Scot, Billy Davies, who had been Brown's assistant. He would bring us as close as Moyes had done to reaching the Premier League, but not in his first season, only finishing 15th. However, the following season would be the most nearly of nearly seasons so far. And consequently the most heart breaking.

We finished fifth at the end of the 2004/05 season which meant we would play Derby in the play-off semi-final. We dispatched them fairly easily to set up a final at Cardiff against West Ham. West Ham had only finished sixth and so on paper we were the favourites, but crucially they had sneaked into sixth place on the last day of the season which meant that they had a certain amount of momentum, but I was still confident that this, finally, would be our year. This was now our sixth attempt at promotion via the play-offs. Surely, after five previous attempts, we would do it this year.

I now had two small children, of five and three years old, as well as an eleven-year-old who would be starting high school soon. It would not be fair to leave my wife at home with all three whilst I went to Cardiff for the day. Basically, I did what my own dad would have done if he'd have been in the same situation as me.

I got both my little ones into their PNE tops, gave them a little PNE flag each and we sat on the sofa, with them waving their flags in anticipation. The truth was that my PMT was more acute than I had ever experienced before. Forget World Cup matches or Champions League Finals. The pre-match tension before this game was almost unbearable.

I had spent the whole day just wandering around the house, unable to concentrate on anything else. This was the day my footballing dreams would come true. I really believed it, and yet there was still that nagging doubt twisting my stomach around. Dad had taken my mum to Cardiff to watch the match, and at least he had the journey down to occupy him. I had nothing to distract me, apart from my kids waving their flags, although they were getting bored already and the game hadn't even started yet.

Once the game started, my PMT did not abate and it changed into DMT (During Match Tension), especially as the game was so tight. Very few chances were created by either side, and by now my kids had got bored enough to go off and play with their toys. Tom went to build a car with Lego, just as I used to do, and Becky went to do the vacuuming with her pretend vacuum cleaner (which always meant that she would pour rice or something on the floor and be amazed when it was still there afterwards, until we cleared it up properly.)

With the score 0-0 at half time, the tension just got worse. We were now only 45 minutes away from the Premiership, the land of sunshine and unicorns, where even pretend vacuum cleaners worked. But within twelve minutes of the restart, it turned back into the Land of Make Believe. I wasn't going to be opening the Bucks Fizz after all.

Before that moment, I had no ill will towards Bobby Zamora at all. He was a decent player and was just trying to make a living like the rest of us. But in the 57th minute, and forever afterwards, I developed a completely irrational hatred of him. His goal was the goal which smashed my dreams into pieces.

It wasn't even a special goal. A simple cross from the left and there he was on the six-yard line to put it in. I had never felt a sense of deflation like the one I experienced then. At that moment I knew we would not come back from this. It wasn't just my heart Bobby Zamora broke, but the whole of our team's collective heart. We looked broken, bereft and ultimately beaten.

Zamora was brought off after 74 minutes so I wasn't even able to vent my fury at him from my sofa any more, and the game fizzled out along with my hopes and dreams. We had lost 1-0, by one stupid, single solitary goal.

I was numb for quite a long time after the final whistle. My wife just told the kids to leave me alone when they tried to cheer me up. She knew that I had to go through this process of numbness before I would come back to them all.

I just stared at the TV screen, not really caring about anything anymore. I still watched West Ham as they were presented with the trophy to confirm that it would be them, not us, who would play in the Promised Land next season. I had to try and purge myself by watching the match coverage right until the end, the tickertape and fireworks, the West Ham celebrations, the post-match post-mortem, the whole lot.

I'm not sure this purging worked, but I eventually moved from the sofa and resumed normal life. But of course this was normal life for me. Disappointment had been part of my footballing life ever since I started watching Preston. The two promotions I had experienced so far had brought a rather fleeting joy, but this feeling of ultimately being not quite good enough was my status quo. "Whatever You Want" never applied to Preston fans and I had to console myself, as I always did, with the undoubtable fact that we would have another chance next season. "There's always next season" has become my motto.

Even though we finished higher in the table the following season, matching our best ever position of fourth, Leeds proved to be too strong for us this time, and we didn't even get to the final. After now seven unsuccessful play-off attempts at promotion, I was starting to think we would be doomed to be the team who never got promoted via the play-offs. It was so unfair, but then again, the play-offs are in their very nature, quite an unfair way of getting promoted.

Very often, the team who finishes third in the table, and so prove themselves to be the third best team in the division, do not get promoted via the play-offs. Before the system was introduced, this team would have been promoted and been rewarded for their efforts over 46 league games. But with the current play-off system, instead of gaining any advantage for their higher position, the playing field is levelled, ironically to make it fairer.

The only advantage, if it even is an advantage the two highest placed teams get, is that they get to play the second leg of their semi-final at home before the final at the neutral Wembley, or Cardiff in the case of 2005. A team that accumulated maybe twenty or so points more than their opponents have literally no advantage in that final. They do not even get the privilege of playing in front of their home crowd. Yes they get the experience of playing at a fantastic stadium, but surely their efforts throughout the season should count for something?

My suggestion to make it fairer is to actually make it unfairer, to tip the balance somehow towards the teams who finished higher in the table. I propose that the further down the table a team finishes, the more games they have to play in order to win promotion. And instead of two legged semi-finals, there should be a one-off game for each tie, to be held at the home of the team who finished higher in the league.

So, to simplify, the third placed team would immediately know that they are in the final, and that game would be played at their ground to give them an advantage, an advantage they have earned the right to have. They would play the eventual winners between the other three teams. Sixth place would play away at the fifth placed team. Whoever won that match would then play away at the fourth placed team's ground, with the winners of that match meeting the third placed team who are already waiting for them in the final. This system would keep giving the higher placed team a better chance of victory, which is only fair seeing as they finished higher after the 46 league games.

A team who finished sixth would have to win three games, all away from home, to eventually win promotion. A team who finished third would only have one match to play, and it would be at their own ground, with more time to prepare etc. If the sixth placed team actually achieved promotion, then fair play to them, as they would have truly earned their moment of glory.

I know this would cause many logistical problems in terms of policing and ticketing, but I'm sure that could be worked out. The main thing is that the efforts of the whole season are not simply nullified as soon as the normal season ends. It makes sense to me anyway.

But of course a system like this would not bring in as much money for the powers that be. They wouldn't be able to sell as many tickets for the Wembley final, and the fans would be denied a chance of watching their team play there, teams that would normally never get the chance of playing at such a fantastic stadium. Maybe some fans would prefer a defeat at Wembley, even if that meant they weren't promoted.

I know what I'd rather have. I know what it feels like to lose a final at Wembley or Cardiff or wherever, and believe me, I'd rather have got promoted than have suffered another glorious failure, only this time in a fancier stadium.

Preston North End v Tottenham Hotspur

Carling Cup Third Round

September 23rd, 2009   Deepdale

Billy Davies would leave Preston after his second consecutive loss in the play-offs, and we decided to give an English manager a try this time. Paul Simpson's only full season in charge wasn't too bad, missing out on the play-offs by one place, before the club went back to a Scot, this time Alan Irvine.

Irvine's first season in charge resulted in a drop down the table, finishing 15th, but in his second season we did what West Ham had done in 2005 and sneaked into the final play-off spot on the last day of the season. But, unlike West Ham, the momentum was not with us and we lost to Sheffield United in the semi-final. If you've been keeping up, that was now eight (eight) play-off campaigns without success. We now held the unwanted record of being the most unsuccessful club in play-off history. Surely there should be some sort of trophy for that.

During Irvine's tenure, we had two big games against not just any old Premier League teams, but two of the biggest in the country: Liverpool and Spurs. The Liverpool match was in the FA Cup Third Round at Deepdale, in January 2009, and a team including Steven Gerrard and Fernando Torres beat us 2-0, but we gave a good account of ourselves. Liverpool certainly knew they had been in a game afterwards, and maybe the score might have been different if we hadn't had a goal ruled out for what was deemed to be a foul by The Beast, Jon Parkin.

At the start of the following season we drew Spurs in the League Cup. Again, if you've been keeping up, you may remember that I had taken my wife to watch Preston away at Luton just after we had returned from our honeymoon in 1998. I also said that after that wonderful experience, she would never go again to watch a match with me. I lied.

As soon as she realised that her club was playing at Deepdale, she was well up for going, and even arranged child care so she could fully concentrate on her team's performance. This was the first time our clubs had met since just before I started talking to her on the train home from work that glorious day in September 1996.

The Spurs team were now managed by Harry Redknapp and this would be the season they finished fourth in the Premier League, qualifying for the Champions League for the first time ever. The team that night included Jermaine Jenas, Jermain Defoe, and a certain left sided player called Gareth Bale, who would go onto become the world's most expensive player for the most successful club in the whole world, scoring in two Champions League Finals for Real Madrid.

Also on the team sheet that night was Peter Crouch. By then he had already scored sixteen times for England and would go onto have a better goals per game ratio for England than our own Tom Finney. He would also beat the ratios of Geoff Hurst, Alan Shearer, Michael Owen, Wayne Rooney, and even Bobby Charlton. Preston's chances did not look good.

My wife and I had seats in the Sir Tom Finney Stand, and discovered that we were in the area of coloured seats which depicted Finney's face. I could now, and forever more, say that my wife had sat on Tom Finney's face (sorry). Deepdale's improvements and renovations were now complete, and we had four magnificent stands now, so at least she and the other Spurs' fans could not sing derogatory chants about our now beautiful and complete stadium.

She was also under strict instructions not to jump out of her seat if Spurs scored. In fact she was not really allowed to show any emotion really, apart from disappointment at the end after her team had been beaten. And only then after we had got back into the car. She had to be on her best behaviour that night as our goal was basically used as target practice.

Crouchy got the fun started for Spurs with his first goal of the night after 14 minutes, before Jermain Defoe doubled the lead before half time. The score remained 2-0 until a mad last quarter of an hour. Crouchy got his second, before we pulled one back, only for Robbie Keane, who had come on for Jermain Defoe, to make it 4-1. Crouchy would complete his hat-trick in added time, but despite this, there was no robot from him that night.

My wife sat with a smug grin on her face all the way home. I hope it was due to the result and not that she had been sitting on Tom Finney's face all evening (sorry again). I didn't really mind. We had been beaten by a much better side and I had my wife with me for the first time since we'd moved Up North eleven years previously. But I can safely say this time that she has never been to a match since, but only because Spurs have never played us again. Unless we got drawn in a cup tie again, either we would have to go up into the Premier League, or Spurs would need to get relegated out of it for us to meet again. The first of these options seemed even less likely the following season, as the Premier League would get further away from us once again.

Preston North End v Swindon Town

September 2ⁿᵈ, 2012   Deepdale

Three months later, after our form had not really improved, Alan Irvine would leave Deepdale and be replaced with not another Scottish legend, but the son of one. Sir Alex Ferguson's son Darren would take over and he would stabilise us to an extent. He kept us up, finishing 17th, with the help of a few loan players from his dad's club, Manchester United. But the following season we were on course for relegation after an awful first half of the season. By December 29th we were bottom of the table and Ferguson was sacked. Strangely enough, Man United recalled all their loan players back to Old Trafford in a rather childish fit of pique from the elder Ferguson.

The younger Ferguson's replacement was Phil Brown, who had famously given his Hull side a half time bollocking on the pitch in front of the bemused and probably a little embarrassed fans. I'm sure the fans weren't as embarrassed as those players though, but hey, he had a lovely tan and a salesman's charming smile, so in times of need, who cared whether he embarrassed his players publicly, losing their trust in the process? If he had a nice tan, then that was good enough for us.

With his squad now depleted, even his smile and tan could not save us. By the end of April we had already been relegated and would return the following season down to League One (the old Division Three) where we had spent so long trying to get out of. All the progress we had made under David Moyes and Billy Davies was gone. Two Championship play-off finals now seemed like a distant memory, as though we were being told off for getting above our station and being put back where we belonged.

However, we did win our final match of the season, a 3-1 win against Watford to ensure we at least did not finish bottom of the table. I mention this because this would be the game my youngest daughter Becky first asked if she could come with me. I'd offered to take her over the previous couple of years but she was still at the stage where making a huge mess around the house and pretending to clean it up was more appealing than sitting in the cold and watching some men run around with a ball.

Now she had turned nine, she had obviously decided that she was much more grown up and would deign to accompany me to Deepdale for the last game of the season, before we would return to League One. Her presence, and Preston's victory, according to Becky, was obviously a sign that she was a good luck charm. I loved her being there with me so suggested she keep on attending next season, which she was only too pleased to do.

The good luck she would bring would not start right away, losing our first match of the season before drawing the next, but obviously that was because she hadn't come to either of those games. She thought it was about time she put a shift in for the team and so she came to the next game with me, which we managed to win 1-0 against Exeter. This was obviously proof enough that she indeed was a lucky charm. Maybe she was, as that game was the start of a run of seven consecutive wins for us, some of which she attended. By the end of September we were second in the table and an immediate return to the Championship was looking quite likely.

When she was with me at the games, she rarely watched the game at all. She would forever be looking around and be more interested in the fans than the game. She would pretend that she was watching though, but usually after the first ten minutes or so, she would whisper into my ear, "Dad, which way are we kicking?" and I would whisper back into her ear that we were kicking that way, pointing to whichever goal we were attempting to score in. After the first few games, I would whisper which direction we were kicking before she would even ask, and she would give me one of her smiles and then continue to survey the crowd, or watch our mascot, The Deepdale Duck's antics on the sideline.

She reminded me of my younger self when I started going with my dad. Most games I would get bored very quickly and would be constantly asking my dad irrelevant questions that had nothing to do with what I was supposed to be watching. I would regularly ask dad how long was left, and I couldn't help but smile to myself when Becky asked me the exact same question, with well over an hour of the game to go. I was almost proud of her. She was being educated, just as I had been, into what being a supporter of a lower league team meant.

Quite often it was boring, but she was undeterred and would keep wanting to come again. I realised that she was doing exactly the same thing as I had done with my dad. I went along with him simply because I would have him all to myself. He was my hero, and spending time with him at Deepdale, even on a cold wet afternoon in November, was our time together, and nobody else's.

I realised that I was now Becky's hero, and she was there sitting next to me not because of the scintillating football, but because of me, and I loved her even more, if indeed that was possible.

Those first few early games with her were lovely, but I was conscious that she was not a proper North End fan yet; she hadn't seen us lose yet. This was to change on New Year's Eve 2011 when Sheffield Wednesday came to Deepdale and beat us 2-0. I was almost pleased that she had seen us lose. It was almost as if she had now been blooded and had grown up to an extent. Ever since that first defeat she has developed an irrational hatred of Sheffield Wednesday, similar to mine for Bobby Zamora.

By then, Phil Brown had been sacked after less than a year in the job. Despite those seven consecutive wins, which had been inspired by my daughter, as she never failed to remind me, we had started losing long before New Year's Eve, when Becky had not been there with me of course.

Brown's replacement was the most baffling of appointments. Graham Westley, who had got Stevenage Borough into the Football League and then into League One with consecutive promotions, was our very strange choice. He never seemed to fit at Deepdale. He brought in new training methods and his own style of players, all of whom frankly were just not good enough.

The most common phrase heard around Deepdale during Westley's first few months was something along the lines of "Who's this bloody southerner coming up here with his poncey new regime? He should sod off back down south!"

As you can see, Graham Westley really endeared himself to the Deepdale faithful and we all embraced him with our northern charm. He could do no better than previous managers, ending up 15th, but after his first pre-season with the players, our prospects seemed better at the start of the 2012/13 season, and the game in question for this chapter was one of our best performances for some time, and certainly one of the best under Westley.

It was memorable not only because of the scoreline and our performance, but also because of the opposing manager's rather bizarre decisions and behaviour. It would also be the start of a tradition that my daughter Becky and I would continue to this day.

We were both due to start the new academic year the following day, and usually I would be in a grump, knowing that the summer holidays were over and I would have to get back to moulding young, and sometimes, rather obstructive and uncooperative minds in the classroom.

As usual, after a rather dismal August in terms of the weather, as soon as September came along the sun came out. That day was a lovely late summer's day. There was a travelling funfair set up in the park opposite the ground, and I promised Becky that we would go on a few rides after the game.

Before the game we had our picture taken next to the statue of Sir Tom Finney which now stood outside Deepdale. "The Splash" depicted in bronze the great man sliding on a soaked Stamford Bridge pitch in 1956. The photograph which had inspired it had won the Sports Photograph of the Year, and the statue incorporated fountains to justify its name.

We had a lovely photo taken of us both, with Sir Tom sliding away behind us as this was our first visit to Deepdale of the season. We have been recreating this photo on our first game of every season ever since. The same positions, same smiles, just different hairstyles, or in my case, less hair each year. The latest instalment came only last week before a comprehensive 3-0 victory over our neighbours Wigan Athletic. That first photo back in 2012 would come before another similarly convincing win for us.

Paulo Di Canio, the fiery Italian and scorer of great goals, was now the manager of Swindon Town, and safe to say, did not enjoy losing. We were 2-0 up after only ten minutes, and then Di Canio decided to make a substitution. He had always been an impulsive player, and his choice of substitute proved this personality trait would continue into his management style.

He decided not to change his team's system, or bring on a different attacking player, but instead he decided to replace his goalkeeper. This was obviously an insult to the keeper who had conceded two goals already through no fault of his own, and he, like the rest of us, stared incredulously when his number was displayed on the fourth official's board. It is fair to say that he neither agreed with the decision, nor was too pleased about it.

As he stormed off the pitch, he and his manager were giving each other quite violent verbal abuse, before he kicked a water bottle that was on the touchline straight at Di Canio. The Italian was not too pleased either about this decision and the keeper marched down the touchline towards the corner where the tunnel entrance is. All the way along the touchline the abuse towards each other continued, accompanied all the way to cheers of derision and hilarity from the Preston fans.

Becky and I were in the Sir Tom Finney Stand that day, opposite to where all the hilarity was happening but even from the other side of the pitch we could hear some of the very very bad words the two antagonists in this farce were screaming at each other. It was the most entertaining thing I had seen at Deepdale for years.

Surprise surprise, the new keeper fared no better than the previous one, conceding two himself in a 4-1 win for us. I kept my promise to Becky and we went to the funfair after the game to continue the entertainment. I didn't know then, as I was whirling around on the waltzers, with my little girl giggling with happiness, that we would both be giggling with a different kind of happiness after a game against Swindon less than three years later. But the next time would be at Wembley.

After this one and only highlight in Graham Westley's year-long reign at Deepdale, our season became yet another disappointing one. We would end up slightly better than the previous season, this time finishing 14th, but by then Westley had been sent packing with his poncey southern ways back Down South. The day before Valentine's Day he was sacked in the most romantic of gestures by our board to their fans. Almost a year to the day later, Preston would lose another member of their club, a much more significant, and certainly more loved member.

On Valentine's Day 2014, at the age of 91, Sir Tom Finney died, and broke all our hearts. The day after, my dad, me, and my daughter, three generations of my Preston supporting family would take part in the most immaculately observed minute's silence at Deepdale. This would also happen at every ground around the country. Not just Preston, but England had lost a true legend. In fact football as a whole had lost one of its legends.

I'm not going to write an obituary or a summary of Sir Tom's achievements. There have been many books doing that, many of which I own and have read. He meant little to my daughter. She was aware of who he was and what he meant to the club. I was more aware and felt the significance of the day more acutely than she did, but to my dad, and subsequently his son and granddaughter, he was part of the reason why we were all there in the first place. Dad was very emotional that day, but just as Finney had touched his life in footballing terms, so he had touched Finney's life, if only for a brief moment, a few years before.

Finney's wife Elsie, before her death in 2004, had suffered from Alzheimer's which meant that her husband became her carer. As the club's president, he still attended games at Deepdale, and at one of these games, in the midst of his new role as carer, my dad saw him just as he was entering the ground. My dad simply went up to him, shook his hand, wished him and his wife well, and told him that he often included them both in his prayers.

It was a simple gesture, but one that touched the Preston legend quite deeply. Dad told me how Sir Tom thanked him for his kind words, and almost had a tear in his own eye, being humbled and touched by this stranger's faith and humility. I hope dad's kind gesture helped sustain him through this difficult period, and even though I do not share dad's faith, he made me even prouder of him because of what he said to Sir Tom that day.

It was a simple moment of kindness between two simple working men, one of whom happened to be possibly the greatest footballer our country has ever produced. And that definitely wasn't my dad.

Another PNE legend with a stand named after him, Bill Shankly, certainly thought that. He had said "Tom Finney would have been great in any team, in any match and in any age ... even if he had been wearing an overcoat", and when asked whether a leading player of the 1970s would compare favourably to Finney, Shankly replied "Aye, he's as good as Tommy – but then Tommy's nearly 60 now". With Sir Tom no longer there, Preston North End would never be the same club again. The most legendary of legends was gone, but would never be forgotten.

Queen Elizabeth School Staff v Morecambe High School Staff

March 2014 Queen Elizabeth School, Kirkby Lonsdale

With the passing of one legend, I now come to the passing of another. Sort of. I had still been playing football on and off for the staff team against other local schools. Just after my son was born, I had moved schools again to be closer to home and now worked in Morecambe. The school I had been working in had a fairly rubbish team; if I was their best player, then it must have meant that they weren't great, but my new school's team was good. We were probably about the same standard as the team I had played for at my first ever school, and once my kids were all past the baby stage I started playing again.

Some staff came and went, being replaced by others, as is the nature of any football team, and by the end of my first decade of teaching at this school we had a couple of very good players in our ranks. I'm not sure I ever saw just how good one of them was, but he was the best in our motley crew of teachers, teaching assistants, and other school associated staff. His claim to fame, if that is possible, was that he had been featured in one of the FIFA computer games.

He was from Denbigh in North Wales and when he was younger, he had played part time for The New Saints, or Total Network Solutions, or whatever they were called at that time, a semi-professional team from North Wales who somehow had managed to win the Welsh league and so had qualified for the Champions League, if only in the qualifying rounds.

As such, the makers of the game needed all the squad details of every participating team, and so my colleague, who would become a very good mate, was included in the game's player selection. Anybody around the world who was playing that particular edition of the game could pick him for their own customised team if they so wished. I have no idea how many people did, if anyone, but at least they had the option.

He was still playing semi-professionally for a local team in Lancashire when he joined my school, and as such I never saw him at his absolute best as we would always play our occasional matches against other schools on Fridays after school, when he would have one of his "proper" games the following day, and so he would always be keeping his best in reserve for the next day. He was easily the best in our team. He even did a David Beckham once and scored from the half way line, straight from the kick off if I remember rightly.

Another lad who played for us was also very good. In his younger days he had played with a couple of players who went on to have half decent professional careers with lower league clubs. These players were not much better than him, if at all, and yet they had gone on to earn maybe two or three thousand pounds a week, whereas he would earn the paltry sum of about eighteen thousand a year as a teaching assistant. It just goes to show the fine lines between making it as a professional player earning very good money, and helping kids to write properly for a pittance.

In the team would also be the lad who had been the captain of my own school team when we had won the District Cup together when we had both been in Year 7, the Ray Wilkinsesque midfielder I mentioned many pages ago. So, we had a decent team, and I was still filling in at right back, although my legs were starting to go by now.

I even got a goal in one game, although it was from only a few inches out. The ball was rolling towards the goal line before I helped it over to claim the goal, rather like Preston's only England player since Tom Finney, David Nugent had done in his one appearance for England, nicking a goal from Jermain Defoe. He never played again for England but in the eleven minutes he was an England player, he can always say he had scored a goal. Not a bad goals per minute record really.

By 2012 or thereabouts, the local schools had organised themselves into a local league of sorts, where we would all play each other and the winners would even get a trophy at the end of each "season". The season ending in 2014 would be our finest hour.

The legend I referred to at the start of this chapter was a man called Alan Alker, or Alks as everyone called him. He really was a legend at our school, having been there since the very start of his career. He was due to retire the following year after 38 years of teaching at the same school. He really was the heart and soul of the school. His assemblies were once seen never forgotten pieces of entertainment, and his whole life was lived for the benefit of the students he taught and the colleagues he worked with.

He had also been a very good rugby and football player in his youth, but by now, in his late 50s, with a new hip and a new knee, he was only used as a sub in our team. He would come on most games and sit up front for the last ten minutes, not doing much. I think he just wanted to be part of a team still, and certainly enjoyed the post-match drinks in whatever pub we went to.

Anyway, the game in question was a crucial one. If we won it, we would go top of the league with only one game to go, putting us in the driving seat to win the league that season. We were playing on the playing fields of the very picturesque site of Queen Elizabeth School in Kirkby Lonsdale, just up the road from where I had got drunk and jumped off Devil's Bridge all those years ago.

The game was very tight and just after half time we snatched the lead with what some might say, our team included, was a rather dubious goal which seemed to have gone in on off a hand and not a legal part of the body. Our opponents were rather disgruntled about this and were putting us under a lot of pressure to try and rectify the dubious scoreline.

With about ten minutes to go it was still 1-0 to us and a couple of us were knackered by now, and would have to be replaced. Alks was on the sideline and jumped, or rather hobbled into action for the final few minutes of the game. His role was to simply stay up front as an outlet from the constant attacks we were under, but Alks had other ideas.

Only a couple of minutes after entering the arena, we were having a rare foray into their half, and the ball was knocked up towards Alks. With his back to goal, he was only meant to hold it up and wait for some of us, certainly not me, to get up to him so he could lay it off again. Instead, he controlled the ball with his chest on the edge of the penalty area, and then swivelled with as much balletic grace as a farmer's son from Blackburn could onto his weaker left foot.

348

Instinctively, he unleashed a shot which rifled into the top corner. None of us, him included, could believe what he had just done. He'd probably never scored a goal like that before, and certainly never would again.

He only lasted another couple of minutes as his dodgy knee went again, not even lasting the game out. But those four minutes on the pitch included one of the greatest moments ever. This 59-year-old cripple had put the rest of us, who were all in our 20s, 30s, or even 40s in my case, to shame. He came on, scored a wonder goal to basically win it for us, then went off to get the first round in at the pub. We had a good session that night it's fair to say.

Our Headteacher, affectionately known as The Boss and another great bloke, was also there to watch and have a pint or two. He would be retiring the following year too and so I wanted to pay my own tribute to them both, but especially Alks who had been at the school for much longer than the Head. Every year after the school Sports Day, the staff would have their own "sports" day too.

The school, just like when I was a student, was divided into four Houses, and every member of staff, non-teaching staff too, were assigned to one. We would all have some sort of House competition, organised by Alks and the Head, ranging from our own version of sports day with the sack race, egg and spoon race, and three-legged race etc.

It wasn't always sports related though. Another year, we would all pile into the school hall and have a huge pub quiz, or bingo session. Another year we went to the local bowling alley, and another we had a snooker, bowls, darts and dominoes tournament in the local village institute.

For his final year the Head wanted to see whether any of his staff actually had any talents, and so organised a talent show, and asked each House to perform a "turn", to use the northern vernacular. One House came up with a surreal and bizarre series of "comedy" sketches, another did some sort of "magic" show, and the Head would decide on a winner.

For my House's act, I wanted to pay my own tribute to both of these great blokes, who were now very good friends as well as highly respected colleagues. A couple of years earlier the Head had introduced iPads into our school. It was the particular educational fad at the time, and we all had to be trained on how to use them in the classroom, for setting homework, writing reports and for keeping our marks and data on etc. Alks was pure old school and it was fair to say didn't think much of these fancy new-fangled bloody iPad things.

A younger, much more tech-savvy Deputy Head had been in charge of persuading us all that this piece of kit was an innovative addition to our teacher's arsenal, but Alks wasn't so sure. He would be retiring anyway so what did he care?

I wanted to affectionately mock Alks' lack of innovation and inability to move with the times. So I changed the words to Victoria Woods' famous and hilarious "The Ballad of Barry and Frieda", in which Barry is not the most accepting of his wife's rather frustrated attempts to satisfy her voracious libido.

My version had these two teachers in a similar, but definitely not sexual way, arguing about the virtues of using these iPads, with the famous chorus being similarly used "But Alks said, I can't do it, I can't do it" etc. About thirty of us all got onto the stage and belted out my version of the song, and it went down a storm if I do say so myself. The other staff members loved it, and the Head and Alks voted it as the winner to everyone in my House's delight.

As another way of paying tribute to them both, I had asked all the students and staff to write down their favourite memory of their time

350

at school, their magic moment, which I would then select and collate into a book called imaginatively enough "Magic Moments" for them both to keep.

Lots of school trips were mentioned, many of which Alks had been on. Many bizarre occurrences, both in and out of the classroom were also mentioned, from staff and students, my favourite being Alks' own memory of when he had had to go to another local school to borrow a large landing mat for our high jumpers to land on. He'd taken the school minibus and a few lads to help him get this mat back, but realised he had no way of securing it to the top of the minibus once he got there. His solution was to get the lads who had accompanied him to sit on top of the padded mat on the roof of the minibus whilst he drove through Lancaster back to Morecambe, in full view of all the traffic and pedestrians. Someone must have phoned the police to notify them of this piece of ingenuity, as when Alks arrived back at our school, thankfully with all the lads still intact on the roof, a police car was waiting for him to have a little chat about his decision. Classic Alks.

My own contribution was a much shorter version of my account of Alks' wonder goal I mentioned earlier, so he had it to take into posterity with him. On his final day at work, I presented him with his own copy of the finished book in front of the whole school. I achieved what I had wanted to do; I had not only paid tribute to him, but I'm sure I made a tear come into his eye as the whole school applauded him for his efforts.

The school was never the same once Alks and the Head left. A new regime came in and took the soul of the school away, which is one of the reasons why I would eventually leave. I would still remain very good friends with them both though, and they both feature in another significant day for me a bit further on, if you would care to continue reading.

But first I think it's about time I got to the greatest season I had ever experienced as a Preston fan, one that deserves its own title again.

Season 2014/15

Preston North End v Manchester United

FA Cup Fifth Round

February 16th, 2015   Deepdale

At the end of this season both Alks and The Boss would retire and I'm so glad they got to share this season with me before they went out to graze. After Graham Westley, the original soft southern wanker, had been sacked in 2013, Preston went back to a tried and tested northerner in Simon Grayson, a tough, no nonsense Yorkshireman.

Despite being born the wrong side of The Pennines, and also having had success with our hated rivals Blackpool, having led them and consequently Leeds and Huddersfield to promotions from League One, it was clear he knew how to get a struggling team promoted in the lower leagues, although he had never been promoted into the Premier League. We knew he could do a similar job for us.

He nearly did it in his first full season with us, finishing fifth and getting yet again into the play-offs, this time to face another team from Grayson's home county, Rotherham United. But obviously we were not content with single figure failures in play-offs. This would be our ninth attempt, and despite Joe Garner scoring one of the best volleys I'd ever seen, chesting it up before firing an unstoppable shot into the Rotherham goal in the first leg at Deepdale, we lost the second leg in Yorkshire and again failed to get to Wembley. We had now extended our unenviable record of play-off losses to nine (nine).

The only way of getting promoted the following season would be to finish first or second. It looked more likely to be a second placed finish as Bristol City became the runaway leaders, even though they could not beat us, drawing at Deepdale and losing to us at Ashton Gate. By the end of March they were ten points clear, with us battling it out for second place with MK Dons and Swindon Town.

But before we would establish ourselves as real promotion contenders, we had the small matter of an FA Cup tie against the team I had most wanted to see us play. As soon as we were drawn at home to face Manchester United, I was ecstatic.

This would be the first time that the two clubs had ever faced each other in all my years of watching Preston, and even though I still had fond affections for the Premier League giants, there was no team I would rather beat than them.

The match was to be broadcast live on BBC1 and was the biggest game at Deepdale for years, maybe the biggest game ever, certainly since I'd been watching Preston. As such, the fight for tickets was one that I would lose. As a season ticket holder, my dad would get a priority ticket, but as for the rest of us, it was a huge bun fight, and one which I would ultimately be unsuccessful in, despite many attempts to get tickets. But at least it would be on the television and I would have my now not so little sidekick, my daughter Becky, on the sofa with me. She was now coming to most matches with me and knew how important this game was.

In the build up to the match, all my non-Man United supporting colleagues and students, all of whom knew how much I cared about PNE, were wishing me all the best. Even one of my good mates who supported Blackpool wished me well. They all wanted my team to be successful, as did every other fan up and down the whole country. If you didn't support United, then you always wanted them to lose, especially if it would be to a plucky little club from League One who had enjoyed similar glories to United, even though those glories had come before United had even been formed as a club.

With the countless well-wishes I felt as though the whole of the school was on my side. My PMT was not so bad as I didn't expect to win, even though United were still in transition, coming to terms with the retirement of Sir Alex Ferguson. They had sacked David Moyes, the ex-Preston manager who frankly should have been given more time to prove himself, and had appointed Louis van Gaal the previous summer. Despite including David de Gea, Angel Di Maria and Wayne Rooney in their team, they were still nowhere near the team they had been under Ferguson and so maybe, just maybe a cup upset was on the cards. Especially as the big donkey Marouane Fellaini would also be playing.

It seemed that way after we incredibly took the lead just after half time. The first half had been tight but in the 47th minute, unbelievably, astonishingly, we scored. A nice lay off from our top scorer that season, Joe Garner, was fired in via a deflection by our left back Scott Laird in front of the rapturous fans in the Alan Kelly Town End stand. Me and Becky were jumping around the living room in disbelief. Whatever else happened in the game, we could at least say we had held the lead against Manchester United, for however long it would last.

We would actually hold the lead for longer than I expected, for almost twenty minutes, and even had a couple of chances to get another, before United thought they had better start playing properly. We were now tiring and were simply not used to the pace of a top Premier League team, if indeed United could still be classed as one.

In the 65th minute Ander Herrera squeezed a shot into the bottom corner with Rooney standing in an offside position just in front of our keeper. Although he did not touch the ball, I am adamant that he was interfering with play as our keeper was unsure whether or not Rooney was going to get a touch, and so dived late. That's my excuse anyway.

United now had the momentum and went onto score another couple, the big donkey Fellaini getting one from two yards out which even he could not miss, before Rooney converted a penalty with only two minutes to go to kill the game off. Despite the defeat, we had shown the country, and a lot of the world, that we were a good side, capable of giving anyone a game on our day.

The following morning I had a similar number of comments from the staff and students as I had received before the match. They all said how well we had played and how many of them had thought of me when we had been 1-0 up. It was lovely to know that a significant number of people had all been thinking of me, and that they had been Preston supporters with me that night. Maybe even the Blackpool supporting colleague of mine had been telling the truth when he said that he wanted us to beat United. Maybe, just maybe.

That game gave us the confidence to make a promotion charge until the end of the season. After losing to United, we would not lose a game until the final game of the whole season, the game which really mattered, the game which would clinch promotion for us, and ultimately the game which would be one game too many.

Colchester United v Preston North End

May 3rd, 2015   Weston Homes Community Stadium

After our phenomenal 18 match unbeaten run, the final day of the League One season dawned with us in second place in the table, and in prime position to win automatic promotion. Bristol City had already been crowned Champions, but if we won our game away to Colchester, we would secure the second place finish we would need to join them in the Championship the following season. However, if we lost and MK Dons won, then they would leapfrog us to pinch that oh so coveted second automatic promotion spot.

MK Dons were at home to the already relegated Yeovil Town, whilst our opponents, Colchester United still had a chance of survival. They would need to beat us to have any chance of staying up. Despite Colchester being near the bottom of the table and us near the top, a victory for us was in no way guaranteed, whereas MK Dons would surely win their game. If we didn't win, we would drop back into the play-offs, and we all know what our record was in the dreaded play-offs.

Both matches would be shown live on Sky and as I didn't have Sky Sports, a trip down to the local pub would be necessary. I'd been there many times before to watch big Premier League games, and it was normally packed full with fans. But that Sunday afternoon, the place was almost empty as Becky and I walked in. The huge clash in Essex was obviously not that important to anyone else in Lancaster.

As so often with Preston, we let ourselves down that day and fell at the final hurdle. We seemed nervous and just not ourselves, and we were agonisingly beaten 1-0. We knew that we'd blown it, and when the MK Dons result came in, thrashing Yeovil 5-1, we had definitely blown our best chance in fifteen years of automatic promotion. The Colchester faithful were going crazy as they had avoided relegation, whereas our team, our fans, and certainly me, felt as though we were the ones who had been relegated, even though we had just finished third in the table.

As I trudged home from the pub I was disconsolate. I knew that most teams who slipped into the play-offs after having had the chance of an automatic spot could rarely recover from such a huge blow. The disappointment and deflation were too great, and the subsequent play-off games would usually be a complete letdown.

We would now have to play Chesterfield over two legs to get to Wembley, and even though we had finished a whole twenty points ahead of them, our only measly advantage would be that the second leg would be at Deepdale. This is where my solution to the play-off system would have been the fairest of outcomes, but as it was, we were basically starting again from scratch.

The following day at school, during the staff briefing which always happened on a Monday morning, I had to make an announcement about a school related matter, and I also had to apologise for my higher-than-usual levels of grumpiness this particular Monday morning. I had never been known for my cheery disposition on any morning, let alone a Monday morning, and definitely not the Monday morning after my football team had just messed up their whole season. Throughout the week I received many good luck wishes again, more in pity than in expectation of Preston's success, and they sustained me somewhat through my week of impending doom.

The first leg would be on the Thursday evening, with the return leg the following Sunday. At least I would be put out of my misery within a week of the Colchester defeat. Throughout the week I received many good luck wishes again, more in pity than in expectation of Preston's success, and they sustained me somewhat through my week of impending doom. But Simon Grayson, with his Yorkshire grit, was not going to allow his team to remain deflated.

357

He had achieved promotion with every other team he had managed and was not about to spoil that record. He breathed new life and belief into his team, if not into me.

We managed to get a 1-0 win down in Essex, with a goal from Jermaine Beckford to put us in pole position to get to Wembley. All we had to do now was not lose the second leg at Deepdale. The following Sunday, we didn't just not lose, but won comfortably, and the game included a goal that would go down in the Preston fans' hearts as one of the best we had ever seen.

Jermaine Beckford had put us 1-0 up before half time to make it 2-0 on aggregate, before Joe Garner had converted a penalty to put us in complete control of the tie. But Jermaine Beckford wanted to send us to Wembley with the ultimate spring in our step.

With just two minutes to go, he received the ball just inside his own half, nutmegged a defender and then just hit it. The ball soared over the keeper and into the net. He had just done a Beckham and scored from the halfway line to complete a 3-0 win on the day, and a resounding 4-0 aggregate win.

We had got to Wembley and would meet Swindon Town, who had finished the season in fourth place. The two teams who should have been there due to points accrued over the season had actually got there. By rights it should be us who should win the final, as we had claimed third spot, but as with many play-off finals, the team who finishes higher in the table does not always win.

Jermaine Beckford, fresh from his wonder goal from the halfway line, had other ideas though. And for what he did at Wembley, he will forever be loved by us PNE fans.

Preston North End v Swindon Town

League One Play-Off Final

May 24ᵗʰ, 2015   Wembley Stadium

If the game in 1989 in which Arsenal beat Liverpool at Anfield to snatch the title from their hosts was the culmination of Nick Hornby's "Fever Pitch" then this game would be the most comparable. Although there was certainly no near orgasmic climax to this game, as Hornby had euphorically witnessed, it would prove to be the greatest day in my life as a Preston fan. And I got to share it all with my daughter.

But first I had the not so small task of a trip to Cardiff the day before the match. I had been doing exam marking for the exam board which provided the GCSE syllabus I was teaching to my students, and every year this necessitated a trip to Cardiff for a marking conference.

Basically this meant that all the examiners would meet at a hotel, and had to be split into groups where we would all look at some sample answers and decide on marks for each answer to ensure consistency across the range of papers we would then have three weeks to mark. Each examiner, me included, would get around 350 scripts to mark before entering the marks on the online system. It was a slog, but the extra money would be a useful addition to being able to take my wife and kids away for a week in the summer holidays.

The conference would be held in Cardiff on the Saturday, the day before Preston's Play-Off Final at Wembley. This meant that I would have to leave school on Friday after work, endure a five-hour train journey to Cardiff, read and mark some scripts about "Of Mice and Men", "To Kill a Mockingbird" and a poem which both I and the students had never seen before, and then get the train back to Lancaster.

This meant that I would not get home until after 10pm, before I would then have to drive down to London the following morning. The kick off at Wembley was not until 5.30pm so at least I wouldn't have to set off at some ungodly hour.

Despite this I could not sleep very well. The train journey back up from Cardiff had been arduous and my PMT had kicked in already. I lay in bed thinking what could go wrong. Not just about what could go wrong on the pitch, after all we had lost nine previous play-offs by now, but also about how my increasingly unreliable little car would hold up on the journey, where I could park, how to get to Wembley, and also the fact that I would then have to start marking 350 exam scripts.

I was awake at about 6am, after only having had about four hours sleep. The car needed petrol so I went to the garage to fill it up and heard a rather worrying squealing sound coming from under the bonnet. This was not what I needed. I checked my oil and water and discovered that they both needed topping up. The squealing seemed to abate, but my car was still not filling me with confidence. It would just have to do.

Becky and I set off around 10am and made a steady journey down towards London. I had planned to pull off the motorway and park near one of the North London tube stations which would then take us to the sacred alter of Wembley Stadium.

Thankfully the car did not blow up, and a very nice, if rather opportunistic man offered to let me park on his driveway for the day if I gave him a certain sum of money. This was fine by me, and we went to get the tube down to Wembley. This was my first ever visit to the new Wembley Stadium and I was probably more excited about it than my daughter. I was doing for my her what my own dad had done for me, although this game was nowhere near as big as the FA Cup Final I had attended in 1985. But back then Preston were not involved; today they most definitely were. It was our equivalent of the Cup Final, with not just a trophy to be won, but also the prize of promotion back to the Championship.

We probably arrived at Wembley Park tube station around 3pm, and so had plenty of time to soak up the atmosphere. We wandered up a now very different Wembley Way, took photos of the statue of Bobby Moore with the new and very impressive Wembley arch as its backdrop, and got ourselves something to eat.

Even though I was completely shattered, I felt more alive than ever. I could feel that today was going to be a good day. Preston were the favourites to win; we had stormed through our semi-final whereas Swindon had struggled to get through theirs; we had finished ten points ahead of our opponents in the league; surely it would be tenth time lucky for us. Surely it was finally our turn.

We entered the stadium and both father and daughter had "that" moment. Wembley is as impressive a stadium as any in the world, and although it was nowhere near full when we saw the pitch for the first time, it was quite a staggering scene. Our seats were on the front row almost opposite the tunnel, with the Preston fans to our left, in the same end as I had been with my dad in 1985. We settled down and waited for the teams to emerge and the game to begin. The stadium was as full as two League One teams could make it, with well over 48,000 fans inside the ground, easily the biggest crowd I had ever been in watching Preston. The scene was set.

Our not insignificant nerves subsided somewhat after only three minutes with Jermaine Beckford continuing his unbelievable scoring form he had started in the play-off semi-final, knocking in one of Paul Gallagher's tantalising in swinging free kicks from inside the six yard box. We knew then that it was going to be our day. Probably.

Only ten minutes later, the nerves almost completely vanished when Paul Huntington, our centre back from Carlisle, who the Preston fans had affectionately named the Cumbrian Cannavaro due to his almost Italian enthusiasm for stopping others from scoring, actually got one himself. An almost identical ball in from Gallagher found Huntington waiting to gleefully tap in after he had stayed up for the corner which had been initially cleared. 2-0 up with less than a quarter of an hour played. One end of the ground was in utter dejection, whilst our end of the ground was in ecstasy. We couldn't believe how easy we were making it seem.

Swindon should have pulled one back, but just as everything we did came off, nothing they tried did. After this slight scare, we just went up the other end and scored a third, Beckford getting his second of the game with a sublime curling finish just before half time. 3-0 up at half time and the beers tasted that much sweeter during the interval.

They tasted so sweet that we didn't get to our seats in time for the start of the second half and almost missed Jermaine Beckford finishing off his hat trick. He had a glorious chance to score but Wes Foderingham, the keeper who had been hauled off the pitch by Paulo Di Canio at Deepdale after only twenty minutes back in 2012, made a fine save. Beckford must have known we weren't in our seats yet, and so very helpfully saved his hat trick goal until the 57th minute.

Another beautiful left foot finish and we were 4-0 up, with Beckford having scored three quarters of the goals. He celebrated right in front of me and Becky, with the photographers capturing the moment, and we even managed to feature in some of the pictures in the papers the next day.

It was at that point that our fans definitely knew it was to be finally our day. The last half hour of the match was just one big celebratory party in our end. It was such an exuberant and friendly atmosphere amongst the thousands of Preston fans who had so often been on the wrong end of results like this. There were no nerves, no tension and no nagging doubts that we could still mess it all up.

The full time whistle blew and after ten attempts, finally, finally we could say that we had won a play-off campaign. We had done it. The Swindon end was already mostly empty, and as the rest of their fans streamed home for the not too long journey back to Wiltshire, we stayed in the ground to watch our heroes lift the trophy and show it to us all, which they obliged us by doing time after time.

Remember when I said that the play-off system was unfair and there was no need for a Wembley Final? I take it all back. That day was the best day ever, and one which I never would have experienced had Preston got automatic promotion. The added stress, tension, and expense of the three play-off games were all absolutely worth it at that moment. This was the best place to win a game and definitely the best place to get promoted.

After years of disappointment and agony, we had done something we had never done before, and I was so pleased I had my daughter there to share the moment with me. I immediately rang my dad, who hadn't gone to the game with us partly due to his health, but mainly due to the game being played on a Sunday, and we both shared a moment of reflection together. I would see him the next day to recount every detail with him, with Becky there to add any details that I'd missed out.

At that point there were three generations of PNE fans, all sharing in the same moment. He still hasn't seen Preston win at Wembley, but at least me and my daughter had. If he wasn't able to have been there, then at least he shared our moment of glory with us down the phone line.

I know he understood how much he meant to me that day, even though he wasn't actually there with me. After all, he could have supported someone else and then I would never have seen that Jermaine Beckford hat trick and Tom Clarke, our captain, lift the trophy on that wearying yet wonderful day out at Wembley.

Even the journey home was great. As the convoy of Preston supporting cars got onto the M1, we all put our scarves out of the windows, allowing them to flutter wildly, just like our emotions had been earlier, taking up all three lanes to everybody else's annoyance. We were all sounding our horns in a cacophony of exuberance, before we went back to abiding the laws of the highway code.

Even when we stopped off at a service station somewhere near Birmingham, there were loads of fans all celebrating, and just then, we saw David Moyes, the man who, as a player had helped get us to Wembley in 1994, and the man who, as a manager, had brought us the League One title in 2000, coming towards us. He had been at the game too and was stopping off for a coffee. He may well have suspected that there would be hordes of PNE fans there, and maybe he also knew that he would be mobbed by us all. He didn't seem to mind. Maybe he wanted to celebrate with us all again as he had done fifteen and twenty one years earlier.

We finally arrived home around 1am and it would take me another few hours until I fell asleep such was the adrenaline and euphoria. I had been to Cardiff and back, as well as Wembley and back in the space of just over 48 hours. It was now my wife's birthday but she did not begrudge me a lie in. It was also Bank Holiday Monday at the start of my half term week so I was due a lie in even if it was my wife's special day. But it was nowhere near as special as the day me and Becky had experienced the day before.

As Becky finally emerged and came downstairs all bleary eyed, she came into the dining room where I was sitting, immediately gave me a hug and said thank you for yesterday. Maybe it was the hug, maybe it was the release of tension from Preston having won, maybe it was the relief that we had made it there and back safely without the car blowing up. Whatever it was, and I don't mind admitting it, but at that moment I cried. I had given my daughter something similar to what my dad had given me, and she loved me for it.

Or maybe I cried as I realised that I hadn't got my wife a birthday present, and I now had only three weeks to mark 350 exam scripts.

Manchester City v Leicester City

February 6th, 2016   Etihad Stadium

If Preston had done something miraculous the season before, then Leicester City would do something not just miraculous, but something which would have been literally unbelievable to anyone in the world had you told them that Leicester City would be Premier League Champions in 2016.

I include this chapter because what Leicester City did gives hope to every other team in the country. Supporters of every club, especially those clubs who have never really had any success can now say if Leicester did it, why not us? It really was a game changing season, or maybe it was just a fluke, one that will never be repeated.

Leicester had never won anything of real note in their entire history. They do hold the record for the most FA Cup Final appearances without winning, having been to Wembley four times and never won any of these four games. They'd won the League Cup three times and a few Second Division titles, but that was about it, and then, out of the blue, just like their shirt colour, they won the biggest prize of all. It truly was a phenomenon, and one which may never be repeated by a club of their size and stature. But they did it once, and so proved it can be done.

The previous season they had to pull off the first miracle of this story by surviving in the Premier League when they looked doomed. They had been at the bottom of the table from mid-November and everyone just assumed that they would go down. By January they had only won four games all season and would not win another one until April. But from then on, they won seven out of their last nine games, drawing once to pick up 22 points from a possible 27.

That run of form was title chasing form rather than relegation battling form, and they ended up avoiding relegation by six points. Their manager, Nigel Pearson, a man who seemed permanently angry with everyone and everything, particularly with his employers, had saved them and started to plan for the following season.

However, his rather tempestuous relationship with the owners of the club came to a head after his son, a youth team player, had been involved in a rather distasteful episode on a post-season tour to Thailand involving Thai girls and a video which had been put out on social media. Both son and then father were sacked after the working relationship with the club broke down. I think the Thai owners had just had enough of him and so decided the club's future would be better served if he was no longer there. However, he was responsible for bringing in some hugely important players before he left.

He brought in Christian Fuchs, Robert Huth, Shinji Okazaki, and most importantly a young French player whose parents had immigrated from Mali and named their son after a King, N'Golo Kante. Leicester's scout, former player Steve Walsh, had found him playing for a little known French team called Caen. Walsh had also been responsible for the signings of Riyad Mahrez and Jamie Vardy,

366

so I think it's safe to say that much of Leicester's success could be down to him.

When Leicester appointed former Chelsea manager Claudio Ranieri to replace Pearson no one expected much from him. Gary Lineker, Leicester's most high profile fan, was certainly not impressed, and like the rest of us, expected the following season to be not that different from many others before; it would be another fight for survival.

The question was whether Ranieri could continue the form they had shown for the last nine games of the previous season. The answer was a most definite yes. They didn't lose until the end of September, and by then Jamie Vardy had begun what would become a record breaking run of scoring in eleven consecutive Premier League games. He simply could not stop scoring.

From the end of August and throughout the whole of September, October and November Vardy scored in every Premier League game that Leicester played. It was a stunning achievement that would come to an end against Swansea in early December, with Vardy not managing to score in a 3-0 away win. Leicester would still win without him scoring, mainly due to Riyad Mahrez who had become a revelation that season. He would go onto become the first ever African player to win the PFA Player's Player award. With Peter Schmeichel's son Kasper becoming almost as good a keeper as his father had been, and that is a huge compliment by the way, Leicester were becoming not only dynamic up front but also hard to score against. The question was would they be able to continue.

Most people thought not, famously including Gary Lineker, who promised to present the first Match of the Day the following season in his underwear if Leicester did go on and win the league. Everyone else, like him, was just waiting for their bubble to burst and then they could maybe fight for a Champions League spot. But the bubble did not burst.

They had an average Christmas period, only taking five points out of a possible twelve, and then went out of the FA Cup to Spurs. This did not seem to bother them as they now had only one competition to focus on. Whereas all their rivals for the title were embroiled in other competitions, both domestic and European, they could relax back into the routine of playing a match at the weekend and then having no interferences in their preparations for the following weekend's match.

After their loss in the Cup, they then beat Spurs away in the league the following week, and this would be the start of their next remarkable run. Within a month they would not only beat Spurs, but Liverpool, which included a truly memorable strike from Vardy, and then Manchester City, at the Etihad, which is the game I have included here.

I could have picked many games from Leicester's remarkable season, but this 3- 1 victory away at City summed up their belief, their ability and their devastating pace, and it made everyone realise that if they could do that to a team like City on their own ground, then they could do it to anyone. It was at this point that I started to think that we could well be seeing Gary Lineker's pants.

Big Robert Huth had put them in front after only three minutes, before Mahrez doubled the lead with another sublime finish just after half time. After an hour they were 3-0 up and out of sight, Huth getting another, before Sergio Aguero got a consolation goal with two minutes left. For a team like Man City to be getting a consolation goal says it all about how good Leicester were that evening.

The following morning I made a beeline for my Man City season ticket holding mate at work. I wanted to ask him just how good Leicester had been. He had been to every game that season at The Etihad and he said that Leicester were the best he'd seen. He actually seemed a little embarrassed about being beaten by Leicester, but he had no reason to be embarrassed. Many other teams would suffer the same fate as City had done.

In fact there was only one team that season that Leicester would not take points from. After beating City, Arsenal would then beat them for the second time, but that would be the last time Leicester would lose all season. Their last twelve games would bring 28 points from a possible 36. They did not just win the title by one or two points; they smashed it, finishing ten points clear of second placed Arsenal and fifteen clear of Man City in fourth place.

And so when they were presented with the trophy in front of their incredulous fans, nobody could blame grown men for openly weeping. I completely understand why they were crying. I would have done by the bucket load. These fans had spent all of their lives never expecting anything even remotely close to what their team had just achieved. And here they were: Premier League Champions 2016.

That year would prove to be a year where many strange things happened. After Leicester's outlandish victory, next came the Brexit vote and Donald Trump's election as US President. None of these things made any sense at all, and I would not have been surprised if Ed Balls had won Strictly Come Dancing either. Thankfully at least the Strictly voters still had their senses about them, but to this day, Leicester's achievement does not make sense.

And that is why football is so wonderful. Its unpredictability and ability to surprise is why we all love it, as well as the fact we all got to see Gary Lineker's pants. An achievement like Leicester's may well never happen again. But that is what we all said before it actually happened. Who knows, if Leicester did it, then why not a team like Burnley, or Stoke, or Southampton, or Crystal Palace, or maybe even a team like Preston.

But first we have to get into the Premier League to even have a chance of winning it. Since our glorious win at Wembley we have had four mid-table finishes in the Championship, and have even flirted with the play-offs again on a couple of occasions. But at least we are in the position now to at least say, as Delboy always said to Rodney, "This time next year we could be millionaires".

Colombia v England

World Cup Second Round

July 3rd, 2018   Spartak Stadium, Moscow

Thank God that Sam Allardyce is a bit of a greedy bastard. After the omnishambles of Euro 2016, when yet another thing did not make sense after England were knocked out by Iceland, leading to Woy Hodgson's rather woeful tenure as England manager coming to an end, the FA, in their infinite wisdom, did the only thing they were good at; they panicked.

We had a struggling team and who better at helping struggling sides out of a hole than Big Sam. The FA sent out the signal, like the signal which would summon Batman, but instead this signal would have a big fat pie as its silhouette. The pie would probably have looked a bit like one of Desperate Dan's cow pies, and we must have been desperate if our only option for the new England manager's job was Sam Allardyce.

He couldn't believe his luck and signed a two-year contract which should have taken him up to the World Cup in Russia, but he only lasted one game. He won his only game in charge against Slovakia after an Adam Lallana injury time winner in our first qualifying match. Sam obviously loved the job too much, especially some of the perks that went with it.

As a result, he fell hook, line and sinker into a trap set by journalists who had posed as Asian businessmen. After his comments to them about how to get around FA and FIFA rules about ownership of players, as well as some not particularly friendly banter about Gary Neville and his predecessor as England manager, he realised that he had stuck his finger into one too many pies, and resigned.

The FA were now scraping the barrel for a replacement, and the only man they could think of was Gareth Southgate, the Under-21s manager. He would be given the job, but only on a temporary basis to see if he could prove himself worthy. He grabbed his opportunity with both hands and won two out of the next three qualifying games, including a 3-0 win against Scotland.

A draw against Slovenia and then a very impressive display in a friendly against Spain, which we should have won but conceded twice in the last few minutes after having led 2-0, were enough for the FA to give him a four-year deal as permanent England manager, and thank God they did. It would seem that with no other choice, the FA finally made the right choice.

Southgate has transformed the England team from a bunch of losers to a team of potential winners; the keywords there being "team" and "potential", as we have not won anything yet, and may still not do, but we are now a team, and not just a collection of talented individuals. His appointment now seems like an inspired one, if only for the fact that nobody had any expectations of Southgate. He'd done an impressive job with the Under-21 side, but managing the full

England team was always going to be different, and yet he has done it with charm, intelligence, astute tactical skill and perhaps most importantly, humility. He never said he would be the messiah, but he almost was once England qualified for the World Cup and then almost got to the final. And he looked quite trim in a waistcoat too.

The build up to the World Cup in Russia was unlike any previous tournament. No one believed we would do particularly well, and just getting into the knockout phase would have been ok, especially as we hadn't done that at the last World Cup in Brazil. Southgate had taken the brave decision to drop Wayne Rooney from the England squad in March 2017 to see how the team would perform without their talisman. The team did not seem to miss him, which no doubt was part of Rooney's decision to retire from England duty the following August.

Without a major star in their team now, expectations for England fell below the radar. There would be no ridiculous predictions coming from anyone in the media, there would be no nationalistic nonsense from the press, there would be no houses covered in white and red, and no ubiquitous England flags flying from cars. It was just the way Southgate wanted it: understated, respectful and humble, reflecting his own personality.

The country finally woke up to our potential after our first match against Tunisia. We won 2-1, but only just, with Harry Kane, who was now becoming our new talisman scoring a last minute winner. And then we would play Panama, who were World Cup virgins. When we beat them 6-1, being 5-0 up at half time, the country started to think we might be onto something.

Our two wins meant we had already qualified for the knockout phase, and so when we lost 1-0 to Belgium with a much changed team, no one cared, especially as that meant we would have a potentially easier route through to the latter stages. We would have to play Colombia in the second round, but this would prove to be much more difficult than we thought it would be, and we would have to do something we had never done before.

This game is memorable for two reasons for me; one, England won their first ever World Cup penalty shootout, and two, I had just cycled through Wales and watched it in a caravan park in Porthmadog. My mates Alks and The Boss were now happily retired and had done a few cycle rides together. Well not together as Alks would cycle whilst The Boss would drive his camper van to the next evening's destination and set up camp for the night. They had already done Land's End to John O'Groats and now wanted to embark on a tour of the Welsh coast, starting in Chester and ending somewhere near Cardiff.

I had by now left my school and was doing supply teaching work. This gave me more flexibility, if not more income, and when they asked me to join them for their Welsh caper, I said I'd be able to do one leg of the trip, from Denbigh through to Porthmadog. My finances and my wife would not allow any more so I had to make the most of these two nights of freedom.

After a few beers watching Belgium cruelly beat Japan, a game we would have been involved in had we won our group, we set off from our campsite and began our not too long but definitely very hot route through to the west coast. We decided to take a short cut and cut out the coastal element of the Welsh coast by going through Ffestiniog and then onto Portmeirion, the weird and wonderful setting for the 1960s TV show "The Prisoner". We had a lovely wander round in our lycra, causing many rather startled looks from the tourists, before the final few miles to the coast would be negotiated.

It was boiling hot that day. In fact Porthmadog would be the hottest place in the country, and as we rolled into our caravan park where The Boss had parked up and unpacked, we dumped our bikes and ran straight into the sea. What a lovely sight we must have been; one man in his early sixties, and one in his mid-forties stripped down to our cycling shorts splashing around with childish glee in the sea, with the hills of Snowdonia as our backdrop.

After cooling down sufficiently, we showered and then got ready to watch the match. We got to the bar/restaurant early to ensure prime position in front of the big screen and got the beers in. A lovely meal was had with great conversation, but then it was time for the conversation to stop; England had the chance to win their first knockout match at a World Cup since they had beaten Ecuador in 2006.

The game proved to be much more tense than it should have been. After the referee finally realised that Harry Kane was getting pulled all over the place from every set piece we had, he finally gave us a penalty which Kane smashed in with his now deadly accuracy. We all thought we would go on and win comfortably, but as usual with England, we would make it hard for ourselves.

We just could not kill the game off and when Colombia equalised in added time, we knew this was going to be one of those nights, especially as we couldn't muster a goal in extra time and we would have to endure another penalty shootout lottery.

But this time we seemed to have a new belief in ourselves, probably due to the fact that Gareth Southgate was the first England manager to not only have taken part in a shootout for England, but definitely the only one to have failed in one. His experience in Euro 96 gave him and the rest of his team the confidence to banish the ghosts of our past failures, and even after Jordan Henderson missed his spot kick, we still believed we could win.

Colombia then hit the cross bar before Jordan Pickford (ex-Preston by the way) saved the next one. It was now up to Eric Dier to score and win us the shootout, which he did with this new found confidence flowing through him.

The bar in that caravan site went wild, with the mostly English clientele jumping around in wild celebrations. We knew that we would have to beat Sweden and probably Croatia to get to our first World Cup Final since 1966, an age ago in modern terms. Both games were definitely winnable and when we dispatched Sweden the following Saturday with ease, the whole country started to believe that football was coming home. Baddiel and Skinner's song from Euro 96 found a new lease of life before the semi-final, but again, just as we had done back then, we failed.

Even though we failed to win, we had not failed at the tournament. We had got further than we ever expected to do, and Croatia were just better than us on the night. Even if he had got to the final, we would never have beaten France, but we could still return home with our heads held high rather than hanging them in shame as we had done at the previous couple of tournaments.

But for all the euphoria, our record at the 2018 World Cup was not that impressive. Yes we got to the last four, but out of seven games we played, including the Third Place Play-Off, we only won three in normal time, and one of those only just. Our only other victory was via a penalty shootout against a team we should have beaten comfortably. We lost twice to Belgium and then to Croatia, two teams who are still not part of the footballing elite, never having won any tournaments yet, so all the raving about a new dawn for the England team may well prove to be both presumptuous and premature, but at least we have hope and expectation back again.

England's impressive performances to get to the final of the Nations League the following season allowed the hope to build, only for us to let ourselves down once again in the final. It will be only when we win matches that really matter against teams that really matter that I will fully believe we are capable of winning a tournament, but there are positive signs for sure.

At least Marks and Spencer know that their sales of waistcoats will be ok as long as Gareth Southgate is in charge. If we get to the final of Euro 2020 or maybe even the next World Cup then maybe I'll even buy one and wear it too.

Ajax v Tottenham Hotspur

Champions League Semi-Final, Second Leg

May 8th, 2019   Johan Cruyff Arena, Amsterdam

By the end of this ridiculous game of football, my wife looked like a prune as she had spent the whole of the second half in the bath. It had nothing to do with her in no way unusual levels of hygiene, but it was all connected with the almost as ridiculous game the previous evening. Allow me to explain.

The previous night, Liverpool were 3-0 down to Barcelona after taking what looked like a hammering at the Camp Nou the previous week. In fact they had played very well and were unlucky to even lose, let alone get beaten by such a margin. It was only due to the mercurial talents of probably the greatest player of all time, the GOAT that is Lionel Messi, with another astonishing free kick that the scoreline was so heavily weighted towards the Spanish giants.

No one really expected Liverpool to overturn this deficit. Some die hard Reds fans may well have believed that they could, but as for expecting it to happen, that was a different matter. I certainly didn't as I turned on the TV to watch.

My wife, an ardent Twitter user who follows the journalist and former Radio 5Live presenter Shelagh Fogarty, kept me updated as to Fogarty's strange behaviour that evening. Throughout the game she had been tweeting about not being able to watch and having to stand outside in her garden. Once Liverpool pulled a goal back early on, she obviously thought that she should remain in her garden as that was helping her team overcome the odds.

When Liverpool pulled level on aggregate with two quick goals in the space of just 122 seconds from Georginio Wijnaldum, there was no question; she was staying in the garden for the rest of the evening and would not see the most stunning comeback in the history of the Champions League. Liverpool of course went on to score a fourth, with Divock Origi latching onto the most brilliant piece of quick thinking from Trent Alexander-Arnold's cheeky corner.

They managed to hold on for a 4-0 victory, overturning the result in Spain and reached the Champions League Final in consecutive years, the first time an English club had done it since Man United did it in 2008 and 2009. It really was the most special of nights at Anfield, a night I thought could never be bettered. It may well never be bettered for those Liverpool fans, and the following day the radio and social media was saturated with scousers who were still in raptures over what had happened the previous evening, many not having had any sleep due to the exhilaration they experienced.

It was the comeback to end all comebacks, and surely the other semi-final, indeed no other game ever, would be able to match the drama and the emotion of what had happened at Anfield. Spurs were 1-0 down after they had lost in their brand spanking new stadium in the first leg, and would need to beat Ajax in Amsterdam. Again no one really believed or expected they would be able to do it. Step up Lucas Moura, and step into the bath my wife.

At first, my wife joined me on the sofa that night to see if her team could at least make a game of it, but after only five minutes they went further behind and then after 35 minutes, when Ajax got a second on the night to go 3-0 up on aggregate, the tie was basically dead.

Liverpool at least had a whole game to pull their tie back. Spurs now had just one half of one game to try and get the three goals they would need to go through on away goals. This was never going to happen. If anything, Ajax looked the more likely to extend their lead, and so as the half time whistle blew my wife went upstairs and started running a bath. She even said that she would try Shelagh Fogarty's tactics by removing herself from the room.

Whilst the bath was running, the Ajax crowd had been celebrating their victory, singing along to Bob Marley's "Three Little Birds" with the famous lyrics of "Don't worry about a thing, cos every little thing, gonna be alright." How wrong they would be? They would have plenty to worry about.

By the time the bath had filled, and my wife stepped in, the second half was just about to get under way. And what an extraordinary 45 minutes she would gladly miss. Actually it was more like 51 minutes, as the added six minutes would prove to be not just crucial, but also the most dramatic few minutes of football I think I had ever seen, rivalling the added time of Man United's Champions League victory in 1999.

After ten minutes of soaking in the bath and channeling her inner Tottenham vibes, my wife was just about to give up and get out. But just at the moment she was reaching for the towel, Lucas Moura, who was only in the team because of Harry Kane's injury, burst through the Ajax defence and pulled a goal back. I immediately shouted up to my wife for her to stay in the bath; whatever she had been channeling for the last ten minutes was obviously working. This was confirmed only four minutes later when a shot from Fernando Llorente was miraculously saved, the keeper then spilled the ball and Moura, with the quickest of feet, managed to spin and slam the loose ball in to make it 2-2 on the night.

Spurs would now only need one more goal and they had over half an hour to get it. In the commentary, Darren Fletcher asked the question whether a Champions League miracle was going to happen again. We all now started to think that it most definitely could.

My wife's bath was starting to get a bit cold by now, but she shouted down that she was topping it up and wasn't moving. The game was now on the sharpest of knife edges. If Ajax scored again, Spurs would need two more; if Spurs scored, then Ajax would only need one. Ajax then hit the post and again the question was asked whether it was going to be Spurs' night, but then they hit the bar and we thought that their chance had gone.

The game trickled into added time and Ajax again should have won it in the third of the added five minutes, with Hugo Lloris making a great save to keep his team's hope alive. Spurs went up the other end but their attack was thwarted, the Ajax keeper holding onto the ball for far too long in his quest to run the clock down. This proved to be crucial as the referee would add this blatantly wasted time on. And then, just as the clock had passed the 95 minute mark, the miracle was completed.

A hopeful long ball was punted up from the back by Sissoko, it fell to Delle Alli who knocked it into the path of the marauding Moura, who slotted the ball past the Ajax keeper to complete his hat trick and send Spurs through. The Ajax defenders were literally sprawled on the ground not believing what had just happened. Even though no one else believed what had just happened, there were no Spurs fans sprawled anywhere, although we all feared for Glenn Hoddle who had just resumed his pundit's role for BT Sport after suffering a huge

heart attack only a few months before. He and the rest of the Spurs'
fans were going absolutely berserk wherever they were. I was
jumping around my front room in utter disbelief and shock, whilst
my wife was emptying the bath without even taking out the plug
such was her manic animation.

There was no time for Ajax to come back and the final whistle blew
to complete the most devastating, the most stupendous, the most
ridiculous comeback ever. The previous evening's game had been
surpassed in terms of drama, and this was seen in the Spurs'
manager, Mauricio Pochettino's face as he wept with emotion not
only on the pitch in front of his fans, but also in the post-match
interview. It was a game which completely overwhelmed not just
him, but anyone who watched it. It was simply stunning, and it was
all down to my wife deciding to take a bath at half time.

We all know what happened in the final when Liverpool and Spurs
met. We all know that it was the dullest, most boring game of
football ever. Even Liverpool fans could not say it was a good game
despite them winning 2-0 to claim their sixth European Cup. It was
as though both teams had used up all their potential for drama in the
two most thrilling games of football on consecutive evenings anyone
had ever seen.

Or maybe Spurs lost because my wife didn't have a bath that night.
We will never know.

Watford v Manchester City

FA Cup Final

May 18th, 2019   Wembley Stadium

And so we come full circle. I mentioned in my introduction that I started this book the day after the latest FA Cup Final, just after Manchester City had won every domestic trophy in one season that they possibly could win. They had just created history. They had shown complete dominance over every other team in the whole country, and had done something no other team had done before. Never before has one team won everything. Now one team has.

The football that the Manchester City team has played over the past two seasons has been as near to perfection as possible. Quite simply, they have taken the game to a higher level, one that no other team has gone to before. They're the Captain Kirk of football teams.

Of course they made history the year before just to add to the phenomenon. And that is what this team are: a phenomenon. To have won the Premier League in 2018 by 19 points, the largest margin ever, and to have accumulated 100 points over the course of one season was their first history making feat. They just upped it a notch this season, even though they only managed 98 points this time.

Forty years ago, just as I'd started watching football, a team like this would have been unthinkable. Their levels of skill, their levels of tactical ability, their levels of physical conditioning are all so much higher. The players back then were just that: players. But now the players are also supremely conditioned athletes. The current Manchester city team are just more supremely conditioned than any team ever before, and who knows, they may even take it up another notch and win a Quintuple (is that even a word?) next year, with the

European Cup thrown in as well. With the way they have played these past two seasons, it wouldn't surprise me any more if they did.

If it hadn't been for another team taking their performances up not just one, but two or three levels, then Man City may well not have achieved what they did. Without Liverpool's own brilliance, Man City would not have had to up their game that little bit more and so maybe would not have been as close to perfection as they needed to be.

For Liverpool to have accumulated 97 points, losing only one game all season, and still not win the Premier league, shows just how good Man City had to be.

Looking at the Premier League results of both teams in a vertical list, with wins in green, draws in yellow, and defeats in red, Liverpool's results look like a very tall sandwich, filled mostly with lettuce, a few strips of cheese dotted here and there, and one slice of tomato right in the middle. Whereas Man City's sandwich is basically lettuce, lots of lettuce, in both halves of the sandwich that has been split into two with a fairly ample layer of tomatoes in the middle, and just a couple of thin strips of cheese towards the top.

I'm not sure I'd want to eat either sandwich but if you love lettuce, then these are the sandwiches for you. Basically both teams won a lot of games and filled their sandwich with a lot of lettuce; Man City just won more than Liverpool and filled their sandwich with two more bits of lettuce than Liverpool did to win the sandwich filling competition. Just. As for the two side dishes for the other competitions, Liverpool had just one solitary stuffed red pepper in each, whilst Man City's overflowed with green ones.

Enough with these bad culinary metaphors; Liverpool were astonishingly good; Man City were even better. And no game showed just how good they were like the last game of the lot; their 6-0 annihilation of Watford at Wembley to complete the full set.

A gospel choir had been brought in to help with the singing of "Abide With Me" and the angels were certainly with Manchester City that day. Their football was indeed heavenly. They won by the biggest margin since good old Bury had beaten Derby in 1903 by the same scoreline. I have no idea how good Bury were that day, or whether they should have scored more, but Man City in 2019 could and probably should have scored ten, despite not really starting to play until the 25th minute or so.

They should have been 1-0 down after Watford missed a glorious opportunity to take an early lead, and survived a penalty scare which could easily have been given, but that just angered City. This just brought out another side of this team which is often ignored; their sheer and almost cruel ruthlessness. They were now going to show Watford how they really could play, and teach them the harshest of lessons for having the cheek to think they had even the slightest chance of winning.

Within twelve minutes of starting to play properly, they were 2-0 up, and the game was basically won by half time. And then, quite frankly, they toyed with their opponents. They scored another couple, and we were all starting to hide behind our sofas by now. It was already a rout, and could easily become a record breaking scoreline, with Watford being reduced almost to bewildered and bamboozled bystanders.

Another couple to make it 6-0, just to make sure. None of the goals were individual stunners, or wonder strikes from 30 yards out. They could do those type of goals too, as they had demonstrated on countless occasions over the season, but this time they were all team goals. Every goal came from within twelve yards, five of them coming from inside four yards, and two were put over the line from literally inches away. They literally walked the ball into the net.

Let's not forget that this wasn't against some lower league team, against, with the greatest of respect, the Bury team of 2019, who, it's fair to say have not repeated the glories of their predecessors of 1903; this was against Watford, a team who finished 11th in the Premier League, and yet City were still able to walk the ball over the line. I've never seen a team so utterly dominant and completely at one with their own individual abilities and those of their team mates. It was maybe not the most dramatic or exciting way to end the season, but it was the most fitting of ways to end a season which had proved to be as close to perfection as possible.

But as I said, they may well just go on and do it again next season, and possibly even improve on it. With Pep Guardiola in charge, maybe anything at all is possible. They could win four, five or even six trophies in one season, including a Super Cup thrown in as a bonus too if they continue to improve. I'm not saying they will, but they might, and that achievement literally could never be beaten. Maybe that's what Pep wants. I'm looking forward to finding out.

But all that's in the future, and now it's time, after all this constant reminiscing, to get my crystal ball out and finally look forward instead of back.

England v USA

Women's World Cup Semi-Final

July 2nd, 2019   Parc Olympique Lyonnais, Decines-Charpieu

This final game encompasses two elements of our wonderful game which most definitely have a future; the women's game, and Video Assisted Referees, which at the moment is a step too VAR.

One of these elements has a bright future which will only keep on improving. The other could also have a bright future, but only if it changes from its current format which is frankly damaging the game it was meant to enhance. I'm sure you can work out which is which. Let's deal with the one which needs no changing at all as it's doing very well indeed already.

When I started watching football, the women's game was just not a thing really. I was aware that some women played football, but as for it having any sort of impact on me, then it was hugely off the radar. It was never on TV and the concept of it being played professionally was laughable. I don't even remember any females watching games back then, maybe a few at Old Trafford, but certainly not at Deepdale. It was an all-male domain and that for many fans was how it should stay.

And yet, Preston had, at one point, the greatest women's football team there had ever been, with some of the greatest female players the world has ever seen. I am proud to say that if my team has not been a world leader in anything else, they pioneered the women's game, and built it to the point that it actually threatened the men's game, before us men got scared by it and simply made it illegal. Good old forward thinking in abundance from us men there.

About fifty yards away from the statue of Sir Tom Finney which stands proudly outside Deepdale, there is another monument to greatness. This is no small plaque tucked away in a corner of Deepdale, but a three and a half tonne slab of granite, six metres wide and four metres high commemorating a team of women known as The Dick, Kerr Ladies. It took us until 2017 to get round to unveiling such a memorial, but better late than never.

The Dick, Kerr Ladies were formed during the First World War, when most of the men who worked at the Dick, Kerr and Co. ammunitions factory in Preston were away fighting in France. The female workers would kick a ball around during their lunch breaks, and were spotted from his office window by a man called Alfred Frankland, who thought the women were good enough to play a proper game. As a way of boosting morale, a game of football was organised between the female workers, and the remaining male workers. The women won.

Their success was the catalyst to play against another team of munitions workers, the Arundel Coulthard Factory, based in Stockport, and it would be played on Christmas Day, 1917 at Deepdale, which Preston North End had been kind enough to allow them the use of.

The game was won 4-0 by the "home" team, despite not even having a home, and was watched by 10,000 spectators. Not only that, but along with some cracking entertainment, a large sum of money (over £40,000 in today's money) was also raised for the local hospital for wounded soldiers.

It was a huge success, and even got a patronising write-up in The Daily Post, where The Dick, Kerr Ladies' attacking play was described as "surprisingly good, with one or two of the ladies showing admirable ball control." I assume the writer of this was referring to a girl called Lily Parr, who was nothing short of a phenomenon, scoring over 900 goals by the end of her footballing career. Had she been playing today, she would have been a superstar.

More games were organised against other local factories, with more money raised for charity, and even when the war ended, the team remained very popular. Even a team of French ladies was invited over to play, and in 1920 the first ever international women's game was played at Deepdale. Other matches in the series were subsequently played in Stockport and Manchester, with the final game being played at Stamford Bridge in London. The trip to the capital really brought the team to the attention of the masses and many more games were arranged. On Boxing Day 1920, the Dick, Kerr Ladies played against St. Helens' Ladies at Goodison Park in front of 53,000 people, but less than a year later, women's football would be banned by the FA.

The FA, in their predictably infinite wisdom, thought that the men's game, the proper game in their blinkered eyes, was being threatened by the popularity of the women, and with the pathetic excuse that the game could be damaging to the women's weak and feeble bodies, they simply stopped it from happening and banned women from playing football at all.

The ban lasted for the next fifty years, and was only lifted in 1971. So, it was no wonder that when I started going to Deepdale, to watch a team of men play ironically in front of much smaller crowds than those women played in front of, the women's game was still in its infancy. Fifty years of potential had been ripped from the women's game, and basically had to start from scratch again.

Back then, the only comparison I can make is with women's tennis. My mum would always watch Wimbledon, and as my only way of bonding with her on a sporting basis, I would watch with her too. She would always prefer to watch the men play, and did not care much for the women's game. Even though Virginia Wade had won

Wimbledon in 1977, my mum found her play airy-fairy, or namby-pamby as she would call it. The women's game was much slower and lacked the power, excitement, and thrills of the men's game, with players like Bjorn Borg, Jimmy Connors and even John McEnroe (although she did disapprove of his manners) being much preferred to the wishy-washy play of the women, despite the efforts of pioneers like Billie Jean King raising the standard of the women's game, and bringing it closer to the standard of the men.

But since then, players like Martina Navratilova, Steffi Graf, and more recently, Venus and especially Serena Williams, have brought the women's game up to a standard comparable to the men's game. Women have become quicker, more powerful and just as exciting.

In fact, to a non-tennis player like me, I prefer to watch women play as I can relate to their game more. The men's game is just too powerful and too explosive, where their obvious skills are almost drowned with speed and power. But in the women's game, although slightly slower and less explosive, their skills are much more keenly observed. The same is true of women's football.

The game played by the women of today is just as technically skillful as the men. Yes it may be slower and at times less dynamic, but that is why the women's skill factors are so high. They are not able to simply power past opponents; they have to pass the ball more efficiently and create goals in a more intelligent way. It is more relatable to youngsters and as such will continue to inexorably grow. The more it is watched, the more TV coverage it gets. The more high profile the players become, then the women's game will naturally become just as important a factor in football as a whole as the men's game already is.

And it's not just female players. Women will also continue to play a greater role in other aspects of the game. Female officials already take charge of men's games. Only last week a female referee officiated at the European Super Cup between Chelsea and Liverpool. No one cared, and those who did will have to just accept this obvious progression in the game as a whole. It will only be a matter of time before high ranking positions are taken up by women within football's controlling authorities like the FA, UEFA and even FIFA. Unless this happens, parity will never be achieved. I don't know when there will be a female President of FIFA, but it will happen sooner or later.

The women's international tournaments will naturally become part of our footballing lives, just as the men's tournaments are now. I watched every England game at the Women's World Cup in 2019, and saw the best and the worst of the game. As far as the worst parts, just look at how the Cameroon team behaved in their second round match against England. When decisions did not go their way, they behaved like small children having a temper tantrum.

This is not what the women's game needs, and Phil Neville, the England manager, quite rightly called the Cameroon players' out for their appalling behaviour. Another game which did no favours for the women's game was the frankly brutal demolition by the USA of Thailand by the remarkable scoreline of 13-0. Results like this make the women's game and the competition look amateurish rather than the professional game it is rapidly becoming.

As for the best, players like Megan Rapinoe and Alex Morgan for the US team, and players such as Steph Houghton, Fran Kirby, Lucy Bronze, Ellen White and Jill Scott for England are all becoming household names, and their skills are finally being recognised as matching those of their male counterparts. They have become role models for not just girls to look up to, but also boys. They may well never achieve absolute parity with the men, but they could get close, just as Lily Parr had done for the Dick, Kerr Ladies a hundred years ago.

As for the match in question, just like the England men's team in their semi-final a year before, we were beaten by a better team on the night. Christen Press headed USA into the lead after just ten minutes, only for Ellen White to equalise nine minutes later with a beautiful finish from the edge of the six-yard box. England were looking as though they could go on and win it, but a sucker punch from Alex Morgan in the 31st minute made it 2-1 to the USA at half time.

The second half was dominated by two incidents which I will go into in more detail later as they were both referred to the VAR officials. We scored what seemed like a perfectly good goal, but it was deemed to be offside, before we were awarded a penalty by VAR. Steph Houghton had the chance to draw us level again, but women can miss penalties too, and her penalty was saved to keep the score at 2-1 and allow the USA to progress to the final which they subsequently won. England would go onto lose the Third-Place Play-Off to Sweden and finished a disappointing fourth, but the fact that we were disappointed will breed the desire to do even better next time.

We lost at the same stage to the same opponents in 2015 too, but with the increase in exposure, I would not be surprised if we win the World Cup at the next tournament. I think the women's team have more chance of winning the World Cup before the men's team does. I now look forward to watching international tournaments not just in the even numbered years, but the odd ones too.

The next Women's European Championships will be held in England, and that is when the game will really come of age in this country, fifty years too late I might add. My crystal ball does not have to work too hard to see that there will be thousands of fans watching the tournament, with the distinct possibility, even probability of England lifting the trophy at Wembley, just as their male counterparts had done in 1966, but failed to do at Euro96. It's going to be great, and I for one cannot wait to see it happen.

***

As for the other element I mentioned earlier which is going to be a major part of both the women's and the men's game, this match provided two clear examples of why the use of VAR needs adjusting. Both decisions, one which went in England's favour, the other against, were so marginal that they could not possibly have been deemed "clear and obvious" errors by the match officials.

In the quest to make football as perfect as possible, VAR is killing off moments which make us want to go to matches in the first place. Only last Sunday on Match of the Day 2, Danny Murphy said that football never has been perfect and never will be, so why try and make it perfect? That pearl of wisdom came after a goal by Gabriel Jesus, which was wildly celebrated by players and more importantly by the fans, which would have won the game for Man City against Spurs, was chalked off for yet another decision which could never be deemed to have been clear and obvious.

It seems that every game in which VAR is used is not being improved, but spoilt because of it. Every highlights show, every post-match analysis, every radio phone-in is now dominated by something which should not even be being discussed anymore. Wrong decisions have always been discussed to the nth degree, and VAR was supposed to ensure we can just talk about the football, but the opposite seems to be true. All we do now is talk about the process of coming to what is still often the wrong decision.

My solution, for what it's worth, would be to learn from other sports such as tennis, but mostly from cricket. Both these sports have systems to review decisions, and both took a few years to get to the point they are at now; a point where all decisions are accepted, and in the case of cricket, even wrong decisions are sometimes accepted.

All decisions in both these sports are always factual. You can prove whether or not a tennis ball landed in or out with the use of Hawkeye. You can prove whether a cricketer should be out in many different ways; whether they were caught before the ball hit the ground; whether they were out lbw; whether they nicked the ball through to the wicket keeper or slip fielder; whether the ball hit the bat or glove and not some other part of the body before being caught. All these decisions can be factually proved. Whether the ball was hit for a 4 or a 6, whether the bowler bowled a no-ball, whether the bat was grounded inside the crease before the bails were removed by the fielding side. The list could go on, and yet every decision a cricket umpire has to make can be verified and checked so that every decision is the perfect one.

In fact, the only real need for there to be an umpire on the field of play, or indeed a tennis umpire on the court at all, is to maintain some sort of order between the players. Their job has basically been made obsolete by technology. And yet they are still there, and in the case of cricket, even decisions which are proved to be wrong after having been reviewed are still allowed to stand in certain circumstances. For an lbw decision to be overturned, the evidence must not just prove the umpire to have been wrong, but it has to prove the decision to be very wrong, i.e. a clear and obvious error.

Cricket made sure to take into account human error, and so the concept of Umpire's Call was introduced. This basically says that even though there was human error, we don't mind as that prevents the game from simply being officiated by technology. It legitimises the human aspect of the umpire, and that is something that should never be taken away from the game. Cricket players and fans alike simply accept this and get on with the game. Otherwise the umpire may as well not be on the field of play at all. Football should also do something like this.

The main lesson we must take from tennis, and particularly cricket, is the fact that not every single decision is checked. That would kill the game by turning it into a series of short waits after every tiny, sometimes meaningless decision had to be made. To counter this, the review system puts the power into the hands of the players and gives them only a limited number of reviews. This puts the onus on the players, rather than the officials to choose which decisions to review and which to just let slide because they may well be too close to call.

If a team challenges a decision and loses, then they have one less review to use for the rest of the game. Once they run out of challenges or reviews, then tough, they should have chosen better.

As such, the players' bad judgements, and not those of the officials are to blame. And we all accept this and still watch these sports in our millions with no complaints about the decisions. Fans do not become bored by the constant and tiresome reviewing, and when there is a review, it very often just adds to the excitement.

Football should do the same and give each team two chances to review decisions they think are incorrect. If they are sure the decision is wrong then they are at very little risk of losing a review. For decisions which are much more dubious, they can still review it, but may well lose that review, leaving them with either one or no reviews left. This will make them think much harder about questioning the referee, unless they believe the decision to be clearly and obviously wrong.

It would also cut down on dissent from players. Instead of mouthing off in an official's face, if a player is so sure that the referee or either of the assistant referees have made a mistake, all they have to do is ask for the decision to be reviewed. If the decision is proved to have been incorrect, then the player can feel all smug with him or herself, rather than feeling hard done by and possibly received a booking. Conversely, if the decision is proved to be correct, then maybe, just maybe the player might even apologise to the official who gave the correct decision in the first place. Probably not actually, but at least they won't have any reason to hurl abuse at the referee.

***

I've always loved songs from the 50s and 60s, and one of my favourites as a kid was Eddie Cochrane's "Three Steps to Heaven". Maybe I've always been a bit of a romantic, but the advice in the song's lyrics have worked for me so far. Step 1: I did find a girl to love (on the train if you remember); Step 2: she did fall in love with me (or so she claims, but I believe her); Step 3: I did kiss and hold her tightly (well, only occasionally, and never on the train). And yes I've been in heaven ever since.

I should really stop this rather indulgent analogy now, but if it worked for me, then maybe it can work for VAR too. So here are my not three, but four steps to VAR heaven. They start off really simple as the first three can all be checked factually. The fourth one is a little more complicated as these types of decision necessitate the use of opinion and not simple facts. But if these steps are followed, simplicity will come from what is at present, the most complicated mess ever. So hit it Eddie…

Step 1 - Ball out of play

If a team thinks that the ball has gone out of play, whether it leads to a goal or not, then it can be checked, just as goal line technology checks whether a ball has crossed the goal line now.

But only if the aggrieved team wants to risk one of their reviews.

Step 2 - Handball

There is some confusion over this at the moment, due mainly to the words "accidental" and "intentional" being a part of the decision-making process. The rule seems to be changing now, but there is still some controversy. There was a time when a foul would only be given if it was deemed to be intentional. That just turns the decision into one of opinion rather than one of fact, and facts can be checked and proved. So the rules on fouls got rid of any concept of intent. Even though most fouls are not committed intentionally, they are still fouls. Most players do not foul an opponent intentionally; they just mistime their challenge and are quite rightly penalised for a foul, whether they meant to do it or not. Everyone accepts this without argument.

The same should be applied to handball. Most handballs are not intentional, but as with fouls, if opinion is taken out of the equation then a factual decision can be more easily arrived at. So, if the ball hits a player's hand or arm, whether they mean to do it or not, which then prevents the ball from taking its natural trajectory, then that should be deemed as handball and could be checked via VAR.

But only if the aggrieved team wants to risk one of their reviews.

Step 3 - Offside

Before VAR, offsides should only have been given if it was obviously offside, because any benefit of the doubt should always be given to the attacking player. The concept of benefit of the doubt has now gone out the window. Even if the fingertip of the attacking player is one millimetre nearer to the goal line than the closest part of any of the defender's body, then it is deemed to be offside. An attacker's feet may well be way behind those of the defender, but they can still be deemed to be offside. This again can be checked and verified factually.

The benefit of the doubt usually results in goals in football's case, or wickets in cricket's case, both of which cause excitement and drama, the very things we watch the games for in the first place. By removing any element of doubt, it makes the game duller. So we need to give the attacking side a fairer deal to try and ensure more of these moments happen.

Offside should only be given if the whole of the attacker's foot which is closest to the goal is in front of the whole of the defender's foot which is closest to the goal. If not, then the attacker should be seen as being level with the defender, and so not be offside. This would ensure more goals, more magic moments and more emotion for the fans to either enjoy or endure. And after all, emotions are why we play and watch the game in the first place. So, if a team still feels that a goal has been scored from an offside position, then it can be checked.

But only if the aggrieved team wants to risk one of their reviews.

Step 4 - Fouls

These are the only types of decision where opinion should come into a decision. Many fouls are clear and obvious ones; many are not. This is where a majority decision should be made. Very often, even after a VAR review, opinion is still divided on whether it was in fact the correct decision. Just look at how many times pundits disagree with each other on the television about whether it was a foul or not.

I propose some sort of mini-jury, with an odd number, let's say three, of video assisted referees, who look at the decision by the on-field referee, and independently, without consulting each other, and without anyone else knowing what their individual decision was, either agree or disagree with that decision. If a team feels aggrieved by a decision for a foul, be it inside or outside the penalty area, they can review it.

The decision is then looked at by the three video referees and they all push say either a red or green button. The majority wins. They may well all disagree with the on field referee, or they may all agree with him. As long as at least two of the video referees push the same button, turning it into a majority decision, and not just the say so of the on-field referee who doesn't have access to various camera angles, then the majority decision wins. As with a jury, justice is then done.

Some people may still disagree with the decision, but they would just have to accept the decision of the majority. End of. So, if a team feels that they should have been awarded a free kick for a foul outside the penalty area, or a penalty if the foul is committed inside the penalty area, they have the right to ask for a majority decision.

But only if the aggrieved team wants to risk one of their reviews.

And to ensure the fans know what is going on, which is definitely not the case at the moment, then the evidence must be presented to them as to why that decision was made. Fans must be shown the video evidence. In the first three types of decision, the factual evidence should be shown. In the case of the fourth type of decision, the evidence must be shown along with the colour of each light the three video referees have pressed. Then there can be no argument, and if there still is, then tough. The majority wins so let's just get on with the game. If a team has lost all their reviews due to their own bad judgement, then tough. They should have been more careful in choosing which decisions to review.

See, I told you it was simple and the way to VAR heaven.

Or maybe it's just not worth all the hassle, and we just carry on as before, and accept that mistakes happen, accept that football isn't perfect, and never will be, so let's stop trying to make it perfect.

It's perfect enough. It's heaven already.

***

So, the future of the women's game looks assured, whereas the future of VAR will hopefully be different. As for all the other possibilities the future has to bring, I have no idea.

In the forty years that this book has roughly covered, so many aspects of the game have changed beyond belief. As such, in forty years from now, I have no idea whether Preston will ever have reached the Premier League, or whether they might even have won it.

I have no idea whether Preston will still even exist as a club or indeed how many of the present clubs will still exist. Only very recently it was announced that Bury FC, a proud club with even prouder fans, no longer exist. And Bolton Wanderers may well be next.

I have no idea whether any team will have won The Double, The Treble, The Quadruple, The Quintuple, or even the Sextuple.

I have no idea if England will win the World Cup again, or if the England Women will win their first.

I have no idea how much ticket prices will be, or whether tickets will even be required.

I have no idea how much players will be earning, and how much the latest TV deal will be.

I have no idea what the world record transfer fee for a player will be.

I have no idea whether a woman will be President of the FA or even FIFA.

I have no idea whether any openly gay players, if any, will be in the men's game.

I have no idea how many ex-players will have developed dementia due to their heading of the ball.

I have no idea whether black players will still be receiving racial abuse, and whether there will be more black managers in the game.

I have no idea how the use of technology and social media will change the game.

I have no doubt that the players in forty years' time will be even more perfectly conditioned in terms of their physical health, but as for their mental health, with the massive pressures they are under, again I have no idea.

And that's why we love this wonderful game so much; it keeps us guessing and we never really know what is going to happen in the last few seconds of a match, let alone the next forty years. Its unpredictability is its beauty so, there's no point trying to predict anything. In the words of Doris Day, probably not the most fanatic of football fans it must be said, "Que Sera Sera". I have no idea even how many of the next forty years I'll be around to see. Hopefully all of them.

As for my dad, he definitely won't see all of them. I have no idea how long he has left. His health is not great and hasn't been for some time now. I could say the same about my mum too. Only a couple of years ago she suffered a near fatal heart attack and ever since has not been her same old self. It also affected my dad, and he rarely goes to Deepdale now. Not because he does not support our team anymore. Preston always have been and always will be his team, but he feels guilty for leaving my mum on her own and doesn't like the idea of not being able to get back in time to help her if she needs it.

He's given me many reasons why he no longer goes. He says he struggles with all the steps or his dodgy knee stiffens up from being cramped in his allocated seat. The drive there and back tires him out even though I very often drive. I'd rather do this anyhow as his driving has become more like a white-knuckle ride at a theme park these days.

He used to love going to watch Preston as he could arrive ten minutes before the game, wander in, pay at the turnstile, and stand and watch the game with a group of similarly like-minded blokes. But now, with the arrival of seat allocations he only sees these blokes he used to stand with dotted individually around the ground like lost children looking for their friends.

With paperless tickets, contactless payments, matches played at all times of the day on any day of the week, international breaks and the general widening of the gap between players and fans, he now yearns for a simpler time where he can just watch football the way he used to watch it.

As such, he gave me his season ticket after only a few games last year, quoting many of the reasons above as to why he could no longer go. I gladly accepted it, but it's not the same without him, even when my daughter comes with me on the odd occasion she isn't working.

Instead, he has started going to watch the closest team geographically to him, Lancaster City, even though they play in the Northern Premier League, seven steps down from the actual Premier League on the pyramid. But this in no way bothers dad; he even prefers it. Lancaster City still play at the rather exaggeratedly named Giant Axe Stadium, the "stadium" I played at when I was twelve and won the District Cup with my school. Here, he can still be home in ten minutes if he needs to be. He can sit or stand wherever he wants. He can get there within minutes of kick off and still get a good view. He can even get a pie at half time without missing the first five minutes of the second half. It is a simpler way for him to watch football.

Of course, the standard of football is not as good, but let's face it, being a Preston fan for over 60 years, the standard of football has never been the highest of his priorities when choosing where to get his football fix.

So, my future for however long he's still with me, is to go with my dad to Lancaster City. Not every game, but maybe once a month. I'll still be going to Deepdale as much as possible, but no doubt Preston North End will still be around when my dad isn't. I'm sure they won't mind waiting for me. Watching football isn't always about who you watch; it's more often about who you watch it with. If going to watch Lancaster City means I'll still be able to watch football with my dad, then I'll follow him there.

I'm ultimately still his boy, who went as a seven-year-old to watch Preston with him not because of the football, but because I would be there with him. I want to do this for as long as we are both able to. After all, as I said in my dedication, none of this journey into mine and my dad's past would have been possible if it wasn't for him.

Our club will always be Proud Preston. I hope I've made my dad proud too.

Printed in Great Britain
by Amazon

41862119R00231